VENI
VEDI
VICI

VENI
VEDI
VICI

WHEN ITALIAN FOOTBALL RULED EUROPE

DOMINIC HOUGHAM

pitoh

First published by Pitch Publishing, 2025

(pitch)

Pitch Publishing
9 Donnington Park,
85 Birdham Road,
Chichester, West Sussex,
PO20 7AJ
www.pitchpublishing.co.uk
info@pitchpublishing.co.uk

A CIP catalogue record is available for this book
from the British Library.

ISBN 978 1 83680 185 6

Typesetting and origination by Pitch Publishing

MIX
Paper | Supporting
responsible forestry
FSC   FSC® C010615

Printed and bound on FSC® certified paper in line with
our continuing commitment to ethical business practices,
sustainability and the environment.

Printed and bound in India by Thomson Press

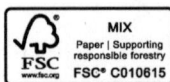

Contents

Acknowledgements

AS ALWAYS, a huge thanks must go out to my family. To my wife Annelise, throughout 29 years of marriage, you have been there for me always, supporting my passions, and every day with you has been special – you are the best. We've spent many trips in Italy together, each of them wonderful, including a full month living in Trastevere. While you may not fully appreciate Italian football of the 1990s, you love everything about the country, as do I. As we always say together, 'You can't get a bad meal in Italy!' Our boys, Jake and Sam, have always been supportive of my football writing efforts, either when watching matches with me or helping me set up a social media page for marketing. It's very handy having 20-somethings around these days when trying to promote your work!

I also need to thank my parents. My lovely mother, who sadly passed away during the pandemic – thank you for engraining a love of Brazilian football in me at an early age. And to my father – for taking me to my first matches, letting me stay up late to watch *Match of the Day*, and endless hours of taking me to the park in all weather, having to be goalkeeper. I still look forward to our footballing chats.

I would also like to thank Omar Saleem at *These Football Times* for publishing my first-ever attempts at football writing during the pandemic and supporting my development along the way, taking me on as a full-time writer for your awesome magazine.

Thank you also to Jane Camillin at Pitch Publishing for publishing my first-ever book and then supporting me on this follow-up, even though it came in originally much longer than expected. *Grazie mille* to you all!

Introduction

IT WAS the best of times; it was the worst of times. English football in the 1980s was a strange beast. I became a teenager in 1978 and it was from that time on that I spent many Saturdays and Wednesdays going to games within London. It was a very different experience from today. You would get to the ground without a ticket – after all, you could just pay at the turnstiles – and then pick your spot on the terracing, maybe behind a crash barrier. If you were lucky, the terrace was covered, but that wasn't a given, especially if you were in the away end. And then you were at the mercy of the crowd, sent flying down in the surges that accompanied moments of drama, trapped in the back-and-forth swaying. Meanwhile, there was always the risk that a group of the visiting fans may have snuck into your end, just waiting for the right moment to create havoc.

Of course, especially to a teenager, a lot of the above made going to a game thrilling. The frisson of danger was part of the attraction. But as we aged, we moved on, tiring of the treatment received within grounds. Sadly, football didn't do the same, allowing dilapidated stadia and hooliganism to thrive. It was inevitable that this would only end one way, leading to the tragic events of Heysel, Bradford and Hillsborough. It was enough to make any English fan question whether it was all worth it.

But as English football sunk to unprecedented depths in the late 1980s, another nation's football rose to the fore. Suddenly Italian football was where it was at. We got glimpses of it on European nights, summaries of games on *Sportsnight*, where we could see these magical sides in action while English teams sat on the sidelines, banned. But what really cemented it first for most was the 1990 World Cup.

This felt like the first modern tournament. The TV coverage seemed brighter, with cool graphics that we hadn't seen before.

Games were being transmitted from incredible stadia such as the San Siro. We had Des Lynam and, of course, 'Nessun Dorma', which still brings chills. The Italian team looked so cool in their *Azzurri* kits, Baggio weaving his magic against the Czech Republic, and Schillaci wheeling away, eyes bulging, after every goal. Statistically it was one of the worst World Cups ever, but visually it was stunning, and England's epic semi-final, along with Gazza's tears, ensured it became remembered with rose-tinted glasses by a whole generation.

And then came the magical moment for many of us. Because of Gascoigne's Italian exploits, he secured a move to Lazio, sparking interest in how he would do there. Channel 4 decided to purchase the rights to show Serie A, so as 1992/93 got underway, football fans in England got the chance to watch top Italian football. For many of us, it was like a veil being lifted from our eyes.

Finally, we had the opportunity to see many of the world's greatest players on a weekly basis. Baggio, Batistuta, Van Basten, Baresi … and these were just some of the Bs! The stadia were awash with sunlight, there were flares, tifos, bouncing crowds. And then there were the kits, those iconic kits of the era. Fiorentina resplendent in purple. Milan in that beautiful Mediolanum-sponsored shirt. The coverage began of a Saturday with James Richardson sipping his cappuccino in a sun-drenched piazza. It was everything that English football was not at that time, enveloped in a hipster vibe, where fellow fans could give each other all-knowing nods on seeing Italian jerseys worn.

For 11 seasons, from 1988 to 1999, Italian clubs dominated Europe. Ten different clubs participated in the big three European competition finals. Transfer records were routinely broken as new owners, flush with cash, looked to outdo one another in a nuclear arms race to the top. Ballon d'Or winners plied their trades within Serie A. Italy themselves were penalty kicks away from winning the 1994 World Cup. It was simply the coolest league in the world.

And then the hangover kicked in. The rise of the Premier League, along with numerous financial and ownership scandals, left many of the clubs in precarious positions. Demotions occurred, *Calciopoli* struck and Italian teams found themselves no longer atop of the European pile, replaced by the likes of Barcelona, Chelsea and Bayern Munich. The words financial meltdown had replaced financial muscle.

But what an 11 years they were. For those of us who lived through them, the memories will always be engrained. Maradona bringing joy back to the city of Naples. The highs and lows of Van Basten's time at Milan. Batistuta inflicting incredible violence onto any football that fell near him. And, my personal favourite, *Il Divin Codino* himself, the one and only Roberto Baggio, weaving through defences with grace and precision.

If you watched it and this book brings back happy memories, then I've achieved my aim. If you were too young, then I hope this book opens your eyes to these great teams and names. YouTube is there for a reason – find the highlights and soak it all in. You won't be disappointed.

Chapter 1

Hanot's Brainchild

*Before we declare that Wolverhampton are
invincible, let them go to Moscow and Budapest.
And there are other internationally renowned
clubs: Milan and Real Madrid to name but
two. A club world championship, or at least a
European one – larger, more meaningful and
more prestigious than the Mitropa Cup and more
original than a competition for national teams –
should be launched.*

Gabriel Hanot, editor of *L'Équipe*

IT WAS a bold statement, but the British press knew how to
sell newspapers. And what better way than by declaring that
Wolverhampton Wanderers were 'Champions of the World'.
They had just beaten Honvéd of Hungary, who contained many
of the players that had been part of the famous Hungarian team
that humiliated England one month before, beating them 6-3 at
Wembley. In the view of the English, any team that could do that
must in fact be masters of the world.

Honvéd were a team stacked with talent: Gyula Grosics, József
Bozsik, Zoltán Czibor, Sándor Kocsis and the great Ferenc Puskás.
The Magical Magyars would lose only one international between
1950 and 1956 within a total of 69 matches. But on 13 December
1954, 55,000 fans packed into Molineux and many more watched
live on the BBC to see whether the English champions, managed
by the canny Stan Cullis, could match up against the Hungarian
greats. Within 14 minutes, Wolves were 2-0 down, but at half-

13

time Stan Cullis asked the ground staff to water the pitch, despite the rainy conditions, presumably a ploy to restrict the Hungarians' passing abilities. It worked; Wolves used long-ball tactics to bypass the boggy midfield and ended up 3-2 winners.

While England celebrated Wolves' 'mastery', some within the rest of Europe begged to differ. The problem was how could anyone definitively determine who was the best side in Europe? Basing the decision of random friendlies seemed inadequate. What was needed was some kind of competition where the top teams in Europe faced each other in a knockout format. And that's exactly what a journalist by the name of Gabriel Hanot sketched out for his colleagues at *L'Équipe*, the French newspaper dedicated to sports coverage. One year later his proposal was put into practice and the European Cup was born.

* * *

The very first European Cup competition comprised 16 clubs, selected by *L'Équipe* as the most prestigious within Europe, although not all champions of their countries at the time. It was the Spanish who took to the competition like a duck to water. Or more specifically, Real Madrid did. They reached the first-ever final, played in June 1956 against French opponents Stade Reims in Paris, and won a 4-3 thriller. It began an unparalleled run of success for the Spanish giants, lifting the trophy five successive times.

Their run eventually came to an end in 1960, ironically at the hands of their eternal rivals, Barcelona. The first round of the 1960/61 tournament saw the pair drawn against each other, Barcelona having won La Liga the season before. The *Blaugrana* won 4-3 on aggregate, thus ending the reign of the *Madrileños* and ensuring there would be a new sheriff in town. But if Barcelona fans thought it would be them, they were sadly mistaken. The centre of European football instead moved west to their neighbours, Portugal.

Benfica, of Lisbon, had developed a strong side, and they swept through the 1961 tournament to face Barcelona in the final, at the splendidly named Wankdorf Stadium in Bern. The Spaniards were no match for the Portuguese, who ran out 3-2 victors. The European Cup had finally left Spain but remained on the Iberian Peninsula.

Obviously, a club as proud as Real Madrid wouldn't take such an event lightly. They tore through the 1962 tournament. Meanwhile, Benfica had added a certain Eusébio to their ranks. The two teams reached the 1962 final in Amsterdam, resulting in a titanic battle. After Real Madrid led three times in the first half, Benfica drew level. Then Eusébio made his impact, scoring twice to keep the European Cup in Portuguese hands.

Despite Real Madrid reaching two more finals before the 1970s, losing and winning, and Atlético Madrid losing in the 1974 final, Spanish football faded into the background. Benfica, though, remained strong for several seasons, playing and losing in three more finals during the 1960s. The remainder of that decade saw European dominance swing to two other countries, first Italy and then the UK.

Italian strength came from two teams based in the same city. Milan had previously lost a final to Real Madrid, but it was the *Rossoneri*, including the likes of Cesare Maldini, José Altafini, Gianni Rivera and a certain Giovanni Trapattoni, who beat Benfica in 1963 to give Italy its first-ever European trophy. But before they could begin a dynasty, their neighbours came along to steal the limelight. The world was about to be introduced to *Grande Inter*, Helenio Herrera and the term *catenaccio*.

Argentine Herrera had limited success as a player in France before moving into management aged 34. After spells in France and Spain, with particular success at Barcelona, Inter Milan came calling. At the time, Inter were living in the shadow of their neighbours. They hadn't won the Scudetto for six seasons, watching as Milan took three titles and Juventus two. Herrera wanted to implement a new system within the team to make them stronger in defence, as the bedrock of his side. He took the traditional four-man defence and added a *libero*, who would play just behind the four and sweep up anything that got through, hence the English term 'sweeper'. This would act as a kind of door-bolt, translated in Italian as *catenaccio*, which became the term synonymous with Herrera's approach.

The combination of this new system and a strong team of players, including Tarcisio Burgnich, Giacinto Facchetti, Luis Suárez, Sandro Mazzola and Brazilian Jair, led to a steady improvement in performance. His first season in charge saw Inter come third, then second, before his third season saw them finally win Serie A. That success led to European Cup competition, where Herrera's approach proved just as effective.

The 1963/64 tournament saw Inter comfortably reach the final, where they faced Real Madrid. Two goals from Mazzola helped Inter to a 3-1 victory and their first European silverware. That was followed by the 1964/65 edition, where Inter controversially eliminated Liverpool courtesy of a 3-0 second-leg home win on a night full of accusations concerning match-fixing and tainted refereeing. The final took place in Inter's own San Siro, where they beat Benfica 1-0, thanks to Jair's goal. However, Inter failed in their attempt at a European Cup treble, faltering at the semi-final stage as Real Madrid exacted revenge on their way to their sixth title.

Undeterred, Inter again reached the European Cup Final the following season, a run that included yet another meeting with Real Madrid, with Inter this time victorious. Their opponents in the final were Scottish champions Celtic.

Inter had shown how defensive football could succeed, but Celtic were completely the opposite. They scored 16 goals over their eight games to the final, with some thrilling performances, so the final would be a perfect match-up of Inter's famed *catenaccio* against Celtic's swashbuckling attack. But the worst thing that could happen in such a match-up took place after just seven minutes when Mazzola converted a penalty for Inter, giving them the perfect excuse to shut up shop. The match became an exercise in attack versus defence, until finally Tommy Gemmell broke through for Celtic in the second half, followed by a winner six minutes from time from Stevie Chalmers.

So, with that, *Grande Inter* was effectively no more. With two European Cups and three Serie A titles added to their trophy cabinet, Herrera moved on to Roma. Spain, Portugal and now Italy had all enjoyed periods of European supremacy – it was time for another new country to rise.

* * *

Celtic's win over Inter marked the first time a team from the UK had won the European Cup, or even reached a final. For Celtic fans, it was all the sweeter that they had achieved what no English team had yet done.

An English team had threatened to succeed once, though. The 1957/58 tournament had seen a strong Manchester United team reach the quarter-finals, where they were drawn to play home and away against Red Star Belgrade. The team had just won back-to-back English league titles under the guidance of manager Matt Busby and, with an average age of just 22, had been nicknamed 'Busby's Babes'. Such a young, talented squad should have meant years of dominance both domestically and internationally. Sadly, fate intervened in the most tragic of circumstances.

A 3-3 draw in Belgrade secured a semi-final spot. Returning to Manchester, the plane stopped over in Munich to refuel. Taking off for the final leg of the trip, their pilot abandoned take-off twice due to engine issues. Snow began to fall but it was decided to attempt it one more time. Hitting slush, the plane skidded through a fence beyond the runway, before striking first a house and then a barn containing a fuel truck, which exploded, killing 20 of the 44 people on board, followed by three more fatalities on the way to or in hospital. Eight were Manchester United first-team players.

It was left to Matt Busby, who only narrowly survived, to try to rebuild Manchester United. The new generation included such greats as Denis Law, Pat Crerand and a young Belfast lad by the name of George Best, and in 1967/68 they were ready for a serious assault on European supremacy.

Cruising through to the semi-finals, Manchester United faced Real Madrid, winning 1-0 at home, before a late Bill Foulkes goal at the Bernabéu sealed a 3-3 draw and a place in the final at Wembley Stadium against Benfica. The final ended 1-1, but in the first half of extra time a magical goal by Best knocked the air out of Benfica, who then conceded twice more in the next seven minutes.

So Bobby Charlton mounted the famous Wembley steps to lift the European Cup – Bobby Charlton who had survived the Munich air disaster, spending a week in hospital. And there to congratulate him was Matt Busby, who had twice received the last rites following the crash. The other survivor playing in the European Cup-winning team was Bill Foulkes, whose goal had sealed their place in the final. In the space of ten years, Manchester United had gone from tragedy to triumph, but would never forget that team of such promise that had perished on a snowy Munich night.

The 60s was to end on a high for Italy, however, as AC Milan won their second European Cup in 1968/69. This success included wins over the champions of the previous two tournaments, Celtic in the quarter-finals, followed by Manchester United in the semi-finals. In the final, Milan met Ajax, the first Dutch team to reach the final, and who were soon to become a European powerhouse. However, on this occasion, Milan were dominant, winning 4-1, with Pierino Prati scoring a hat-trick. But this would be the last Italian success for over a decade.

* * *

The first half of the 1970s continued the trend of shifting European dominance as two new countries gained control. First came the Netherlands, as Feyenoord lifted the European Cup in 1970, defeating Celtic after extra time. This success was merely the appetiser for what the Netherlands had in store next. In Amsterdam, a revolutionary manager by the name of Rinus Michels was about to change how football was played.

In 1965, Rinus Michels was appointed manager of Ajax of Amsterdam, a team that included an 18-year-old Johan Cruyff. Together they would work on a new system of football – one that became known as Total Football – which at its crux relied on the interchangeability of players, requiring a technically diverse team and an intense press.

After taking Ajax to three successive Dutch league titles, Michels led them to the 1969 European Cup Final, the aforementioned 4-1 defeat to Milan. But just two years later they returned for the 1971 final, facing Panathinaikos of Greece at Wembley Stadium. This time Ajax won comfortably, 2-0, to keep the trophy in the Netherlands. But that was just the start.

Not since the first days of European competition and Real Madrid had any team managed to win a hat-trick of European Cups. Ajax set about changing that. Michels had moved on but his team marched on to the 1972 final, where Cruyff's two goals were enough to defeat Inter. Then Juventus were the victims in 1972/73 in Belgrade, Ajax winning 1-0 to seal their place in footballing history.

The third title would be the end of an era, though, as Cruyff left at the end of the season to join Michels at Barcelona, resulting in a 22-year wait for their next European Cup.

Many of the Ajax squad played for the Netherlands in the 1974 World Cup Final, a defeat to West Germany, whose starting XI also included a concentration of players from one club. That club was Bayern Munich, the next team to dominate Europe. Like Ajax, Bayern had a squad with some young talent, including Franz Beckenbauer, Sepp Maier and Gerd Müller. Defeated by Ajax in 1972/73, Bayern came back the following year and took the baton from the Dutch, securing the European Cup in dramatic style from Atlético Madrid, a last-minute equaliser earning them a replay, which they won 4-0. And just like Ajax, Bayern would go on to win a hat-trick of European Cups. Next, Leeds United were defeated in Paris, a game that was marred by crowd trouble as Leeds supporters felt a couple of major refereeing decisions had gone against them unfairly. Then Bayern beat Saint-Étienne, a favourite of 1970s hipsters, at Hampden Park to seal their third title in a row.

As European football, and the European Cup in particular, moved into the mid-1970s, a pattern had emerged of each major nation having a period of domination. After Bayern's third success, the question was: which way would the pendulum swing next? Although the Netherlands and Germany seemed all-powerful, there were signs of another nation beginning to emerge. One country was now about to go on an unparalleled run of success, led by one team in particular, while Italian football would enter the doldrums during this period, the era of *Grande Inter* fading rapidly into the past. The English were coming.

Chapter 2

Rule Britannia!

My idea was to build Liverpool into a bastion of invincibility. Had Napoleon had that idea he would have conquered the bloody world. My idea was to build Liverpool up and up until eventually everyone would have to submit and give in.

Bill Shankly, Liverpool manager

LIVERPOOL FC's period of domestic and European supremacy began under Bill Shankly in 1972/73. Winning their third First Division Championship under the great Scot's watch, they also enjoyed success in Europe, lifting the UEFA Cup. Liverpool had enjoyed a first taste of European glory – and it would be by no means their last, although Shankly realised the need to evolve their game, as they failed to make an impression on the European Cup.

But it would not be Shankly that would oversee this change. At the end of the 1973/74 season, he shocked Liverpool and the footballing world by announcing his retirement. Deciding to promote from within, assistant Bob Paisley stepped out of the Boot Room and into the limelight, and the Reds never looked back.

The total British domination of Europe's premier competition began with Liverpool in 1976/77. The final saw the Reds travel to the Eternal City to meet Borussia Mönchengladbach. There they won their first European Cup, 3-1. It was the first won by any English club since Manchester United in 1968, but more English success would soon follow. In 1977/78 Liverpool progressed to the final again, this time at Wembley Stadium, where they faced Club

Brugge. Having sold their talisman, Kevin Keegan, to Hamburg SV, Liverpool had bought Kenny Dalglish from Celtic, and it was he who scored the only goal to give the Reds their second successive European Cup.

Everyone expected Liverpool to make it a hat-trick in 1978/79 but Nottingham Forest also entered the competition as English league champions. Unfortunately for England, their two representatives were drawn against each other in the first round, and it was Forest who took bragging rights over the two legs. Could they now shock Europe and go all the way? The answer was a resounding yes.

A famous comeback to salvage a home 3-3 draw against Köln in the semi-final was followed by an equally impressive one-goal victory in Germany, taking them to a final against Swedish champions Malmö FF. Earlier in the season, Forest had broken the British transfer record, making Trevor Francis the first British £1m player. He had so far been ineligible for the European Cup fixtures but was able to play in the final at the Olympiastadion, Munich. Scorer of the only goal, Francis quickly paid back his record-breaking fee as Nottingham Forest became unlikely European champions, the third English team in succession.

Like Liverpool, Forest then made it two in a row in 1979/80. Having beaten Ajax in the semi-finals, Forest faced Hamburg in the final at the Bernabéu in Madrid. Although Hamburg dominated, Forest stole a 1-0 victory courtesy of a John Robertson goal. Incredibly, Nottingham Forest were now two-times European champions.

With Liverpool once more winning the First Division title, England again had two representatives in the 1980/81 European Cup. Forest went out in the first round but Liverpool progressed to the final thanks to a heroic 1-1 draw away at Bayern Munich in the semi-final. Their opposition in the Paris final would be the mighty Real Madrid. With eight minutes remaining, Liverpool won the game through the unlikely scoring boot of left-back Alan Kennedy. Five successive European Cups to two English clubs – the rest of Europe could only look on jealously.

Domestically, the surprise package of Aston Villa had won the First Division, so they and Liverpool entered the European Cup

21

in 1981/82. Liverpool crashed out in the quarter-finals, but Villa, whose manager Ron Saunders had resigned halfway through the season, reached the final in Rotterdam under his assistant Tony Barton. There they faced three-times winners Bayern Munich. Against the run of play, a Peter Withe header saw them surprise *Die Roten* to keep the European Cup in England for the sixth successive season. It was starting to become almost tedious, unless you happened to be English.

Finally, the 1982/83 European Cup saw an end to English success as both holders Aston Villa and league champions Liverpool fell at the quarter-final stage. A new country would be able to claim the trophy, and it was Hamburg who stepped up to win their first-ever title and take the trophy back to Germany. At least an Italian team had reached the final for the first time in ten years, but Juventus failed for the second time, going down 1-0.

Italian football was, though, beginning a revival, as Roma reached the final of the 1983/84 European Cup, where they had the advantage of playing at their own Stadio Olimpico. But they faced the toughest of tasks, as they confronted Liverpool. The same Liverpool who had won three of the previous seven instalments. It promised to be quite the contest.

Off the pitch, this was a night that's said to have laid the foundations for what happened the following season at the Heysel Stadium in Brussels. English fans in general suffered from a poor reputation throughout Europe, created by several incidents of hooliganism from various supporters. Liverpool's knew they were travelling into the heart of the beast, where they could not expect a warm welcome. They were herded into a corner of the stadium, high up in the stands and surrounded by a significant police presence and a sea of red and yellow. The Liverpool players could sense the tension in the stadium but they went into the coliseum and fought like gladiators.

With a goal apiece, there was little to separate the teams as they moved through extra time and on to penalties, where Alan Kennedy coolly converted Liverpool's winning penalty to leave the Reds once again as European champions.

Roma's fans did not take the defeat well. Police protection seemed to evaporate as the small pocket of Liverpool fans had to endure attacks from knives, sticks and bottles. Just trying to get to the coach outside the ground was an ordeal. It was a horrendous evening as Roma fans stalked them all night throughout the city in cars and on scooters amid a swirl of tear gas – more than a dozen stabbings were reported, a warning of the risk of trouble between English and Italian clubs that would come back to haunt the game.

The victory meant that, as the 1984/85 European Cup commenced, English teams held almost complete dominance over the competition. Seven titles in eight years – a period of supremacy that no other country has been able to match since, the closest being Spain through Barcelona and Real Madrid between 2009 and 2018 – and what made it more remarkable is that all three teams were purely made up of British and Irish players.

Hamburg of Germany were the only team to break the English stranglehold, but Italian teams had reached the last two finals. While Roma had their brief moment in the sun, Juventus would become the much more successful outfit. *La Vecchia Signora* was emerging from her slumbers.

Chapter 3

The Old Lady Rises

*Juve are like a dragon with seven heads, you
cut off two but another five remain. You can't
kill them off.*

Giovanni Trapattoni, former Juventus manager

THE YEAR is 1899, and a new business venture, *Fabbrica
Italiana di Automobili Torino*, which roughly translates as the Italian
Automobile Factory of Turin, better known by its initials FIAT, is
established, led by an Italian entrepreneur by the name of Giovanni
Agnelli. Within six years, an Italian powerhouse has been created
and, before long, Giovanni Agnelli has become a very rich and very
powerful man.

Agnelli's son Edoardo wanted to become involved in other Turin
ventures, and therefore his eye turned to a recently formed local
football team. Turin at that time had two footballing alternatives:
Juventus, who had been formed in 1897 and had recently adopted
black-and-white striped jerseys in tribute to English side Notts
County, and FBC Torino. The lucky team to receive Edoardo's
funding would be the former, as he was elected the club president in
1923. With his financing, Juventus became the major force in Italian
football during the 1930s, until Edoardo's sudden death in a plane
crash in 1935. However, the Agnelli family continued to control the
majority ownership of the club, which became affectionately known
as *La Vecchia Signora* (The Old Lady).

During the 1960s, the AC Milan team that had lifted two
European Cup trophies had included a defensive midfielder who had
turned his attention to coaching, taking charge of the Milan youth

team for a couple of years before then being appointed first-team coach in 1975 at the age of 36. It was ahead of the 1976/77 season that Juventus turned to this young, relatively untested manager to take charge. The coach was Giovanni Trapattoni – a man who would gain legendary status with *La Vecchia Signora*.

While English teams were dominating the European Cup, domestically Trapattoni's first two seasons saw Juventus win the Scudetto back-to-back. With Dino Zoff in goal, a defence bolstered by the fearsome Claudio Gentile and classy Scirea, a midfield containing a young Marco Tardelli and Franco Causio, combined with a fearsome strike force of Roberto Boninsegna and Roberto Bettega, they swept aside the previous Milanese dominance. But while successful within Italy, their record in Europe during the same period was more limited. They did lift the UEFA Cup in Trapattoni's first season as Athletic Bilbao were defeated on away goals over two legs, their first-ever European silverware, but failed to reach another European final until 1983.

Having lost to Arsenal in the 1979/80 Cup Winners' Cup semi-final, the Juventus management, including Trapattoni, had been impressed by Arsenal's midfield genius, Liam Brady. They saw him as the kind of player who could add a spark to their already strong team, a creative player who could play in the space between midfield and attack, known in Italy as a *trequartista*. When Arsenal lost in the final, Brady felt it was time to move on, so he became Juve's first foreign signing. Previously, foreign signings had been prohibited, in a vain attempt to improve the Italian national team.

And what an effect the magical Irishman had. Joining a Juventus side that had not won the Scudetto during the last two seasons, 1980/81 got off to a slow start, but Juventus rallied to take the title. Brady was the club's top scorer – not bad for a midfielder. Therefore, 1981/82 saw Juventus enter the European Cup, but to their great disappointment they exited during the second round to Anderlecht. With attention turning back to the domestic league, Brady continued to start as Juve's only foreign import, as they battled for the title with Fiorentina. With three games remaining, Juventus and Fiorentina were joint top of Serie A.

There then occurred two significant events for Juventus ahead of the season finale. The first was the return of Paolo

Rossi, a player who had started his career with *I Bianconeri*, before moving on to Vicenza under a co-ownership deal. There Rossi made his name, earning him a place in the 1978 Italian World Cup squad, where he scored three goals and received the Silver Ball as the second-best player of the tournament. He seemingly had the world at his feet, until becoming embroiled in the 1980 *Totonero* scandal.

In Italy, the only way to bet on games legally was through the *totocalcio*, which required correctly picking the results of 12 matches, making single match-fixing redundant. But, of course, illegal betting on single matches was widespread. Two businessmen, who owned a popular restaurant in Rome frequented by Lazio players, decided to enter deals with those players to throw games for a cut of the winnings. Unfortunately for them, the games didn't always end as hoped and they soon owed huge amounts to decidedly unsavoury characters. Panicking, they turned themselves over to the authorities, and soon 13 players were under arrest from various clubs – the most well known of which was Paolo Rossi, who had been on loan at Perugia at the time. While claiming innocence, a three-year ban was handed down to him, which would see him miss the 1982 World Cup.

Conveniently for the *Azzurri*, the ban was later reduced to two years, which left him eligible for the tournament. It also meant that he was available for the last three games of the 1981/82 season with Juventus, who had bought him a year earlier, despite his ban.

The second significant event was a rumour that Juventus were looking to sign emerging Polish star Zbigniew Boniek from Widzew Łódź, which was soon confirmed. The Italian Football Federation had expanded the one foreign player rule to two for the upcoming season. But then the major bombshell dropped – not only were Juventus signing Boniek, but they were also signing French star Michel Platini from Saint-Étienne. Three foreign players and only two starting spots – not surprisingly Brady felt enraged and aggrieved.

Going into the final day of the season still level with Fiorentina, Juventus held the superior goal difference. All they had to do was travel down to Catanzaro and come away with a result that matched that of Fiorentina, who travelled to Cagliari. With 15 minutes remaining, Juventus were awarded a spot kick for handball. The question was, who would take the vital penalty? Throughout the season, it had been Liam Brady, but given recent events the players had decided that the duty should move across to striker Pietro Paolo Virdis. Unfortunately, he had already been substituted, so Brady picked up the ball. He sent the keeper the wrong way and Juventus retained the Scudetto. The Irishman would subsequently leave for Sampdoria as Juventus said farewell to their first foreign hero of the 1980s – but with the arrival of Boniek and Platini, their reign of success was gathering momentum.

Trapattoni had now put together a fearsome side. In goal was Dino Zoff, one of the greatest goalkeepers of all time, while the defensive line-up of Sergio Brio, Antonio Cabrini, Claudio Gentile and Gaetano Scirea was famed for its strength. In midfield, Marco Tardelli would now be joined by Platini, while the strike force contained new boy Zbigniew Boniek along with Paolo Rossi. If further proof was needed, the Italian national team travelled to Spain for the 1982 World Cup, coming home with the trophy after beating West Germany in the final with a starting XI containing six Juve players, one of whom, Paolo Rossi, scored six goals in the tournament, including the famous hat-trick against Brazil, to earn the Golden Boot. The third-place play-off was contested between France and Poland, Platini and Boniek being the key players for each side. This was a Juventus team to be feared throughout Europe.

While Paolo Rossi was expected to be the goalscoring star, 1982/83 saw Platini dominate in front of goal, despite being nominally a midfielder. The Serie A campaign saw the Frenchman end with a staggering 16 goals, earning him the *Capocannoniere*, of which 14 came in the last ten matches alone. However, a slow start to the season as the new players settled in cost Juventus, who fell behind Roma early on and could never quite overhaul them, ending four points behind. In Europe, though, Juventus did show that Italian football should still be respected.

Overcoming Hvidovre of Denmark and Standard Liège of Belgium, Juventus then defeated reigning champions Aston Villa in the quarter-finals of the 1982/83 European Cup. With Liverpool falling at the same stage, the trophy would finally be wrested from English hands and Juventus took a step nearer when beating Liverpool's conquerors, Widzew Łódź, in the semi-finals to set up a showdown against Hamburg. Sadly, they failed to show up on the big occasion, losing to a Felix Magath goal on the night, despite being pre-game favourites. It was hugely frustrating for the Italians but reaching the final had shown how much the team had progressed under Trapattoni.

Platini, meanwhile, had demonstrated his worth to the Old Lady, his performances earning him the 1983 Ballon d'Or. He had a Gallic coolness about him, often starting moves from midfield before bursting into the box to score. It felt like time slowed around him, never looking rushed before picking out the perfect pass. Juve had secured themselves the best player in Europe.

Losing the Serie A title to Roma meant no European Cup place for Juventus in 1983/84; instead they would enter the Cup Winners' Cup. Having reached the semi-finals, they were drawn against Manchester United, representing a rare chance for Juventus to try to overturn the English dominance in Europe. After a drawn first leg at Old Trafford, the scores were level again in Turin and the tie appeared to be heading into extra time. Then Juventus got a huge piece of luck. A free kick fell to Scirea just outside the United area, and his shot was charged down, only for the ball to break loose to that arch-poacher Paolo Rossi. As quick as lightning, Rossi pounced, slipping the ball past the keeper to take *I Bianconeri* into a European final for the second successive season.

It had been seven years since an Italian side had tasted European glory – seven years in which British clubs had lifted eight European trophies. The last success had been Juventus when they overcame Athletic Bilbao in the UEFA Cup, as Trapattoni was just starting to build his iconic side. The opponents this time would be Porto at the St Jakob Stadium in Basel.

It took only 12 minutes for Juventus to take the lead – a pass from Platini finding winger Beniamino Vignola, who fired a great shot into the corner. However, against the run of play, Porto equalised when a shot from António Sousa took a nasty bounce over the diving Stefano Tacconi. Boniek then latched on to a Vignola pass to stab the ball past the Porto keeper to give Juventus the lead once again. It was scrappy but it proved enough to give Juventus, and Italian football, that first European trophy after a long drought. Trapattoni had his hands on a second piece of European silverware.

Juventus now turned their sights back to the big one. The ultimate test for any European club was still to raise the European Cup – the competition that pitted the best against the best. Juventus had taken the Serie A title back from the capital, finishing two points ahead of Roma to reclaim their crown. Incredibly, the *Capocannoniere* for the season had once again been midfielder Michel Platini, banging in an impressive 20 goals for the *Bianconeri*, one ahead of the legendary Zico at Udinese. He also secured his second successive Ballon d'Or. That title allowed Juventus another crack at the trophy they most desired – the trophy that had sat in English hands for seven of the last eight seasons and currently resided at Anfield once again. It was going to be a mighty task to wrench it away from those Liverpudlian hands.

As the 1984/85 European Cup got underway, Juventus faced a first-round tie against Finnish champions Tampereen Ilves, while Liverpool were drawn against Polish champions Lech Poznań. Neither side were greatly troubled as Juventus emerged victorious 6-1 on aggregate and Liverpool 5-0. The second round sent Swiss champions Grasshoppers to the Stadio Comunale. Juventus secured a 2-0 win, which was then cemented by a 4-2 win in Zürich, putting Juve into the quarter-finals. It was a last eight that wasn't particularly strong, with German champions VfB Stuttgart and Spanish champions Athletic Bilbao already eliminated. But all eyes in Turin would have noted that there was still one other powerhouse among the eight – Liverpool were on their usual march through Europe, as a hat-trick from the relentless Ian Rush helped them negotiate a strong Benfica side. As each round progressed, it felt like, at some stage, Juventus were going to have to overcome Liverpool if they wanted to ascend the throne. The question was when?

The two giants avoided each other in the quarter-finals, as Juventus drew Czech champions Sparta Praha. A first-leg 3-0 victory in Turin meant a nerveless passage into the semi-finals, Rossi grabbing his fourth of the tournament. But, once again, Liverpool appeared in Juve's rearview mirror, joining them in the semi-finals after seeing off Austria Wien easily, 5-2 on aggregate. The European Cup was now down to just four teams: current holders Liverpool, Italian giants Juventus, French champions Bordeaux and Greek champions Panathinaikos. As the four teams went into the pot, would this be the moment that Juventus would finally have to face the mighty Reds?

Not yet. Juventus were matched up with Bordeaux, while Liverpool would take on Panathinaikos. At the Comunale, Boniek gave Juventus an early lead. Meanwhile, at Anfield, Liverpool scored their opening goal. As both games broke for half-time, it was advantage Juventus and Liverpool. Within five minutes of the second half kicking off, Liverpool had virtually put their tie to bed, with two Rush goals. It was then Juve's turn, as another precision pass from the halfway line by French maestro Platini fell perfectly to Massimo Briaschi, who calmly placed it into the corner. The provider then turned scorer when three minutes later the classic combination struck again, this time Boniek weaving down the wing before crossing for Platini to volley home Juve's third. Both Liverpool and Juventus were cruising – a final between the giants looked inevitable.

With five minutes remaining, Liverpool added a fourth, so as the final whistle sounded in England and Italy, both teams had considerable first-leg leads, meaning it would take something extraordinary to prevent either from heading to Belgium for the final. And nothing extraordinary did occur; Liverpool won 1-0 in Athens to give them a 5-0 aggregate win, while Bordeaux did threaten after taking a 2-0 lead after 80 minutes in France, but Juventus hung on.

For the second time in three years, Juventus had reached the promised land, but if they wanted to achieve greatness this time, they would have to earn it by beating current champions Liverpool – the team that had won four of the previous eight tournaments. The final was scheduled for 29 May, to be played at the Stade du Heysel in Brussels, more commonly referred to as the Heysel Stadium.

JUVENTUS (1976-1984)
European Cup runners-up – 1982/83
UEFA Cup Winners' Cup winners – 1983/84
UEFA Cup winners – 1976/77
Serie A champions – 1976/77, 1977/78, 1980/81,
1981/82, 1983/84
Coppa Italia winners – 1978/79, 1982/83

Chapter 4

The Heysel Disaster

It wasn't until we were leaving the ground and there were ambulances everywhere and blue lights flashing, and lines and lines of soldiers and policeman, that it became clear it was something serious.

Lifelong Liverpool supporter John Mackin

THE WORDS of John Mackin attempt to crystallise the horrors that he had just witnessed. The occasion was the 1985 European Cup Final, UEFA's annual showcase event, played on 29 May at the Heysel Stadium in Brussels, Belgium. A game pitting the champions of England, Liverpool, against the champions of Italy, Juventus. Close to 60,000 supporters had travelled by road, sea and rail to watch their beloved teams compete for Europe's highest honour – fathers and sons, friends and couples. Thirty-nine would never return to their families or loved ones.

The Heysel Stadium had been selected, despite being 55 years old and in poor condition. Maintenance had been minimal for many years, and fans spoke of the old terracing literally crumbling around them. It had been a somewhat surprising choice – both Real Madrid's Santiago Bernabéu and Barcelona's Camp Nou were available and would have made much better venues. Senior management at both Liverpool and Juventus had asked UEFA to consider moving location, especially given that the final would involve two teams with significant fanbases, but unfortunately UEFA couldn't be swayed, despite it being often highlighted by others that the stadium was antiquated and a shambles. It was a decision that would have deadly consequences.

As with any major final, the ground had filled early, with most fans sporting Juventus black and white, given the easier trip from Turin. Huge banners were unfurled by the *tifosi* as they created their usual electric atmosphere, set to the sounds of drums and chants of 'Juve', drowning out the normally vociferous Liverpool following. Two hours ahead of kick-off, the teams came out to taste the atmosphere, still dressed in their club suits, as anticipation continued to build. After soaking up the mood, both sets of players headed for the changing rooms, and it was at this stage that the first hint of trouble arose.

Each end behind a goal had been designated to one set of fans. Juventus fans occupied zones M, N and O, while zones X, Y and Z were at the Liverpool end. But while Liverpool fans crowded into zones X and Y, zone Z had been reserved for neutral Belgian fans. The problem was that, while zone Z was in theory a neutral section, many of the tickets had been sold to Italian ex-pats within Brussels or on the black market, where again the majority had been bought up by Juventus' huge fanbase. There was therefore a section of Juventus fans placed right next to the Liverpool supporters, rather than being properly segregated.

Section X bordered section Z, separated by temporary chain-link fencing and a poorly policed no-man's land in between. With the ground being dilapidated in many places, there were pieces of loose concrete easily available, and soon Liverpool fans began to hurl those into zone Z. Some supporters later claimed that they had seen Liverpool fans stranded there being attacked by Juventus fans, so wanted to protect their colleagues. The police charged with keeping order within that area had no previous experience in combatting hooliganism and could only watch as Liverpool fans finally broke into the section, causing fans therein to either flee across the terrace or spill onto the running track surrounding the pitch. Those Italians crossing the terrace found themselves trapped against a wall in the lower corner, and panic started to set in as fans began to trample upon each other. Crushed against one another, supporters remember feeling their shoes sucked from their feet, bodies suspended in mid-air unable to move a muscle. Then, at 7.31pm, came the first emergency radio call – a wall had collapsed in section Z, the wall against which the Juventus fans had been wedged. Cameras showed fans spilling over in a heap of bodies, those at the top scrambling to safety over those trapped beneath.

The collapse of the wall had at least allowed those being crushed to now escape; the pressure finally released. The problem was that, as those fans spilled out, many were trapped beneath the stampede, slipping over and consumed by the throng. As the chaos continued, police struggled to control the situation, panic taking over as fans continued to pour over the damaged wall in a heaving mass. Those that escaped the commotion joined those on the running track as the crowd built around the pitch, confusion filling the air for both watching viewers and most supporters within the stadium as to what was occurring. The police eventually managed to clear Liverpool fans from zone Z, but that didn't reduce the panic by the wall. Fans continued to spill onto the pitch, many in blood-soaked clothes, stumbling in shock or trying frantically to find friends and family.

There now came the shocking sight of police using barriers as makeshift stretchers to carry motionless bodies from the scene, while medical officers were seen administering CPR on prostrate bodies. It was at this time, around 8pm, when most TV stations began their scheduled coverage of the final. As viewers tuned in expecting to see the build-up, they instead found themselves watching presenters trying to explain the chaos surrounding them. The BBC coverage commenced with a solemn Jimmy Hill announcing, 'I'm afraid the news is very bad from Brussels. Hooliganism has struck again and I'm afraid the scenes are as bad as anything we've seen for a long, long time.'

Italian TV coverage, meanwhile, wrestled with the question of whether to mention names of those who were safe to reassure loved ones back home, but decided against it as they couldn't mention everyone, and any names not mentioned would create the assumption of injury.

By now, many of the Italian fans who had escaped from section Z had made their way to the Juventus end, where they shared stories of what had occurred with fellow supporters, anger rising. As the rumours spread, Juventus fans started to invade the pitch, running across towards the Liverpool end. The scene evolved into clashing fans on the pitch, the local police trying to regain some control with heavy use of batons. When that didn't work, police on horseback were eventually escorted onto the pitch, creating a standoff between them and fans.

The big question now facing UEFA and the police was whether to cancel the game. While it may seem obvious now that the match should have been postponed, there was a fear that this might cause more problems between the two sets of fans. The players themselves were in the changing rooms, unaware of what exactly was occurring outside, receiving instructions from officials to remain where they were for now. But some started to leave the dressing room and quickly got a sense of the unfolding disaster as fans came past, asking for help and water while discussing what they had seen. Those players that made it to the pitch to witness the carnage were swiftly told to return, where they were then stunned to see riot police filing past.

Liverpool manager Joe Fagan asked his players to stay put while he went outside to try to talk to the supporters, but it was a fruitless exercise within the din and chaos. On the Juventus side, president Giampiero Boniperti asked his coach not to mention to the players what had occurred and not to allow any outsiders into the changing room. But it was futile – the dressing room was infiltrated by distressed Juventus fans from section Z, resulting in the Juventus players going out onto the pitch to try to calm the situation, telling their ultras that the situation wasn't as bad as they may suspect. Many fans appealed to the team not to play, and it was a stunned squad that returned to the changing room, many in tears.

* * *

An hour after the collapse of the wall, the full extent of the disaster became clear as the police announced an official death toll of 35. No decision had been made about whether to play the game or not as police continued to clash with fans from both sides. VIPs were huddled within the stadium, discussing possible courses of action, and finally it was decided to stage the match once extra police had been brought into the stadium, as immediate evacuation was seen as potentially more dangerous. Boniperti disagreed with the decision, stating that he would take his team from the stadium immediately, but the other VIPs eventually wore him down. A UEFA delegate was charged with informing the players that a serious incident had occurred, resulting in injuries, but to avoid mentioning deaths.

At 9.40pm, two hours and ten minutes after the tragedy, the two team captains were asked to tell fans over the loudspeaker system that the game was going ahead. Liverpool skipper Phil Neal was led onto the pitch, where he was stunned at the sight surrounding him as fighting continued. Broadcasters prepared to cover the match, except for German TV, where the announcers stated: 'ZDF has decided not to broadcast this game, because it has only one aim, not to play the European Cup Final but to prevent further mass hysteria, to calm the fans down as much as possible.'

At 9.45pm, the two teams came out onto the pitch, despite Juventus players' continued protestations. Unsurprisingly, the first half was a muted affair as both teams seemed to play at half-pace. At half-time, the names of missing people were read over the PA system, adding to the chilling atmosphere. The second half got underway and, after just 13 minutes, a long ball from Platini found Boniek through on goal. He appeared to be fouled just outside the penalty area but the referee felt otherwise and awarded a spot kick, which Platini dispatched before wheeling away in celebration. That was to be the only goal of the night. As the final whistle blew, many Juventus fans rushed onto the pitch to celebrate. Authorities made sure to escort the Liverpool fans out of the stadium and back home as quickly as possible, which ensured no further clashes between the two sets of fans, while Juventus players celebrated with their supporters within the stadium, carried away by their victory.

* * *

In the following days, the official death toll was revised to 39, with around 600 others injured. The blame game then began, with UEFA stating that English fans had been responsible but ignoring the deplorable condition of the stadium and their decision to stage the match there despite many warnings. There were calls for English teams to be banned from European competition and, trying to get ahead of any official ban, on 31 May 1985, British prime minister Margaret Thatcher asked the Football Association to withdraw English clubs from Europe. But it wasn't enough – just two days later

UEFA announced that English clubs were banned from European competition for 'an indeterminate period of time'.

It would be six years before an English team stepped out in a European tie again. After years of discussion, April 1990 saw UEFA finally confirm that English teams could rejoin its competitions, commencing with the 1990/91 season; however, Liverpool were omitted from that decision, and wouldn't be permitted back until the following season. Ironically, Liverpool won the English league in 1989/90, so, although the ban had been lifted on all other English clubs, there was no English entrant in the 1990/91 European Cup due to Liverpool's extended ban.

The prohibition on English clubs immediately changed the European footballing landscape. They had played in nine of the previous 11 European Cup finals, lifting the trophy seven times. The most dominant nation was now out in the cold – their teams no longer benefitting from the experience of playing in Europe, with its two-leg format and differing styles. Players who wished to test themselves at the highest level were no longer attracted to England, when instead they could play in Germany, Italy or Spain and be part of the most prestigious competition. As England became isolated, continuing to wrestle with its problems of hooliganism and deteriorating stadia, the rest of Europe continued to evolve. There now existed a vacuum, and the question on everyone's lips was which country would next become the centre of power within Europe.

Chapter 5

An Argentine in Napoli

[Despite the lack of a] mayor, houses, schools,
buses, employment and sanitation, none of this
matters because we have Maradona.

Local Naples newspaper

IT SHOULD have been a dream combination. Following on from the 1982 World Cup, Barcelona announced a blockbuster deal – they had signed a young Argentine for $7.6m, a world record transfer fee, from Boca Juniors. The player had represented Argentina during the World Cup but had generally disappointed, albeit suffering from tight marking and some questionable tackles. The pressure had eventually got to him, leading to his sending-off in the final minutes as the *Albiceleste* trailed their arch-rivals Brazil 3-0, as he violently retaliated by kicking opponent Batista in the stomach. Despite this setback, his play for Boca had made him the most exciting prospect in world football, and Barcelona were delighted to capture such a talent. The player's name was Diego Armando Maradona.

There was an element of risk in the signing. Maradona was still only 21. He had never played outside of his homeland – the Spanish La Liga would be a whole different ball game, but it would represent a statement purchase for the Catalans, showing that they could compete with rivals Real Madrid for the brightest and the best. The Camp Nou had recently been renovated and it was important to the Barcelona hierarchy to keep the fans entertained. Under manager Udo Lattek, they had just lifted the Cup Winners' Cup in front of 100,000 in their own stadium, but their last league championship had been back in 1974. They had since watched as Real Madrid dominated the late 1970s before the pendulum then swung to the Basque region, where Real Sociedad took the first two titles of the new decade. Something had to change, and Barcelona gambled $7.6m that Maradona would be that change.

On 28 July 1982, Maradona was presented to the Barça faithful in front of 50,000 elated fans. But it didn't take long for cracks to appear in the marriage as Maradona began to build an entourage around him, creating friction between him and the club. His agent was Jorge Cyterszpiler, a lifelong friend who he trusted completely and allowed to oversee much of his off-field lifestyle. As Maradona's agent, it was almost part of the job description to clash with Barcelona's senior management as he protected his client's interests, but it reached a point where even Lattek, a known disciplinarian, had to ban him from attending training seasons.

Maradona suffered a pulled muscle early in the season, angering Barcelona's management when bringing in his own medical representative, Dr Oliva, to treat him rather than using the club's medical staff, and then compounding this by using his own personal trainer, Fernando Signorini, to cover his recuperation. Then there was his growing retinue, many hanging out at his palatial Barcelona villa, encouraging him to enjoy a party lifestyle, a world away from the conservative Barça management, who heard stories through the grapevine of the shenanigans occurring therein, the most concerning of which was alleged snorting of cocaine.

While Maradona's early relationship with the club was troubled, Bernd Schuster, the German who had been with the club for two years and had achieved cult status, also had his own issues, specifically with Lattek. Barcelona continued to impress in the league, reaching the top of the standings in early February 1983, but as Lattek's relationship with both Maradona and Schuster deteriorated, that wouldn't be enough to protect him. On 4 March 1983, Barcelona made a big call – club president Josep Núñez announced that Lattek was out, replaced by Argentine legend César Menotti, the man who had masterminded the *Albiceleste*'s 1978 World Cup triumph.

Menotti's management methods were much more to Diego's liking. While Lattek had scheduled morning training sessions, Menotti's attitude was more laid-back, often commencing training in the late afternoon, allowing Maradona to recover from any prior night excesses. Barcelona's league form fell away as Athletic Bilbao continued the Basque domination. Barcelona finished fourth, but could take solace in winning the 1983 Copa del Rey. Maradona ended the season as Barça's top scorer, with 11 league goals and 23 across all competitions, but Barcelona's management were still unconvinced – were those goals worth the world record fee and accompanying heartache of dealing with him?

The aim for 1983/84 was to overcome Athletic Bilbao and to finally bring the La Liga title back to Barcelona. The fixture list dictated that on week four Barcelona would be hosting the Basque champions at the Camp Nou. Athletic Bilbao were managed by Javier Clemente, who had put together a no-nonsense team that played with an aggressive style, and the tension was ramped up by an ongoing war of words between Menotti and Clemente, with neither a fan of the other's tactical approach. The match was hugely anticipated and would not disappoint. From the kick-off, Barcelona took the game to the champions, outplaying them to take a 2-0 lead into the break in front of an ecstatic crowd. But then came the moment 12 minutes into the second half for which the game would be forever remembered.

Maradona picked up the ball in midfield and started to run forward, unaware of an incoming tackle from Bilbao's Andoni Goikoetxea. As the crowd watched in horror, Goikoetxea flew into him, a scream emanating from the Argentine genius. It was a horrendous challenge, resulting in a broken ankle for Maradona, who was stretchered from the pitch in tears. Amazingly, Goikoetxea escaped with just a yellow card, although Spanish authorities would later throw a ten-match suspension at him. But all that was of little solace to Barcelona and Maradona, who would undergo three months of therapy before being able to play again, worsened by a bout of hepatitis.

Upon his return, Maradona hit a fine run of form, scoring nine goals in his first eight league games. A frustrated Barcelona finished third, just one point behind champions Athletic Bilbao and Real Madrid. There was fury within the club at what could have been if Maradona had not been sidelined by that Bilbao tackle, which of course was exasperated by the fact that Bilbao went on to claim their second successive title. To make things worse, both teams had reached the final of the Copa del Rey, the last game of the season, a powder keg that could easily spark into violence.

The teams lined up in front of 100,000 fans packed into the Bernabéu. Bilbao took an early lead, scoring after just 14 minutes through striker Endika, a lead they held until full time through resolute defending. Unsurprisingly, the Barcelona players were fuming at the end, having lost again to the team that they viewed as 'anti-football'. As the players milled around the pitch, Bilbao substitute Miguel Sola threw a 'fuck-off' sign at Maradona. The red mist descended, and Diego punched Sola, after which mayhem reigned. Flying kicks and punches were exchanged as both teams went to war, including Goikoetxea, who once again aimed his violence at Maradona. Barcelona officials could only watch in horror as their players degenerated into a mob in front of King Juan Carlos, Maradona being dragged off the pitch with his shirt in tatters.

It was the straw that would break the camel's back, leading president Núñez to state, 'When I saw those scenes of Maradona fighting and the chaos that followed, I realised that we couldn't go any further with him.' Diego Armando Maradona was now persona non grata in Catalonia – Núñez had put up with his demanding personality for two seasons, won nothing and was now publicly ashamed and embarrassed. The problem was who might be persuaded to take him off their hands.

* * *

Under a smouldering volcano sits the city of Naples, home to Società Sportiva Calcio Napoli. A city obsessed by football, Napoli fans had suffered disappointment for decades, only winning two trophies of note during their existence: the Coppa Italia twice. But they had never lacked in ambition and had recently come under new ownership when local construction magnate Corrado Ferlaino took over as club president, supported by sporting director Antonio Juliano, a Neapolitan through and through, born in one of the poorest areas of the city before playing for Napoli almost 400 times over the space of 16 seasons.

The season of 1983/84 had seen Napoli flirt seriously with relegation, eventually ending 11th in Serie A, just one point above relegated Genoa. While Juventus continued to dominate Italian football, Napoli weren't even a close runner, having finished in the top three in only one of their last nine seasons. Needless to say, they were not a team on many people's radar throughout Europe, and certainly not one that would have entered people's minds as a possible destination for the world's most high-profile footballer.

However, as rumours spread about the discontent between Barcelona management and Maradona, Juliano went to Ferlaino with an ambitious suggestion. If Napoli really wanted to make a splash, and become serious contenders, why not look at bringing Diego to the Stadio San Paolo? Worryingly, they had heard whispers that Juventus may be interested and, if that were to occur, it could only mean continued Juve dominance. Several secret meetings were held in the summer of 1984 to see whether a deal could be struck. As the closing date approached for Italian league transfers, Ferlaino flew to Barcelona to see whether he could hammer out final details with Barcelona vice-president Gaspard, whose latest improved contract offer had been rejected by Maradona.

Eventually a £6.9m world record transfer, another involving Diego, was agreed. The announcement stunned world football and immediately threw Napoli into the limelight. While English teams continued to dominate Europe, they did so almost entirely with homegrown talent. Now this minor team from the Italian south had suddenly bought the world's hottest property. Diego-mania was to sweep the south-west coast of Italy as Napoli fans rubbed their eyes in disbelief. Interestingly, no one stopped to ask too many questions about exactly how this record fee was being financed – after all, why spoil a good story. As Maradona departed for his new destination, he proclaimed, 'I expect peace, the peace I didn't have in Barcelona. But, above all, respect.' If it was peace he wanted, he would soon find that Naples was not the place to go.

Maradona's arrival in Naples is brilliantly captured in Asif Kapadia's excellent documentary *Maradona*. From the airport, Maradona is driven through city streets at high speed while paparazzi give chase. Frenzied fans converge on the San Paolo for his unveiling, over 70,000 packed in. They don't care that he had endured a disappointing 1982 World Cup and suffered a stint at

Barcelona plagued by issues – he is a saviour, come to lift them to great heights – a poor kid from a shanty town with whom they can relate. His mother is even Italian. When he finally enters the stadium, dressed simply in T-shirt and tracksuit trousers but sporting a Napoli scarf, he juggles a ball while looking slightly embarrassed. 'Good evening, Neapolitans. I'm very pleased to be here with you.' Ferlaino and Juliano look on with pride at their coup.

A later press conference provided Maradona with his first taste of the environment in which he was now encased. A French journalist asked if he knew that his transfer had been funded in part by Camorra money. It's doubtful that Maradona knew what the journalist was alluding to, but Ferlaino most certainly did. In simplistic terms, the Camorra were the Neapolitan Mafia, who had a strong influence on the politics and economy of Naples. To bring them up now obviously angered the club president. He bristled as he shouted, 'Your question offends us. Naples is an honest city. As president of the football club, I ask you to leave.' Unsurprisingly, the French journalist was swiftly escorted out.

* * *

On 23 September 1984, Maradona made his debut at the Stadio San Paolo, against Sampdoria, slotting into a forward line that included fellow countryman Daniel Bertoni, who had scored in the 1978 World Cup Final, alongside a couple of lesser-known Italian strikers. The team had lost its opening match away at Verona 3-1, where Maradona was introduced to the shocking northern views of his new home: 'We went up north and, wherever we went, they put up banners that said: "Wash yourselves." It was disgusting. They were all racists.' Napoli fans were familiar with such abuse, however.

Now Napoli's fans were getting a first home view of their new hero. In the 62nd minute, Maradona's moment came. A penalty was awarded to Napoli and Diego took responsibility, calmly slotting into the corner before celebrating with a knee slide near the corner flag. The love affair had commenced.

That affair was consummated in the fifth game of the season when Napoli travelled to the Stadio Olimpico to face Lazio. One goal down early in the second half, Maradona played a beautiful one-two with Bertoni, receiving the return ball on his chest before volleying it into the corner. For the Napoli faithful, it confirmed that they were now in the presence of genius.

As the season progressed, the Napoli *tifosi* fell deeper in love. Maradona looked sharp once again, having lost weight, and enjoying the adulation being heaped upon him. Napoli didn't set Serie A alight but they did finish in eighth place, a marked improvement on the previous season's flirtation with relegation. Maradona scored 14 goals over 30 appearances, which in the tough Italian league was enough to end the season as the third-highest Serie A goalscorer, behind Juventus's Platini and Inter's Alessandro Altobelli. In a surprising season, it was Hellas Verona that won their one and only Serie A title.

It was also at the end of this season that the Heysel disaster occurred, leading to the indefinite ban on English clubs. If ever there was a time for Napoli to strengthen, it was now, as Europe looked for new leadership.

* * *

While eighth was a definite improvement, Maradona demanded more. Flexing his muscles, he instructed Ferlaino to 'buy three or four players, and sell the ones the crowd whistle at. If not, start thinking about selling me, because I'm not staying like this.' The chequebook was swiftly extracted – Claudio Garella, Alessandro Renica and Bruno Giordano, the latter an experienced and prolific goalscorer for Lazio over the past ten seasons, were purchased.

The following season saw Napoli again improve, sitting in second place for the first half before dropping to finish third, behind champions Juventus and Roma. In November 1985, Maradona scored the only goal as Napoli beat Juventus at the San Paolo. With 18 minutes remaining, Napoli won a free kick within the penalty area and, with Juventus placing a six-man wall and little room between the free kick and goal, Maradona flicked a beautiful shot into the top corner. Napoli fans could hardly believe their eyes – their hero had led them to beat the strongest team in Europe – creating a delirium that caused five fans to faint and another two to suffer heart attacks within the stadium.

Maradona was again Napoli's top scorer for the season, with 11 goals, but Giordano also pulled his weight, scoring ten. In

Maradona's two seasons in Naples, he had helped to take Napoli from narrowly avoiding relegation to UEFA Cup qualification. The question being asked around Italy was: could he take them even further? But before that question could be answered, Maradona, and many others within Serie A, were off to Mexico to contest the 1986 World Cup.

* * *

The 1986 World Cup saw Maradona at the height of his powers. Ironically, Argentina and Italy were drawn together in Group A, meaning Maradona would face those same players that he had just battled against all season. Italy's squad included experienced defenders Antonio Cabrini and Gaetano Scirea, both of Juventus, along with Giuseppe Bergomi from Inter. The midfield was powered by captain Marco Tardelli, now playing his football at Inter, but otherwise relatively inexperienced players such as the emerging Carlo Ancelotti from Roma and Antonio Di Gennaro coming off his successful year with Hellas Verona. With Paolo Rossi unable to play due to injury, Alessandro Altobelli led the line, a prolific goalscorer with Inter who was approaching the sunset of his career but could still find his way to goal. Enzo Bearzot was charged with once again leading the *Azzurri*, now remarkably in his 11th year as coach, an iconic sight on the bench with pipe in mouth, contemplating the game.

While Argentina won their opening match comfortably, defeating South Korea 3-1, Italy could only draw with Bulgaria, their solitary goal coming from Altobelli. That set up the Argentina against Italy clash. Napoli fans had been in love with Maradona to date, but now would have to watch him represent the opposition. Everyone wondered how his two seasons of experience playing against Serie A defenders would help him.

The game was just six minutes old when Italy were awarded a controversial penalty. No matter; Altobelli took responsibility and netted his second goal of the tournament to give Italy an early lead.

Maradona then gave his first flash of brilliance. Picking up the ball on the right, and faced immediately by two Italian defenders, clever footwork took the little magician right through them before firing a shot narrowly wide. It was clear that he was growing into the game, and after 34 minutes he made his mark. A ball into Jorge Valdano on the edge of the area saw him immediately flick it over the Italian defence to where Maradona was running, marked by Scirea. Not bothering with a first touch, Maradona used his left foot to pass it into the corner past a stranded Giovanni Galli in goal, his prior experience against Italian defences paying off.

The game ended one apiece, Conti coming closest to breaking the deadlock with a low shot that rebounded back off the post. Both sides then won their final group matches, but the Italians saw their defence of the World Cup come to an early end, beaten 2-0 by France in the round of 16. For Maradona, however, his World Cup was only just starting.

This chapter is about the relationship between Napoli and Maradona, rather than Maradona himself, but it is still worth taking a moment just to recall how incredible he was during the latter stages of that tournament. After Argentina negotiated Uruguay by a single goal in the round of 16, there followed one of the most famous World Cup matches of all time when Argentina faced England in the quarter-final at the iconic Estadio Azteca in Mexico City. It was that game that launched Maradona into a worldwide phenomenon, following his two goals within five minutes. The first, of course, was the infamous 'Hand of God' goal, scored by jumping with England goalkeeper Peter Shilton, punching the ball into the net, and wheeling away in celebration, his actions unnoticed by either referee or linesman. The second was one of the greatest goals of all time when, receiving the ball in his own half, Maradona proceeded to beat half of the England team before rounding Shilton and slotting the ball home – a goal of pure genius.

The semi-final against Belgium saw Maradona score twice again, the first a beautiful run and flick with the outside of his foot, the second a dribble past three defenders into the penalty area before scoring while falling off balance, leading his side to a 2-0 victory. That led to a meeting with West Germany in the final, where Maradona was more subdued due to the close attentions of Lothar Matthäus. A two-goal Argentina lead was wiped out by two German goals in the 74th and 81st minutes, before, with just six minutes remaining, Maradona got loose for just a second. It was enough time to hit a perfectly weighted through ball for Jorge Burruchaga to break the offside trap and score the winning goal.

Argentina were champions of the world and Diego Maradona was now a global superstar, finally delivering on all the promise he had shown in bursts up until that point with Boca Juniors, Barcelona and Napoli. His life would never again be the same – he was the player who had almost single-handedly (no pun intended!) delivered the ultimate trophy to his home nation. When he departed for the tournament, he was a hero to Neapolitans; when he returned to Italy, he was the best-known footballer on the planet. If his life had been under a microscope before, that was nothing compared to now.

* * *

Having delivered for the *Albiceleste*, what Neapolitans wanted to know now was could Maradona perform a similar miracle for them. With their steady improvement over the past two seasons, the next aim was to overcome Juventus and Roma to fight for the championship. But now they had the best player in the world, they could dream of payback. Also, having brought in Bruno Giordano the previous year, Napoli chairman Ferlaino continued to invest in new talent, strengthening the attack by signing Andrea Carnevale from Udinese, while bolstering the midfield by bringing in Fernando De Napoli from Avellino. An expanded squad was needed as Napoli now had European football to contend via the UEFA Cup.

Maradona's return as all-conquering hero saw him take the pitch for Napoli's season opener, away at Brescia, where just before half-time he gave fans a taste of what they could look forward to for the next nine months. Receiving the ball just outside the penalty area, man-marked, he chested the ball down, turned his marker and set off into the area, dribbling past another challenge before firing in the only goal of the match.

Four years since their last European competition appearance, Napoli entered the UEFA Cup, where they were drawn against Toulouse of France. Just three days after the Brescia game, so only Napoli's second competitive match of the season, the French club came to an expectant Stadio San Paolo, Napoli fans hoping for a deep run in Europe. The atmosphere was volcanic, both ends of the ground ignited ahead of kick-off by red flares, more resembling

Mordor than Naples. To everyone's surprise, Toulouse proved much stiffer opposition than expected. They frustrated Napoli, keeping the first half goalless, until Carnevale finally made the breakthrough after 55 minutes, heading in a cross from Bagni at the far post to give *Gli Azzurri* the lead and set off another eruption of fire across the stands. A second goal wouldn't come, however, allowing Toulouse to take a narrow deficit with them back to France.

Two weeks later, the two teams lined up for the second leg. Maradona was captain, giving an impromptu display of his ball-juggling skills as he waited for the kick-off. As the whistle went, he took the ball forward, only to be wiped out by a cynical foul after just three seconds – Toulouse were obviously trying to get inside his head from the start, while in true 1980s fashion no yellow card was deemed necessary. After just 15 minutes, a well-worked move down the right led to a cross that was scrambled within the Napoli penalty box before being struck home by Yannick Stopyra, putting Toulouse even on aggregate. The score remained unchanged after 90 minutes, meaning penalties were required to settle the tie.

Toulouse went first and Stopyra saw his attempt blaze over the bar, after which Giordano converted to give Napoli the early advantage. The next four penalties were scored to keep Napoli ahead. Toulouse's fourth penalty fell to Jean-Jacques Marx, who coolly slotted it into the corner, before Salvatore Bagni saw his shot saved by Toulouse keeper Philippe Bergeroo, bringing it back to all level after four penalties apiece. It would come down to two Argentines, as first Alberto Tarantini scored for Toulouse, leaving Maradona needing to convert to avoid elimination. Among a cacophony of whistles, Maradona struck to the keeper's right. It hit the inside of the post, bounced back against the keeper and away from the goal. Napoli had been felled at the first fence; a devastated Diego surrounded by celebrating Toulouse players. Napoli's focus would now have to turn 100 per cent to domestic competition.

By the seventh week of the season, Napoli were top of Serie A, and from that point on *Gli Azzurri* were on fire. Going into the new year, they were unbeaten over 13 league matches, Maradona having scored five times, and that run included a statement victory over Juventus, 3-1 in Turin. After a 3-1 defeat to Fiorentina in Florence in January, Napoli then went on another eight-game unbeaten streak, winning six, before losing away at Inter. They had retained the top spot in Serie A during this whole time – 17 weeks of sitting atop the standings – with the main competition coming from Juventus, their next opponents, at the Stadio Sao Paolo. This could be the championship decider, the key game that would decide whether Napoli would continue their season dominance or Juventus could apply enough pressure to break them.

The Napoli faithful filled the stadium, undergoing all their famous superstitious rituals. Never had they been this close to a potential championship. As the crowd whipped themselves into a frenzy, Maradona waited to kick off, bouncing in anticipation while clad in that iconic sky-blue shirt sponsored by Buitoni. Juventus included Michel Platini, now in his fifth season with *I Bianconeri*, and Michael Laudrup, the Danish midfielder, part of the 'Danish Dynamite' team that had so captivated world football over the past four years.

With just 14 minutes gone, Napoli scored from a free kick around 15 metres outside the Juve penalty area, Juventus keeper Stefano Tacconi allowing Alessandro Renica's low shot to squirm through his grasp. Juventus equalised five minutes into the second half through Aldo Serena but Napoli's response was swift and scruffy. Maradona crossed the ball into the danger area, where it eventually fell to midfielder Francesco Romano to slide home. The final whistle blew to signal a famous victory. Napoli remained top, in touching distance of their first-ever Scudetto, with just six games remaining. It had been a statement win.

A shock third loss of the season, away to Hellas Verona, increased nerves but the remaining four games of the season became the Andrea Carnevale show. The run-in commenced with the visit of Milan, Napoli's second stiff test within a month and the hardest remaining hurdle to surmount in their championship bid. Maradona showed himself to be in the mood early on, dribbling and weaving with impudence, but Milan had the better of the early opportunities. Then, after 33 minutes, a cross into the box fell perfectly to Carnevale at the back post, and he powered his header home, giving Napoli a priceless lead.

As half-time approached, it appeared that Napoli would go in with their precious one-goal advantage, until a moment of pure

Diego magic that doubled the lead. Bruno Giordano received the ball on the left wing and cut towards the middle, before looking up and seeing Maradona making a run towards the area. Hitting a perfect lofted pass, the ball fell right at Maradona's feet while at full pace with the keeper rushing out to meet him. With one touch, Maradona rounded the Milan keeper before slotting home just ahead of the defenders sliding back to intercept. It was a goal fit to win a championship and beat one of Italy's best teams. Milan got one goal back in the second half but Napoli held on for a famous victory.

The Scudetto was within sight – just three games remained. First was an away trip to picturesque Como, where Napoli suffered a scare as their opponents took a surprise lead, before Carnevale again came to the rescue, equalising to secure a point, meaning Napoli needed just one more to be crowned champions.

So it was back to Napoli, to play a struggling Fiorentina in front of a frenzied crowd. Fans poured to the stadium, traffic grinding to a halt near to the ground, gridlocked, but no one cared – it was a party atmosphere. The game was scheduled as a 4pm kick-off but the gates opened at midday and just 15 minutes later all tickets had been sold out. Once inside, the noise was deafening. Outside the stadium, Naples was a ghost town, the whole population seemingly in or around the ground.

Just before the half-hour mark, Maradona slotted a ball from midfield to Carnevale, who took it on the run, shook off a marker, exchanged a beautiful one-two and slid the ball home. As half-time approached, Napoli gave away a free kick on the edge of their own area, which Roberto Baggio curled around the wall and into the bottom corner, his first-ever Serie A goal. The second half saw both sides create chances but then all eyes turned to the referee as the final seconds counted down. After what felt like an eternity, he raised his whistle to his lips and Naples exploded into a paroxysm of unbridled joy. For the first time in their history, SSC Napoli were Italian champions.

Napoli flags were waved around the bouncing stadium, filled with smoke, noise and flame, as press and photographers spilled onto the pitch, mainly congregating around Maradona. Eventually the players broke away, heading around the running track on a lap of honour, almost overcome with emotion. Maradona stood like a god, arms outstretched to the Napoli faithful who had adopted him as one of them. An interviewer managed to grab an emotional Diego for a moment to ask his thoughts:

> Diego: This is the greatest moment in my life, honestly, because I've won a few things, but …
>
> Interviewer: You're the World Champion!
>
> Diego: No, the problem is that I didn't win it in my country, you see? They took away my chance to be a part of Argentina's victory in 1978, in my country, that's why this is the most important celebration of my life …
>
> Interviewer: What does Naples mean to you now?
>
> Diego: It's my home, my home for sure.

Fans surged back into the centre of town where the noise from honking car horns was ear-splitting. In John Foot's excellent *Calcio*, he states: 'By 7:30 along the sea front … there was a single wave of Napoli flags, a long singing, dancing, jumping blue snake.' Old, young, male, female danced in the streets clad in blue and white to a backdrop of flares and firecrackers, making the town look like a war zone, fans atop of buses, while motorcycles buzzed maniacally around. Every surface was blue and white – even dogs were dressed in Napoli colours – as fountains became makeshift baths, fans from seven to 70 dancing in the streets. A famous shot showed a banner placed outside a cemetery, which read: 'E non sanno chese sò perso', translated as 'You don't know what you missed', for all those deceased relatives that had followed Napoli for so long but never saw them victorious.

The festivities would continue until the start of the next season – the city characterised by impromptu street parties, free food and fireworks. It was also during this period that the famous murals of Maradona began to appear on building walls, some even comparing him to the patron saint of Naples, San Gennaro.

One cannot underestimate what winning their first-ever Scudetto meant for the city and people of Naples. It's a one-club city, unlike Rome or Milan, so everyone supports the team, from the highest politicians to shop owners and street cleaners. For so long, they had been looked down upon by the cities of the north, scorned as those provincial southerners who were considered backward in their ways. It was viewed as a poor club in a poverty-stricken city. And that's part of the reason why they took Maradona to their hearts so strongly. He presented himself as a streetwise rogue, a kid who had been raised in a shanty town in Buenos Aires and fought his way to the top through both skill and cunning. He was like them – a fighter who had beaten the system.

It could be argued that, although he probably had no idea at the time of signing, Napoli and Maradona were a perfect match. Remember that when Maradona joined Napoli, they had only just avoided relegation, and now three seasons on they were lifting the Scudetto – he had pushed, improved and inspired the players around him to lift their game with his presence. He's sometimes thought of as a luxury player but for three years he was nothing of the sort – he worked hard to help Napoli achieve that Scudetto. Maradona himself wrote:

> We built Napoli from the bottom: it was proper workmanship. The Scudetto belonged to the whole city, and the people began to realise that there was no reason to be afraid: that it's not the one with the most money who wins but the one who fights the most, who wants it the most.

It is important to remember when discussing Maradona and his achievements at Napoli that he was playing against some of the toughest defenders in the world. Players would think nothing of going right through the back of an opponent, as well as employing various dark arts to rile and provoke. So Maradona being top scorer for Napoli this season with ten goals was a much better achievement than it may sound. And Maradona tended to receive more 'attention' than most on the pitch.

If Neapolitans thought the Scudetto was reason to celebrate, their lives became even better just a month later when Napoli stepped out to contest the Coppa Italia in a two-legged affair against Atalanta. Napoli had won all 11 games en route to the final, with Giordano netting nine and Maradona another seven. The first leg was at the Stadio San Paolo, where three second-half goals in the space of just ten minutes saw Napoli as good as clinch the cup. Six days later, Napoli weathered the storm in Bergamo before a late goal by Giordano sealed the deal, maintaining their 100 per cent record.

Napoli had clinched the double – Scudetto and Coppa Italia – to underline their dominance of the 1986/87 season. It turned out to be just another excuse to continue the party.

* * *

When the celebrations finally ended after two months, the collective hangover having worn off, with hundreds of newborns in Naples christened Diego and Diega, Ferlaino turned his attention to further bolstering his squad ahead of the 1987/88 season. His gaze turned to Brazil, where a young striker by the name of Careca had been lighting up the league for São Paulo, scoring 54 goals in 67 appearances, helping his team win the Brazilian championship in 1986 while being voted Brazilian Footballer of the Year. He would be placed into the attack, along with Giordano and Maradona, where they would go on to earn the nickname 'Ma-Gi-Ca'.

The obvious benefit from winning their first Scudetto was that Napoli could look forward to playing in the European Cup for the first time. There was great anticipation as to who would be their first-round opponents. Back in the 1980s there was no seeding in the competition – 32 teams went into the hat from around the continent and were randomly drawn against one another. Anyone could draw anyone – in theory the champions of Spain could draw the champions of Italy in the first round and one of them would be immediately eliminated. And that's exactly what befell Napoli, to their horror – paired up against the mighty Real Madrid. Napoli, playing their first-ever European Cup tie, against Real Madrid, in their 100th, in the first leg at the Bernabéu.

It was a draw that would have a profound effect on European football. While many neutrals salivated at the idea of these two heavyweights clashing, many others saw the madness of such an arrangement, including one Silvio Berlusconi, who couldn't believe that one of the favourites would be forced out at so early a stage. He had recently become the owner of AC Milan, saving them from bankruptcy, and was horrified that first-round elimination could befall his new toy in the future. It placed the idea in his head of a European Super League, something that Berlusconi championed and, although never realised to date, did provide the blueprint for the future Champions League.

The tie also had another peculiar quirk. The previous year's European Cup had seen Real Madrid make it to the semi-finals, where they were drawn against Bayern Munich. Having lost the first leg in Munich 4-1, the atmosphere in the second leg soon turned ugly, and after just a few minutes French referee Michel Vautrot had to suspend the game for several minutes due to objects being thrown onto the pitch, including golf balls. When the game finally got back underway, Real Madrid were eliminated, before salt was added to their wounds by UEFA imposing that their next European home game would have to be played behind closed doors. And so it was that when Napoli travelled to Madrid on 16 September 1987 for the first leg, no fans were there to see it.

This was a Real Madrid team that had just won the Spanish league for the second year running, having also won the UEFA Cup in 1985 and 1986, before that European Cup semi-final exit to Bayern Munich. It contained Emilio Butragueño, Míchel and Rafael Martín Vázquez, all graduates of Real's youth academy, La Fábrica. Within the strange atmosphere of near silence, Real Madrid took the lead through a penalty after 18 minutes, converted by Míchel, before Fernando De Napoli had the misfortune to score an own goal 14 minutes from time, giving Real a two-goal advantage to take to Naples.

Two weeks later, the teams reconvened in front of over 83,000 rabid fans, buoyed by the return of Careca to the starting line-up. Unlike the eerie first leg, the stadium was a cauldron of noise and colour, blue, green and white smoke billowing around at kick-off. While Napoli fans could cheer the return of Careca, Real fans were also cheered by the return of their ace marksman, the Mexican Hugo Sánchez, who had been suspended for the first leg.

The match started at a furious pace as Napoli took the game to their opponents, looking for an early breakthrough, and after just nine minutes they got it – a cross found Careca, whose second attempted header fell to defender Giovanni Francini. His header was saved, but Francini bundled in the rebound. The stadium exploded in celebration.

Napoli continued to dominate the first half, although suffering one scare when Sánchez went close with one of his trademark overhead kicks. The best chances fell to Careca, who had a golden chance to double the lead when he ran on to a low cross in the six-yard box, only to see his shot well saved by Real's keeper Francisco Buyo. Then, just as half-time approached, disaster struck for Napoli. Míchel intercepted the ball in midfield and played it first time to Sánchez. Looking up, the Mexican saw Butragueño setting off on a run into the area on the blind side. Holding the ball just long enough, Sánchez slipped a perfect pass through to allow 'the Vulture' to beat the offside trap, and he did the rest, chipping over the onrushing keeper. It was a devastating blow to Napoli, who had been so assertive for 44 minutes, giving Real Madrid a vital away goal. Requiring three goals in the second half was always going to be a tough task, and so it proved as there were no further goals. So just like that, Napoli's European Cup dream ended before it had even really begun, falling victim to the vagaries of the European Cup knockout format.

Once again it was back to the league, where Napoli had started with a bang, winning their first three games. With focus now on domestic competition, Napoli continued to fly, going unbeaten through to the new year, winning nine and drawing the other three, with Maradona receiving scoring support from both Careca and Giardino. They sat on top of the standings throughout this period, with the only significant challengers being Milan, and it was to the San Siro that Napoli travelled to kick off 1988, facing the *Rossoneri* in a vital head-to-head.

After just ten minutes, Napoli continued their hot form with a Careca goal, but they then faced their first setback of the season when Ruud Gullit set up an equaliser for Angelo Colombo, before a solo effort by Pietro Paolo Virdis five minutes later gave Milan the lead. After the interval, Gullit rounded Napoli keeper Claudio Garella for Milan's third before Roberto Donadoni put the icing on the cake with a fourth, helped by a Garella howler.

It was Napoli's first league loss of the season and against the one team that could challenge them for the title, but they were still top of the standings. Shaking off the disappointment, they then went on a seven-game winning streak, with the 'Ma-Gi-Ca' combination firing in 13 goals over the run. With two thirds of the season done, Napoli were still top of Serie A, five points ahead of Milan. Just ten games left, and everything was pointing towards a second successive Scudetto.

Napoli suffered a wobble when Roma came to the Stadio San Paolo and left with a 2-1 victory but then two wins and two draws saw them stabilise. Their points gap over Milan was reduced by just one point over the five games, so they were still in great shape with only five matches remaining. But then the wheels came off the bus in spectacular fashion, leading to a host of conspiracy theories that still exist to this day.

* * *

It all began with a trip to Turin on 17 April 1988 to face fifth-placed Juventus. After 19 minutes, Antonio Cabrini headed Juve into the lead from a corner, which is how it still stood at half-time. The second half saw Napoli pressurise, before ex-Liverpool legend Ian Rush scored a second and Luigi De Agostini converted a penalty to give Juve a 3-0 lead. Careca did get a consolation goal back, but it was too little, too late.

With their lead now two points, Napoli next went to eighth-place Verona, where they came away with a draw courtesy of a Maradona goal. But with Milan winning the *Derby della Madonnina* 2-0, Napoli's lead was now just a precarious single point with three games remaining. And as fate would have it, the next match was Napoli at home to Milan – a game that had now become a virtual title decider. All eyes within Italy turned to Naples to watch the great Maradona and Careca battle reigning Ballon d'Or winner Gullit and Marco van Basten – they would not be disappointed as a classic match materialised.

Maradona had made his thoughts on the game clear beforehand, stating: 'I don't want to see a single Milan flag at the San Paolo. We are at home and for them it must be like a graveyard. Here they must die. I want to see the San Paolo all blue.' With so much at stake, it was a cagey start to the match as both sides shadowboxed, until nine minutes before half-time when Carlo Ancelotti went on a lung-busting run through the heart of the Napoli midfield. Brought down close to the penalty area, the resulting free kick was deflected into the path of Pietro Paolo Virdis, who slid Milan into the lead. Napoli needed a response before half-time and, just before the break, they got a free kick of their own just outside the Milan area. Cometh the hour, cometh the man – up stepped Maradona to hit it perfectly into the top corner. So, all square and all to play for.

The second half saw Van Basten join the fray from the bench and, 21 minutes into the half, Milan regained the lead, Gullit firing a perfect cross for Virdis to head home. Napoli's season was collapsing and, as they threw men forward seeking an equaliser, they left themselves open to the counter. A throw from the Milan keeper started a move that saw Gullit pick up the ball in his own half and run at the Napoli defence. He remained unchallenged all the way into the penalty area where, faced by the onrushing Napoli keeper, he simply slipped it to an unmarked Van Basten, who couldn't miss. Eight minutes that looked like upending the whole title race.

The drama was not yet over, though, as Careca scored with a header just two minutes later, giving Napoli 12 minutes to find a precious equaliser. But the Milan defence held strong and as the final whistle sounded their players fell in a heap of celebration, the title now up for grabs thanks primarily to an outstanding display by Gullit. Napoli, after 27 successive weeks at the top of Serie A, had surrendered that spot for the first time, with Milan leapfrogging them with a one-point advantage and just two games left. The game had a crushing psychological effect on Napoli, whose only hope now was that Milan would have to face fourth-place Juventus next, while they would be travelling to Florence to take on ninth-place Fiorentina. The famously superstitious Neapolitans would be lighting many votives over the coming days.

Napoli had pushed Maradona through the previous games despite an injury but were going to have to pay for that decision, unable to field him for the vital last two matches. He would only be able to watch and pray from the bench.

Juventus travelled to the San Siro and held Milan to a goalless draw, meaning the path to the Scudetto was reopened for Napoli, providing they could come away from Florence with a victory. But they got off to the worst possible start, conceding after just eight minutes. Ciro Ferrara brought Napoli back into the game after 24 minutes and that's how the first half ended, all square.

Fiorentina continued to dominate after half-time and retook the lead. Then things got even worse for Napoli as *La Viola* grabbed their third. Napoli were now staring at a third defeat in four games and, although Alessandro Renica pulled one back in the last minute, it wasn't enough. Napoli had taken one point from the last possible eight and now trailed Milan by two points with the same goal difference. They had to win at home to fourth-place Sampdoria and hope that Como could pull off a shock at home to Milan.

The Napoli fans came out to encourage a miracle but, after just two minutes, that began to fade as news came through that Virdis had struck early for the Milanese. Five minutes later, Carnevale headed Napoli into the lead to provide a glimmer of hope, and the two games remained that way until half-time. Almost immediately after the second half kicked off, Salvatore Giunta drew Como level, allowing the superstitious Napoli *tifosi* to think maybe, just maybe, it could happen. But just as that thought entered their heads, Napoli once again went into full self-destruct mode. Firstly, Luca Pellegrini hit a long-range screamer into the top corner to pull Sampdoria level, before an emerging young striker by the name of Gianluca Vialli grabbed his tenth league goal of the season with 23 minutes remaining. And with that goal died Napoli's dream of successive Scudetti. They had blown the 1987/88 title in stunning fashion.

* * *

To this day, the 1987/88 season creates tales of suspicion and conspiracy theories. Napoli had strengthened from the previous year with the 'Ma-Gi-Ca' trio in full force, they had been eliminated early from European competition, allowing them to focus solely on the league, in which they had been flying. In fact, at the turn of the year, they were unbeaten and had only trailed for a total of 29 minutes. But then they had taken just one point from a possible ten over the last five matches. Obviously, anytime you're closing in on a league title there's pressure, which can get to players, but this team had been there the previous year and coped – they had experience of closing out the season successfully. So why failure this time around?

One of the theories that has received most attention over time is that of the murky world of the criminal underworld within Naples. Since the 17th century, the city had been under the influence of the Camorra crime syndicate, and the 1980s were a particularly brutal era of their impact. The Camorra derived their revenue from a variety of sources, one of the most lucrative being illegal gambling, known in Italy as *totonero*. This had been the cause of a huge scandal within Italian football during 1980, when Paolo Rossi was notably caught up within the disgrace. State-run gambling allowed citizens to bet on football, but it was wrapped up as *totocalcio*, whereby you could only bet on correctly picking the outcome of 12 matches, betting on any single game being prohibited. For single-game bets, punters had to turn to the *totonero*, which in Naples was run by the Camorra.

It was reported that the people of Naples had placed a lot of money early in the season on Napoli retaining the Scudetto and, as that looked increasingly likely, the Camorra stood to lose a serious amount. So did the Camorra influence some players to 'throw' the Scudetto? There were some incidents reported in the press towards the end of the season, such as Maradona's car being vandalised and Salvatore Bagni having his house broken into twice, which some saw as possible links.

Maradona himself said that he didn't believe that any players had been compromised, stating in his autobiography that 'there was talk of the Camorra, of *totonero*, the Italian football betting system. I couldn't stand being accused and I was willing to leave Napoli if I thought there were any players who sold out. I don't accept it today and I didn't accept it then.' He had a much more down to earth explanation for what he felt went wrong: 'Bianchi, the wanker, had started experimenting and left Giordano out, and everything went to shit.'

It was true that Bianchi had left Giordano out of the vital Milan match, and also true that he had faced a coup due to this, with four players – Moreno Ferrario, Salvatore Bagni, Garella and Giordano – signing a letter calling for his removal after the Fiorentina defeat. Bianchi had also decided to play Maradona during Coppa Italia games, increasing the strain on his crumbling body and his over-reliance on cortisone. Ferlaino sided with his coach, however, and the four signees left the club over the summer. Unfortunately, that created tension between Ferlaino and Maradona, as the Argentine felt that Bianchi was to blame for the collapse and should be punished rather than the four players. It was the start of worsening relations between Ferlaino and Maradona, the president realising that his star player now held the balance of power with fans in the relationship.

Whatever the cause of Napoli's late-season collapse, they still ended the season in second place, earning a spot in the following season's UEFA Cup. A second Scudetto had been so close – but objectively it was still another great season – the question would be how they would react to such a disappointment during 1988/89.

* * *

The summer saw the addition of another Brazilian to the Napoli squad – Alemão from Atlético Madrid – a strong yet technically gifted player, excelling as a defensive midfielder who could start attacks after winning back the ball deep. The squad was set for another tilt at the title, again with Milan as likely foes.

The first 11 games leading up to the end of 1988 saw Napoli regain their mojo, winning eight, while losing only two, away at Lecce and Roma. There were some notable early victories: thrashing Pescara 8-2, with a hat-trick from Carnevale and two goals apiece for Maradona and Careca; winning 5-3 away at Juventus, including a Careca hat-trick; and battering champions Milan 4-1 at home, with a double from Careca and a Maradona goal.

Careca especially was on fire, scoring nine goals across the 11 matches. But Napoli found themselves second at the end of this run. How could that be after such a strong start? The answer lay in Milan, but not with AC Milan, but instead their neighbours Inter. They were unbeaten over the same period, winning nine and drawing the other two. This was an Inter managed by the legendary Giovanni Trapattoni, powered by two Germans in Lothar Matthäus and Andi Brehme, fired by the goals of Italian striker Aldo Serena. The 1988/89 season was being dominated by these two sides.

For Napoli though, the season wasn't just about the Scudetto. Having been eliminated so early from the previous season's European Cup, this time they were determined to have a decent tilt at the UEFA Cup. By the end of December, they had progressed to the quarter-finals, courtesy of eliminating PAOK of Greece, Lokomotive Leipzig from behind the Iron Curtain and Bordeaux of France. However, from now the opposition was going to get much stiffer.

January and February saw Napoli unbeaten in Serie A across eight games, winning five and drawing three, with one of the draws being at home to rivals Inter, who also enjoyed a strong couple of months, remaining top of the standings despite their first defeat of the season in a 4-3 thriller in Florence. The end of February saw Inter just two points ahead of Napoli. It was looking like a two-horse race.

March brought about the quarter-finals of the UEFA Cup, in which Napoli had been drawn against rivals Juventus. The first leg in Turin saw over 46,000 cheering on *La Vecchia Signora*. An early goal from Pasquale Bruno and an own goal right on half-time by Giancarlo Corradini gave Juventus a precious two-goal lead to take back to Naples two weeks later. With a two-goal deficit and no away goal, the odds were stacked in Juve's favour, but still over 83,000 turned up to see whether Napoli could perform a minor miracle.

Napoli looked to have got off to a bad start when Michael Laudrup scored, only for it to be ruled out for offside. But this early scare provoked a reaction from Napoli, who were awarded a penalty ten minutes later. Maradona stepped up to send the keeper the wrong way and give his side just the start they were hoping for. They continued to dominate the first half, and Carnevale rifled in a second just before the break to send the Napoli fans into ecstasy. Half-time and all square on aggregate.

It would remain that way after 90 minutes, meaning extra time at the San Paolo, where both sides struggled to create clear chances. As the 120th minute came along, with fans starting to prepare for the agony of penalties, Carnevale broke down the right before sending in a cross that was headed in by defender Alessandro Renica. Napoli had snatched victory over their northern rivals with a last-minute winner. As the Juventus players slumped to the ground, Renica ran the length of the pitch in celebration, ending up hugging his keeper. Almost immediately the final whistle sounded, allowing the players and fans to break into wild partying, a place in the semi-finals in April clinched.

Before those semi-finals, however, Juventus managed to gain some revenge. Travelling to Napoli for a league game on 2 April, they inflicted only the third defeat for Napoli all season, coming away with a 4-2 victory. With Inter on a hot streak, they now held a six-point advantage over the southerners and, given their form, it was hard to see them losing that lead. It seemed that Napoli's season now boiled down to the UEFA Cup, as well as the Coppa

Italia, where they were due to play Sampdoria in the final in June.

* * *

The UEFA Cup semi-finals were German-dominated, with Bayern Munich and Stuttgart representing the West, while Dynamo Dresden flew the flag for the East. Napoli received probably the toughest draw, Bayern Munich, with the first leg to be played in Naples. On a wet Neapolitan night, it took 40 minutes for Careca to fire Napoli ahead. They doubled their lead 15 minutes into the second half through Carnevale and it ended 2-0, giving Napoli an advantage to take back to Munich, with a first-ever European final in sight.

As the teams warmed up for the second leg, there occurred a moment that would live on in the memory longer than the game itself. 'Live is Life' was a popular song by Austrian band Opus, released in 1984, and it was playing across the Munich speakers. Maradona couldn't resist, proceeding to juggle a ball in time to the music, in perfect harmony as thousands of fans looked on in admiration. It was a display of incredible coolness before a major match – one that has attained cult status through YouTube clips.

The first half saw both keepers make incredible saves as well as Maradona having a goal chalked off for offside to keep the match goalless at half-time. The breakthrough finally came in the 61st minute when poor Bayern defending allowed Maradona to roll the ball across for Careca to tap in. It was the vital away goal, meaning Bayern now needed four goals to eliminate Napoli.

Bayern gave themselves a flicker of hope, equalising two minutes later, but in pushing for four goals, they were always going to leave gaps at the back. And sure enough, with 14 minutes remaining, a fast break saw Maradona put Careca through on goal once again. He completed his brace with a low drive into the corner. There was still time for Bayern to grab an equaliser but as the final whistle sounded Napoli were off to their first-ever European final, driven by the ruthlessness of Maradona and Careca. Leaving the pitch, they found out that their opponents were to be Stuttgart, with the first leg to be played in Naples on 3 May.

As the first leg of the final approached, Inter maintained their league advantage over Napoli, six points with just eight games remaining. Try as they might, Napoli just couldn't reduce that deficit, Inter still only having lost just once all season, so Napoli's full attention turned to European silverware and the visit of Stuttgart.

Unlike Napoli, who had to eliminate both Juventus and Bayern Munich to reach the final, Stuttgart's progress had been easier, their main hurdles having been Real Sociedad in the quarter-finals and Dynamo Dresden in the semis. The Germans had been powered by the scoring prowess of Karl Allgöwer and Fritz Walter but also included a young striker who had been making quite the impression in the Bundesliga for the prior four seasons, having scored 75 goals for Stuttgart over that time. That striker's name was Jürgen Klinsmann but, thankfully for Napoli, he wouldn't be available for the first leg of the final.

Over 81,000 packed the San Paolo to witness Napoli's first-ever appearance in a European final, a testament to just how far they had progressed over the last five years. Since the start of the 1970s, Italian teams had only won four European competitions, three of which had been landed by Juventus, including the tainted 1985 European Cup. Italians had watched on the sidelines as Dutch, German and British teams had dominated, until now, when Napoli had the resources and the strength to challenge for Italy once again. It was a seminal moment for Calcio.

After just 17 minutes, Stuttgart were gifted a goal when Napoli keeper Giuliano Giuliani could only parry a free kick into the roof of the net. A deathly silence fell around the stadium. With no further goals before the break, the second half kicked off in a cloud of blue smoke, flares burning around the periphery of the pitch, Napoli fans desperate for their team to get back into the game. They started the half at a furious pace, creating several early chances that they just couldn't convert, Maradona in the thick of everything. Then came a moment of controversy that changed the game.

The ball was crossed into the Stuttgart area, where Carnevale won the header, the ball falling to Maradona. The Argentine took a moment to bring it under control before his shot was deflected out by the hand of German defender Günther Schäfer. It was handball and the referee awarded a penalty, but the slow-motion replay showed that Maradona's touch to initially control the ball had also involved his hand – probably the 'Hand of God' intervening once again.

Despite German protests, Maradona took responsibility for the kick, calmly sending Immel the wrong way to give Napoli a much-needed equaliser.

Napoli pressed on, aware of the importance of taking a lead back to Stuttgart. Just as it appeared that time was running out, a moment of Maradona magic saw him beat a defender before crossing for Careca to bundle the ball home. Napoli had managed to turn the game around in the second half to take a slim advantage back to Germany, with Maradona involved in both goals, albeit with a slight whiff of deception about the first.

With the second leg two weeks later, Napoli returned to league action with an away game at Bologna. Following on from his midweek heroics, Maradona declared himself unfit on the eve of the game, citing a recurrent back injury. This was repeated a month later before another away game, at Ascoli, a stomach complaint this time being cited. With Napoli's league campaign fizzling out, it seemed like Maradona was crying off some games, heightening the tension between him and Bianchi. The suspicion was amplified the next weekend when Napoli played Pisa at home and Maradona asked to be substituted with a muscle strain after just 17 minutes. To his surprise, the move resulted in whistling around the stadium. An enraged Maradona swore after the match that he was ready to leave Naples in protest.

But first, on 17 May 1989, Napoli travelled to the south-west corner of Germany, where the big news of the night was the return of Klinsmann to the Stuttgart starting XI. The Germans started like a team possessed, tearing into Napoli, but, completely against the run of play, Alemão burst through the Stuttgart defence and poked the ball past Immel to give Napoli a vital lead and an away goal. Stuttgart immediately returned to peppering Napoli's goal and after 27 minutes their breakthrough came from a corner, as Klinsmann rose to head in at the far post. The emerging German superstar had brought Stuttgart back into the tie.

With half-time approaching, Maradona again changed the game with a moment of magic. A long pass was fired over to him, as he stood out wide. The logical thing to do was to control the ball and whip in a cross, but Maradona liked to defy logic. Watching the ball fall, he instead powered an incredible header, acting as a cross into the box, which Ciro Ferrara thrashed into the goal. It was a great piece of improvisation that gave Napoli a 4-2 aggregate advantage at the break, and two away goals. Stuttgart would need to score three unanswered second-half goals to prevent the UEFA Cup travelling to southern Italy.

Once again Stuttgart pressed but Napoli held resolute. With half an hour remaining, they took advantage of Stuttgart committing men forward to launch a swift counter-attack, which saw Maradona burst forward before setting up Careca to slide home a third. The travelling Neapolitans started the party, safe in the knowledge that Stuttgart were unlikely to score four in the next 30 minutes.

They did have a go, though. With 20 minutes remaining, a Gaudino shot was deflected into his own goal by the wonderfully named Fernando De Napoli, after which Stuttgart scored again in the last minute through an Olaf Schmäler header. But it was to be Napoli's night, wild scenes breaking out at the final whistle, manager Bianchi celebrating with his backroom staff as the players hugged on the pitch. Bianchi, who had suffered so much tension at the club, could finally permit himself some pleasure. The trophy was handed to an elated Maradona to raise into the German sky, signifying that Napoli had won their first-ever European trophy, an Italian team once again rising to the pinnacle of the continental game. The pain of the previous season's late-season collapse had been erased to some degree.

* * *

With the UEFA Cup in the trophy cabinet, Maradona told Ferlaino that he felt he had now done all he could for Napoli. It was time for him to move on and seek new challenges, preferably away from the glare of the Italian league and media. He reminded Ferlaino that, before the Bayern Munich tie, Ferlaino had told him that 'if we win the UEFA Cup, I promise I'll let you go to Marseille'. But now Ferlaino was insisting that Maradona honour his contract, which ran until 1993. 'I wanted to smash the [UEFA] cup over his head,' wrote Maradona later.

The relationship between Ferlaino and Maradona deteriorated further as Maradona felt that Ferlaino was keeping him a prisoner in Naples against his will. His mood was worsened by the swirling rumours that he wasn't giving 100 per cent to the team anymore, dedicating more time instead to the Naples nightlife. He came out swinging against the Italian media, who just saw his rants as paranoia – there was no love lost between the two anymore.

The season ended with disappointment on the two domestic fronts. In the league, the key game towards the season's end was Napoli's trip to Inter, although at that time Inter virtually had the title sewn up, sitting seven points ahead of Napoli with just five games left. Inter won 2-1 to clinch the championship. Then Napoli's season ended with the two-leg Coppa Italia Final against Sampdoria, which saw Napoli take a 1-0 lead to Genoa after the first leg, before being swept away in the second leg 4-0.

So Napoli finished this historic season as runners-up in the league and Coppa Italia, but noble holders of European silverware. Once again, Italian football could stand proud, four years after the tragic events of Heysel. It was a season that demonstrated the firepower of Careca, Maradona and Carnevale, each scoring double figures across all competitions. Careca had an especially strong year with 25 goals, compared to Maradona's 12. It's easy to think of Napoli in the late 1980s as the Maradona story but, while he was the catalyst for all around him, they were by no means a one-man show as amply demonstrated by Careca in 1988/89.

The question facing this great team now was whether they could return to the pinnacle of Serie A during the following season, as well as attempting to retain the UEFA Cup. Milan and Inter had each pushed them into second place following on from that historic first Scudetto in 1986/87 – it was time for Napoli to push back again against the Milanese royalty.

* * *

The summer saw Maradona return to Buenos Aires for a break as his war of words with the Italian media escalated. His camp issued a statement that Maradona felt intimidated by the Napoli fans, especially during his substitution during the Pisa game, and that his sister's apartment had been broken into and one of his cars also damaged. If it was an attempt to appeal to Napoli supporters and regain their love, it failed – while they loved him for the success he had brought, his antics were beginning to irritate them. Maradona turned up late to pre-season training, leading to various explanations from differing sources. There were shades of his time at Barcelona resurfacing.

The season saw a new coach, as Ottavio Bianchi decided to call time on his successful spell in Naples and move on to a new challenge with Roma. Somewhat surprisingly, his replacement was announced as Alberto Bigon, who had succeeded in bringing AC Cesena back into Serie A in 1987 before narrowly keeping them up the following season. In wanting to break the two-year Milanese monopoly, Ferlaino dipped into the transfer market yet again. His next discovery would involve one of the most colourful, and infamous, characters in Italian football. It's at this stage when Luciano Moggi first enters our story.

Luciano Moggi was born into a working-class family near Siena and while he loved football as a child, he showed no aptitude for the game. Leaving school at 13, Moggi eventually found employment with Italy's state-owned railway company where, in the early 1970s, he met Juventus's managing director, Italo Allodi, who saw something in him and brought him to help with the club's scouting network. Moggi eventually fell out with Juventus's president Giampiero Boniperti, after which he landed at Roma, before spells as general director at Lazio and coordinating transfers at Torino.

On 22 June 1987, Ferlaino hired Moggi to look for talent for Napoli, and in 1989 he noticed a young striker playing for Serie C club Torres, based in Sardinia. The 5ft 6in forward had scored 11 goals during 1988/89 while still only 22 years old, technically gifted for his age with potential to develop into something valuable. He was signed for £2m and placed into the squad to understudy and learn from Maradona. The player's name was Gianfranco Zola. Napoli were ready to battle Milan and Inter again for the top spot.

Napoli started the season at a blistering pace, winning four and drawing two of their first six games, before their first major test when they hosted Milan at the Sao Paolo. Sweeping aside the *Rossoneri* with two goals from Carnevale and one from Maradona, Napoli climbed to the top of Serie A, vaulting over Inter. Napoli's next home game saw them take on Inter, where once again they were victorious, with a goal apiece from Careca and Maradona. They continued to hold the top spot throughout the rest of 1998, not losing until 30 December when Lazio defeated them 3-0 in Rome.

Things were not so straightforward in their defence of the UEFA Cup, however. After scraping past Sporting Lisbon on penalties and then narrowly eliminating Swiss side Wettingen, Napoli came up against Werder Bremen. A back-and-forth battle in Naples saw Bremen take a two-goal lead before Napoli pulled level, only for Bremen to grab a last-minute winner. Two weeks later, Bremen slaughtered Napoli back at the Weserstadion, inflicting a humiliating 5-1 defeat and aggregate 8-3 drubbing.

The next six Serie A games saw Napoli continue unbeaten before the crunch month of February, which would see successive away matches at first Milan and then Inter – two games that would have a huge influence on the Serie A title and both to be played at the famous San Siro. First up was the *Rossoneri* on a muddy afternoon that saw a goalless first half, after which Milan exploded, scoring three unanswered second-half goals. The result saw Milan take top spot from Napoli for the first time in 18 matchdays, albeit only on goal difference, meaning Napoli's game against Inter took on increased importance.

Things couldn't have started better – Careca scoring a fine solo goal after just seven minutes. The lead was maintained until half-time, despite heavy Inter pressure, but then, just like two weeks earlier, everything fell apart for Napoli in the second half. Firstly, Ferrara headed into his own goal just four minutes in, before Inter hit two more in quick succession. Three goals in the space of nine minutes and Napoli had lost two successive away games to their Milanese rivals. Eight games to go and Napoli now sat in second, two points behind Milan and just three ahead of Inter.

Napoli's next vital home game was against Juventus, where they got back on track with a 3-1 victory, Maradona stepping up with two goals. And then came an infamous trip to Bergamo to face mid-table Atalanta. Needing another win to maintain their momentum, it was scoreless with 15 minutes remaining. It was then that a coin entered folklore, kicking off a multitude of theories, depending which team you supported.

Standing near the touchline, Brazilian Alemão suddenly fell to the floor, holding his head. As the cameras zoomed in, bleeding could be seen, although it didn't look like a particularly nasty wound. It transpired that he had been hit by a coin thrown from the Atalanta stands, although the perpetrator was never identified. The Napoli physio, Salvatore Carmando, theatrically dabbed cotton wool on the area, which remained stubbornly white. But it seemed enough for him to insist that Alemão be rushed to hospital.

Under Serie A rules, the fact that a Napoli player had to leave the pitch due to the actions of the Atalanta fans meant that the game would be forfeited, and Napoli awarded a 2-0 win – a vital victory in the league run-in. With Milan suffering a goalless draw at Bologna, the extra point was huge and, unsurprisingly, Milan weren't happy. They appealed the decision, even hiring a speechreading professional to watch the footage, who claimed that Carmando had whispered to Alemão, 'Just stay down,' as he started to rise. Napoli officials insisted that Alemão had been genuinely injured, Carmando visiting the Brazilian in hospital and saying that his player couldn't even recognise him, so bad was the concussion.

Milan's appeal cut no ice with the Italian authorities, who stuck by the rules and awarded Napoli a vital 2-0 win, allowing them to draw level with Milan with three games remaining. The following weekend saw both teams win, Napoli beating Bari with a goal apiece from the deadly trio of Maradona, Carnevale and Careca. Next up for Napoli was a tricky away game in Bologna but there was never any danger as they swept into a 3-0 lead after just 15 minutes, Careca and Maradona again striking, before ending 4-2 winners, Alemão adding the fourth, having seemingly recovered from his concussion.

Meanwhile, Milan visited the beautiful city of Verona, its team lingering near the foot of the table. Despite Milan taking an early lead, Verona fought back to equalise, in a match where the *Rossoneri* had two penalty appeals turned down. As Milan's players became more frantic in search of the win, tempers rose to boiling point. First, Frank Rijkaard received a second yellow card and his marching orders, then Marco van Basten received a straight red. Milan had completely lost the plot, down to nine men with three minutes remaining when in need of a goal. Unsurprisingly, Verona went on to snatch a last-minute winner. To add insult to injury, there was still time for Milan defender Alessandro Costacurta to also get his marching orders.

Milan's defeat meant that Napoli only needed one point from their final match, at home against Lazio, to lift their second Scudetto. So, on 29 April 1990, a packed San Paolo came to see whether their heroes could do the unthinkable and win a second title. Lazio had nothing to play for – they were sitting exactly mid-table – but that also meant they had nothing to lose and could just enjoy the game.

If nerves were jangling, then they were soothed when Maradona floated a free kick into the Lazio area, headed home by Marco Baroni, one of only two goals he ever scored for Napoli. News came through from Milan that they had hit four second-half goals past Bari, giving them the superior goal difference. But provided Napoli didn't concede two goals, the trophy was theirs. And they didn't, the game petering out as both sides settled for the result. The referee took the ball from Napoli's goalkeeper, blew his whistle and cued the start of pandemonium. A giant Italian flag was carried around the stadium as fans balanced precariously on the edge of the stands, several feet above the seats below, cheering the players on. Napoli had secured a second Scudetto in four years.

What makes this achievement more remarkable is how Maradona even functioned during this season. He was now in his full alcohol-and-cocaine-fuelled existence, along with a colourful nightlife that rarely saw early nights. His modus operandi would be to play for Napoli on a Sunday and then party until the middle of the week, when he would then sweat out all toxins in training before the next match. His body was starting to look more ravaged, less slim, but he still produced moments that could take your breath away. He finished the season with 16 Serie A goals, placing him third in the scoring charts. It seemed that even a 75 per cent functioning Maradona was better than most mortals.

* * *

While Maradona was obviously the centre of attention, Napoli's success in winning the UEFA Cup in 1988 and then a second Scudetto in 1990 was not purely down to him. Football is a team sport and we've seen too often that simply buying a superstar does not guarantee success. Maradona needed skilful team-mates and he got that, primarily through Careca, who deserves much praise for his part in the Napoli success story.

Careca endeared himself quickly to the Napoli *tifosi*, striking up an immediate understanding with Maradona, where many others may have been overwhelmed by such a famous partner. Maradona was a genius at finding space in the midfield, allowing Careca to draw defenders before the Argentine played a killer pass for the Brazilian to convert. The speed with which Careca acclimatised to Italian football is demonstrated by his 18 goals across all tournaments in his first season, placing him second only behind Maradona in the Serie A goalscoring charts. The following season saw him improve further, banging in 27 across all tournaments as he became part of the UEFA Cup-winning side. It's very easy when talking of Napoli's success in the late 1980s to just think of Maradona, but Careca should be celebrated as well, along with many of their other team-mates.

No one knew at the time, but the 1989/90 Scudetto would represent the apex of Napoli and Maradona's relationship. Most Napoli *tifosi* probably believed that the good times would roll on endlessly. They had the best player in the world, they had a team of winners – what could possibly go wrong? The answer, sadly, was much.

Following on from the events at Italia '90 (see next chapter), Maradona returned to Napoli a changed man. The way he had been treated by the Italian public during the tournament was, for him, inexcusable. That resentment combined with his various addictions to start his career on a downward trajectory, beginning in 1990/91. His cocaine addiction was now becoming common knowledge, as well as the questionable company that he kept, primarily members of the Camorra with whom he had been photographed. Napoli's management had tried in vain to keep everything under wraps – but while they could try to monitor Maradona's behaviour, they couldn't change it. He had won them the Scudetto twice, he had won them European silverware, he was practically a deity in the eyes of the Napoli fans – in his own mind, Maradona was above the law and above regular player requirements. Like the Roman emperors of old, the rules did not apply to Diego.

Napoli got off to a horrible start that season, losing two of their opening three matches and drawing the other. After a first win, against Pisa, came three draws and two losses, leaving Napoli in

12th place. Maradona scored only twice during that period, both from the penalty spot, as his form dipped alarmingly. Thereafter, Napoli settled as a mid-table team, then their whole world turned upside-down.

The game itself was nothing special. Napoli scraped a 1-0 victory against Bari through a goal from the emerging Zola and, as usual, a player from each team was chosen for a drug test. Maradona was taken aside to provide a sample, which was sent off to the lab, and thoughts turned to Napoli's next game, away at Sampdoria. Their relatively poor form continued as Sampdoria thrashed them 4-1, Napoli's sole goal coming from the boot of Maradona with yet another penalty. And then came the news that shocked the footballing world.

On 29 March, the Italian Football Federation announced that Maradona's sample from the Bari match had tested positive for cocaine. A second test had been conducted, yielding the same result, and therefore Maradona was to be suspended from playing in Italy for up to two years. The ban was extended to apply within FIFA's jurisdiction, meaning Maradona was also ineligible to play for Argentina. The cocaine habit that Napoli management had tried so hard to hide was now public information – their star player had finally flown too close to the sun.

The news was sensational and immediately the world's media converged upon Maradona's Naples residence. Desperate to escape the frenzy, Diego slipped out and flew home to Argentina, facing a career in ruin. In his mind, it was all a conspiracy – after all, he had been taking cocaine for years, but the positive test came around after his 1990 World Cup vilification. Napoli's *tifosi* were in shock – their saviour had departed, leaving them to pick up the pieces. Napoli limped to the end of the season, powered now by Careca and Zola, but without Diego Armando Maradona – the thrill had gone.

Napoli haven't won another European trophy. It would take them another 22 years before they won more silverware, that being the Coppa Italia, and another 33 years to finally win a third Scudetto. One man may not make a team but, when Maradona left the city, they were never the same again. He had contributed to a golden six-year period when a fanbase had learned to dream once more, putting the southern Italian city into the limelight, rising from the shadows of their northern compatriots. A period when Napoli had shown that Italian football could once again win European silverware. It was a base that other Italian teams would build upon over the next decade.

NAPOLI (1984–1990)
UEFA Cup winners – 1988/89
Serie A champions – 1986/87, 1989/90
Coppa Italia winners – 1986/87

Chapter 6

Italia '90

*Maradona, Naples loves you but Italy is our
homeland.*

Diego in our hearts. Italy in our songs.

Banners displayed during Italy's semi-final clash against
Argentina in Naples

ZÜRICH – 19 May 1984. The FIFA Executive Committee meet
in the bucolic Swiss city to decide who should host the 1990 edition
of the World Cup. In those days, the tournament swapped back and
forth from Latin America to Europe, and 1990 was a European
turn, meaning that eight countries initially submitted bids: USSR,
Italy, Austria, England, France, Greece, West Germany and
Yugoslavia. Four withdrew shortly after the submission deadline,
leaving USSR, Italy, England and Greece, which a few months
later became just two: USSR and Italy. On the eve of voting, the
Soviets announced their boycott of the 1984 Olympics, so the next
day the 1990 World Cup was awarded by 11 votes to five to Italy.
The most prodigious tournament in world football was returning
to Italia for the first time since 1934, when they had won in front
of a watching Mussolini.

The timing was perfect. Serie A dominated world football as
anyone who was anyone strutted their stuff in Italy. The country was
the shining jewel of world football – and now all eyes would turn
to it again, making the country the centre of footballing attention.
But much of the glow of Italian club football had been provided by
bringing in overseas stars. For example, Napoli fielded Maradona
and Careca, Inter had Lothar Matthäus and Andreas Brehme, Roma
included Rudi Völler and Thomas Berthold, while Milan contained

Ruud Gullit, Marco van Basten and Frank Rijkaard. The question was whether such overseas talent was strengthening Italian clubs at a cost of homegrown talent? Was the Italian national team, rather than just the Italian league, among the world's best?

Hosting the tournament meant that Italy automatically qualified, so the squad was built over a series of friendlies. The coach was Azeglio Vicini, who had managed both Italy U23s and U21s before taking the reins of the senior team in 1986, replacing Enzo Bearzot. Under his watch, Italy had reached the semi-finals of the 1988 European Championship before being eliminated by the USSR. As the tournament approached, it became obvious that a strong Italian squad had a key weakness in attack, as just two goals in seven games ahead of the World Cup showed.

Elsewhere the Italian squad looked impressive, making them favourites in many eyes to win the World Cup on their home turf. Walter Zenga was the goalkeeping pick, while the defence was always Italy's strong spot, and continued to be with Franco Baresi, Giuseppe Bergomi, Riccardo Ferri and a young Paolo Maldini to pick from. The midfield contained the talents of Nicola Berti, Carlo Ancelotti, Roberto Donadoni and Fernando De Napoli, as well as the mercurial talents of Roberto Baggio.

The attack would rely upon Napoli's Andrea Carnevale as well as a young Gianluca Vialli, Roberto Mancini and Aldo Serena. That left one more spot to allocate for a striker. Surprisingly, Vicini's pick was a player who had only made his Italian debut three months ahead of the tournament, his only game for the *Azzurri* – a Sicilian striker who had played for Messina in Serie B until 1989 before moving to Juventus, where he had broken out by scoring 21 goals in all competitions for the Old Lady'across the 1989/90 season. The final attacking spot went to Salvatore 'Toto' Schillaci.

Italy were drawn into Group A as hosts and therefore top seed, paired with Czechoslovakia, Austria and USA, and all the *Azzurri*'s group games would be played at the Stadio Olimpico in front of a passionate Roman crowd. The World Cup kicked off with defending champions Argentina, led by Maradona, facing Cameroon, which resulted in a stunning loss for the South Americans as the Africans won by a single goal, despite ending the game with just nine men. As Italy lined up to face Austria in their opening game the following day, the Cameroon result must have been in their minds as a reminder not to take anything for granted.

Vicini decided to go with the known and dependable, starting Vialli and Carnevale up front, while keeping Baggio and Schillaci on the bench. Over 73,000 packed in to cheer on their beloved *Azzurri*, the atmosphere slightly muted by the presence of a running track separating the fans from the pitch, although the noise was still considerable. The first key chance fell to the Italians when Carnevale was played through by Vialli, only to see his shot saved by the feet of Austrian keeper Klaus Lindenberger. Vialli then had a great goalscoring opportunity when a loose back pass put him one-on-one with the keeper, but he poked it narrowly wide. Ancelotti next came close before Carnevale again missed a great chance, meaning the teams went in at half-time goalless before a frustrated fanbase.

The irritation continued as Vialli again fired narrowly wide. So, with just 15 minutes remaining, Vicini decided to change things up. Overlooking Baggio, he instead turned to Schillaci for his second-ever appearance, replacing Carnevale in attack. It would prove to be a moment of either great genius or great luck for the Italian coach.

Three minutes later, Donadoni played a through ball for Vialli to chase down the edge of the penalty area. Holding the ball momentarily, he turned the marking defender and whipped in a cross from the byline. The cross dropped perfectly between two defenders, where Schillaci had positioned himself, allowing him to power a header past Lindenberger. Italy had the breakthrough they desperately needed, Schillaci celebrating wildly before being mobbed by team-mates. As the final whistle went, giving Italy an opening win, the English commentator described it as 'a dream start for substitute Salvatore Schillaci'. The Italian nation had uncovered a new hero.

Next up for the *Azzurri* were the USA, who were viewed as the weakest team in the group. It was hoped that this game would provide a springboard for a stronger Italian performance, and once again Vicini stuck with his attacking partnership of Carnevale and Vialli, with Baggio and Schillaci available off the bench. And once again Italy struggled to impress, despite going ahead after only 11 minutes through midfielder Giuseppe Giannini. The remainder of the first half saw them huff and puff to no avail, with Vialli striking a penalty against the post to deepen his gloom. With the Carnevale-Vialli partnership clearly not working, Vicini again brought on Schillaci for Carnevale, this time with 39 minutes to make an impression. Despite dominating, Italy couldn't extend their advantage – in fact only a superb double save by Zenga prevented an embarrassing draw. The end was accompanied by a smattering of whistles from the *Azzurri* faithful – yes, Italy had two wins from two, but it wasn't pretty, and they weren't firing on all cylinders.

With qualification for the knockout stages assured, Vicini finally felt emboldened to shake up the attack for the final group game against a dangerous Czechoslovakia. Out went both Carnevale and Vialli, not even named to the bench, and in came Schillaci and Baggio. It would be an opportunity for the two of them to stake their claims.

It took just nine minutes for Schillaci to make his mark. Donadoni swung a corner to the edge of the area where Berti attempted an ambitious volley. Hitting the ball into the ground, it bounced into the Czech area, where Schillaci was first to react, heading into the roof of the net to give Italy an early lead. Once again, the world was treated to his wild celebrations, eyes wide in an image that would become an iconic part of the tournament. With Schillaci endearing himself to Italian hearts, the next question was whether Roberto Baggio could also take his opportunity to impress. A player of great talent, Baggio could be enigmatic, often drifting in and out of games but capable of sublime genius. Everyone wondered which Baggio would turn up against the Czechs. The answer came with 12 minutes remaining.

Giannini picked up the ball in the midfield and played it out to Baggio, hugging the touchline at the halfway line. Baggio started to cut inside, playing a quick one-two with Giannini to take out two Czech midfielders in one move. Continuing to move in, Baggio evaded a challenge, keeping the ball glued to his feet, before being faced by defender Miroslav Kadlec. Dummying to the outside, Baggio then cut inside before stroking the ball under keeper Jan Stejskal and wheeling away to lie on his back, face looking up to the heavens, arms wide in delight.

In the words of John Motson: 'Giannini ... Baggio ... and still Baggio ... and he's taking them all on ... that's a fantastic goal!

That's the goal they've all been waiting for.' Suffice to say, the Italian commentary was probably even more effusive. It was a stunning piece of individual skill – one of the goals of the tournament – and suddenly Italy's striking problems seemed to be solving themselves. Italy were through to the knockout stage with a 100 per cent record, along with no goals conceded, while Schillaci and Baggio were demonstrating their potential. Poor Carnevale wouldn't even see the substitutes' bench for the remainder of the tournament.

Finishing top of their group provided Italy with a round of 16 tie against Uruguay, managed by Óscar Tabárez and captained by the great Enzo Francéscoli, who had scraped through as the worst third-placed side to reach the last 16 courtesy of a stoppage-time winner against South Korea. Italy would once again be playing in front of a packed Stadio Olimpico and, given Uruguay's poor form in the group stage, were expected to win comfortably.

Schillaci and Baggio were again partnered up front, relegating Vialli to the bench. Uruguay, as they often do, proved to be stubborn opposition, frustrating Italy with a physical approach that drew three yellow cards in the first half. Schillaci was creating chances, though, coming especially close eight minutes into the second half when only a great save by Uruguayan keeper Fernando Álvez denied him an opener. Álvez then made another great save from a wonderful De Agostini free kick as Italy turned the screw further. Finally, with 25 minutes remaining, the pressure paid off, Schillaci latching on to a ball just outside the Uruguay area and lashing it past Álvez. The relief was palpable around the stadium.

The result was put beyond doubt with seven minutes remaining when Serena headed home a Giannini free kick. It hadn't been a classic by any means, but the *Azzurri* had once again got the job done, Schillaci grabbing his third goal of the tournament, and the Italians still yet to concede a goal.

* * *

Elsewhere in the round of 16, the Republic of Ireland beat Romania on penalties to prolong their fairy-tale tournament under big Jack Charlton, placing them as Italy's quarter-final opponents. But the bigger story concerned Argentina. Following on from their shock opening-match defeat to Cameroon, they had beaten the Soviet

Union before drawing with Romania to scrape into the round of 16 as a third-place side. Their football was significantly poorer than 1986, Maradona helping to drag an uninspiring team this far. Next up for them was Brazil, the classic South American rivalry.

Brazil dominated, with Argentina managing to hang in the game, clearly looking second best. But, with just nine minutes remaining, Maradona produced a piece of magic. Picking the ball up at the halfway line, he drove forward before releasing the perfect slipped pass to Claudio Caniggia for him to round Brazilian keeper Cláudio Taffarel to give Argentina an against-the-odds win. But it was afterwards that the controversy really started. During the game, Brazil's Branco had taken water handed to him by one of Argentina's training staff while an injured player was being tended to on the pitch. Branco claimed that the water was laced with tranquillisers, affecting his performance – a claim that sounds outlandish until you consider that Maradona said on Argentinian television that it was true, ironically calling it 'holy water', while coach Carlos Bilardo said, 'I'm not saying it didn't happen,' before subsequent denials. What the win did mean, though, was that should Italy beat the Republic of Ireland and Argentina defeat Yugoslavia in the quarter-finals, they would meet in the semi-final – a game that was scheduled to occur in Naples of all places.

And that's exactly what happened. Despite Ireland's visit to see the pope, divine intervention didn't occur and the Stadio Olimpico again saw Italy keep a clean sheet, while Schillaci fired home his fourth goal – another poor game but a place in the semi-finals achieved. Argentina's match against Yugoslavia was also a grind, remaining goalless for the whole 120 minutes before Argentina edged the penalty shoot-out 3-2, despite Maradona having his weak attempt saved. Thus, a semi-final between an Italy yet to concede a goal and an Argentinian side that had ground its way through was set for Naples. Maradona would be facing the *Azzurri* on what he regarded as his home patch.

In Maradona's head, he couldn't imagine why the Napoli fans would want to cheer on Italy as opposed to him. After all, the north of Italy was famous for looking down on the south, so why should the south cheer for the nation? With this in mind, Maradona declared, 'The Italians are asking Neapolitans to be Italian for a day, yet for the other 364 days in the year they forget all about Naples. The people do not forget this.' It was a bold attempt to sway the *tifosi*, which worked to a degree – while most fans were still cheering for Italy, they were respectful of Maradona and the Argentinian national anthem. He had, after all, won them two Scudetti and enjoyed god-like status in the city.

The scene was set – 3 July 1990 saw the two nations line up under a Neapolitan evening sky. Vicini made one key change, dropping Baggio and returning Vialli to partner Schillaci up front, and the partnership struck after just 17 minutes when Vialli's shot was parried by Argentina's keeper Sergio Goycochea, only for Schillaci to sweep home the rebound. The second half saw Argentina, and especially Maradona, begin to press and, after 67 minutes, he played a ball out wide to Julio Olarticoechea, whose cross saw Caniggia get a backward flick just ahead of the onrushing Walter Zenga to level the scores. Shortly after, Vicini threw Baggio into the heat of battle as the game moved into extra time.

Baggio so nearly broke the deadlock with a trademark free kick during the first period, Goycochea superbly saving his effort. Shortly after, Baggio went down in an off-the-ball incident with Ricardo Giusti that the TV cameras failed to pick up. After consultation with his linesman, French referee Michel Vautrot showed Giusti red to an accompaniment of complaints, led by Maradona. Italy failed to take advantage of their man advantage during the second period of extra time, meaning that Naples would witness a penalty shoot-out for a place in the World Cup Final.

Italy went first and both sides converted their first three kicks. Fourth up for the Italians was Donadoni, who fell to his knees after seeing Goycochea save his attempt. Of course, for drama, it just had to be Maradona next. To a chorus of whistles, Diego calmly stroked his kick home to give Argentina the advantage. It was left for Serena to score to keep Italy alive – but once again Goycochea guessed correctly. A stunned Naples, and Italy, looked on in shock. Argentina and Maradona were moving on to a final against West Germany – Italy were out.

It always seems a cruel twist of fate that the teams that are eliminated in the semi-finals must remain to play a meaningless third-place play-off. Does anyone ever really remember who comes third in a World Cup, and do they really care? The players would surely prefer just to leave and start to heal from being so close to a final rather than subject themselves to another 90 minutes. But the third-place match still exists, so in 1990 Italy went down to Bari to face England.

Baggio and Schillaci reunited up front one more time. The match came to life in the 71st minute when England keeper and captain Peter Shilton, making his 125th appearance for his country, received a back pass on which he lingered a moment too long, allowing Baggio to steal the ball before exchanging passes with Schillaci and scoring. Ten minutes later David Platt equalised with a header to continue his fine form over the tournament, before the final word went again to Schillaci, who was brought down for a penalty with just four minutes remaining. He converted it himself to give Italy a third-place finish. But it was small consolation for a country that had hoped to lift the World Cup in front of its adoring public.

In scoring his sixth goal of the tournament, Salvatore Schillaci earned himself the Golden Boot award, the second Italian to win that honour, joining Paolo Rossi in 1982. The All-Star team, chosen by journalists, included five Italians: defenders Paolo Maldini, Giuseppe Bergomi and Franco Baresi, midfielder Roberto Donadoni and striker Salvatore Schillaci. Italy had only conceded two goals in open play throughout the whole tournament but had to watch Argentina and Maradona face West Germany. With the final being played in Rome, most Italians were rooting for the Germans, as probably were most neutrals, given Argentina's insipid path to the final.

The final was a dreadful affair. Argentina's national anthem received a loud chorus of boos from the Rome faithful. If Maradona was in any way hoping for some Italian support, he wasn't getting it in the capital and, as the camera panned along the players during the anthem, he could clearly be seen growling 'hijo de puta' twice, Spanish for 'son of a bitch'. The game then went along the expected pattern of Germany pushing forward while Argentina hung in, a game plan that worked effectively for 85 minutes, despite Argentina being reduced to ten men after 65 minutes when Pedro Monzón became the first player ever to see red in a World Cup Final. With most spectators praying not to have to watch another 30 minutes of this dross, the referee finally put the world out of its misery by awarding West Germany a penalty, which Andreas Brehme thankfully converted.

This just incensed Argentina's players further, and they lost any semblance of self-control and discipline. Almost immediately after the goal, striker Gustavo Dezotti earned their second red card for throwing Jürgen Kohler to the ground with an arm around the neck off the ball. The referee was surrounded by protesting players, led by Maradona, jostling him until he gave the captain a yellow card. Finally, he ended the game, and the world watched as Maradona wept while Lothar Matthäus received the trophy the Argentine had held four years prior. It was a sad end to the tournament, but West Germany were worthy champions.

* * *

For Italy, it had been a frustrating World Cup. Played in their own country, and with Serie A so strong, it had been seen as a real opportunity to bring the trophy back home. They had stuttered during the tournament, saved by the discovery of Schillaci, but had reached a semi-final against a weak Argentina, only to fall on penalties. But they had showed that, despite the influx of foreign talent into the domestic league, the national team was still strong.

Overall, especially when reviewed in hindsight, Italia '90 was one of the worst World Cups in terms of entertainment. It averaged just 2.21 goals per game, still an all-time low. The matches were overly defensive, with several decided by penalties and a record number of red cards shown – so poor was it, in fact, that subsequent analysis of the tournament led to eventual rule changes, including three points for a win and the imposition of the back-pass law. But cold analytics don't tell the whole story. Many people remember the competition fondly for several reasons, but mainly the glamour of Italy hosting it.

At the time, Italy was the epicentre of world football, so the coolest place to host the tournament. There was the San Siro, lit up like a futuristic spaceship. There were the modern TV graphics. For English fans especially, there was Des Lynam's smooth introductions, a feel-good performance, Gascoigne and, most notably, Pavarotti's 'Nessun Dorma'. A whole nation of people who had never been to or listened to opera became enamoured by that song, which still gives goosebumps to that generation. The football may not have been the best, but as a spectacle it was beautiful, as most things in Italy are.

All'alba vincerò!
Vincerò!
Vin ... ce ... rò!!!

ITALY (1990 WORLD CUP)
Third place

Chapter 7

The Shoe Salesman
from Fusignano

I never realised that in order to become a jockey
you have to have been a horse first.

Arrigo Sacchi

IN A scene straight out of *Apocalypse Now*, the three helicopters came down from the heavens, accompanied by Wagner's 'Ride of the Valkyries', as the crowd looked on in awe. The Milan faithful had never witnessed anything like this, all eyes turning to watch the occupants step out – club directors, the first-team squad, the coaches – and a businessman with slicked-back hair emerging into the sunlight. The man's name was Silvio Berlusconi and he had just become the latest owner of Associazione Calcio Milan, better known to all as AC Milan or, more simply, just Milan. Italian and European football were about to undergo a seismic change.

Berlusconi was born in Milan in 1936 and as a young man studied law at Milan university. To make ends meet after graduating, he spent some time as a crooner on board cruise ships, but eventually realised that it was time to turn his attention to more serious pursuits. To this end, he started in construction and real estate, becoming involved in a successful project known as Milano Due, a luxury compound built with all amenities north of the city, which earned Berlusconi his first fortune.

Even at a young age, Silvio had a charisma that rubbed off on all those around him. Well dressed and with a permanent tan and smile, he could charm anyone and used those skills within his business relationships. With money in his pocket, he turned his eye to the world of media, when in 1973 he bought a small cable television company named TeleMilano, the first private television channel in Italy. Importing US television shows such as *Baywatch* and soap operas, he watched his subscriber base grow, restricted only by the wrinkle that he could only operate locally and not take the channel to a wider Italian public. But Berlusconi was not a man who worried about obstacles and how to get around them – he was a man who saw obstacles and just ploughed over them.

Berlusconi started more TV companies, each restricted to a certain area but in effect giving him national coverage to rival the national broadcaster Rai. Following complaints from the RAI, a relationship with the Italian prime minister, Bettino Craxi, meant that decrees were passed allowing Silvio's TV network to expand across Italy. And just like that, the obstacle was removed, although it may not have all been down to Silvio's famed charm but also connected with $17 million that ended up in secret offshore bank accounts owned by Craxi, who would later move to Tunisia after being convicted of corruption.

But whatever the reason, Berlusconi's empire expanded hugely overnight. He suddenly had money to burn and was looking for something new to invest in – something that would win him popular support from the masses as his thoughts turned to an eventual political future. Berlusconi was nothing if not hugely ambitious. But what could a man born and raised in Milan buy that might earn him that kind of coverage?

* * *

The early 1980s had been a tough time for Milan. Everything had seemed so perfect when, on 6 May 1979, they were able to celebrate their long-awaited tenth Scudetto following a goalless draw at the San Siro against Bologna. It was the perfect way to cap the stellar career of Gianni Rivera, who retired from football at the end of the season, having played over 500 Serie A games for Milan over 19 seasons, scoring 122 goals to become a legend at the club. However, as the celebrations took place, no one could foresee the storm brewing that would have huge implications for the club.

The earlier chapter on Juventus mentioned Paolo Rossi's involvement in and subsequent punishment resulting from the

Totonero scandal of 1980. But he was only one of many participants caught up within the affair. In fact, 27 players and 13 clubs were included in the files that were given to Rome's public prosecutor, across both Serie A and B. Just 22 days after receiving these files, the Guardia di Finanza shocked fans and officials by arresting 13 players literally as they left the pitch following the final whistle on that matchday. Milan were especially affected, with their owner, Felice Colombo, also arrested.

The punishments handed down included five-point penalties for five teams, to be applied to the 1980/81 season, but the headline was that both Lazio and Milan were relegated to Serie B. For Milan, this would be their first experience of playing at this level. Not surprisingly, they instantly won promotion, heading Serie B for most of the season, but the club was now out of sorts.

Back in Serie A, Luigi Radice was hired as the new coach but 1981/82 started badly for Milan, as they quickly fell into the relegation zone. The players were unhappy with Radice, the fans were unhappy with the players, Franco Baresi was sidelined with a rare blood disease – whatever could go wrong was going wrong. By late January, Radice was out, his place taken by Italo Galbiati, while the president of the club was also changed, Giuseppe Farina taking over. With five games left, Milan were second from bottom, with the final three to be relegated. But then came some spirit as they won two, drew two and went into the final match with a chance of safety. They needed to beat Cesena away but with 23 minutes remaining were 2-0 down, before an incredible fightback saw them score three goals in the space of 14 minutes. If Napoli beat Genoa in Naples, Milan were safe.

It was all going so well. Despite falling behind in the first half, Napoli rallied to take a 2-1 lead. Then, with just five minutes remaining, came one of the strangest incidents to befall Italian football. The Napoli keeper, Luciano Castellini, had the ball unchallenged in his area. He decided to throw it out – and somehow managed instead to throw it behind for a corner. Inevitably, a Genoa header from the corner went towards the edge of the six-yard box, where Mario Faccenda slid in to write himself into Genoa legend and send Milan back down to Serie B. As so often in Italy, a thousand conspiracy theories were launched.

Again Milan came straight back up as champions, under the captaincy of 22-year-old defender Franco Baresi, after which 1983/84 saw them finish an unremarkable eighth. It was the season that will always be remembered as the first for new signing Luther Blissett, bought from Watford. Blissett had ended the previous season as the top scorer in the English First Division, bagging an impressive 27 goals for Graham Taylor's surprise package. Sadly for him, his time at Milan wouldn't work out so well, returning to Watford after one season with just five Serie A goals. Following his departure, Blissett's place was taken by another new English signing: Mark Hateley, bought from Portsmouth. He registered eight Serie A goals during 1984/85, a season that saw Milan finish a disappointing fifth.

So as 1985/86 got underway, Milan had spent the last six seasons with a highest finish of fifth, along with two seasons in Serie B. The championship won under Nils Liedholm's guidance back in 1979 felt like a distant memory as Juventus dominated the early 1980s and Milan fans despaired about whether their beloved *Rossoneri* could ever return to prominence.

Matters weren't helped by Milan's third-round elimination in the UEFA Cup in December 1985 to SV Zulte-Waregem of Belgium, hardly a renowned European superpower. The fans' patience was wearing thin, with protests aimed at chairman Giuseppe Farina as it became apparent that the club's finances were a mess. They had taken on considerable amounts of debt and faced the possibility of bankruptcy if repayments couldn't be met on time. Fans' attention turned to Berlusconi; a huge banner unfurled at a December game urging him to buy their club. The pressure built until Farina could take no more – on 12 January 1986 he resigned as chairman. Rosario Lo Verde was elected as his replacement and charged with finding a buyer for Milan who could pull them out of their turmoil. And it's at this point that Silvio Berlusconi seized the opportunity to make himself the new face of his hometown club.

On 20 February 1986, just over a month after Farina's resignation, Berlusconi bought AC Milan for around £6 million, immediately paying off their considerable debts and saving the club from bankruptcy. His business vision was instantly apparent as he stated that 'Milan is a team, but it's also a product to sell; something to offer on the market', a new approach that also saw him open an apparel shop near the famed Milan Duomo where fans could purchase match tickets. He installed Adriano Galliani as the new CEO and settled in to see his new investment finish seventh under manager Nils Liedholm, who had returned after five seasons at the helm at Roma to try to restore Milan's glory.

Berlusconi brought a modern, business-like approach to various parts of the organisation. A psychologist was hired for the players, a dietician came in to improve eating habits, the training facilities were updated and advanced. He also paid the players generously, implementing bonus incentives for results. But that could only help so much – Berlusconi knew that he needed the right personnel in place as well as an improved squad – and the summer of 1986 saw him make his first material dips into the transfer market, signing midfielder Roberto Donadoni from Atalanta as well as both forward Daniele Massaro and goalkeeper Giovanni Galli from Fiorentina.

* * *

Excitement rose in Milan for this new era of ownership, with season ticket sales jumping from 36,624 in 1985/86 to 52,520 for the upcoming campaign. However, Berlusconi's first full year of ownership was unremarkable – Milan finishing 1986/87 in fifth place – but it was the Coppa Italia that had a seismic effect on Milan's future. At this time, the Coppa Italia was run under a split format rather like the current Champions League, a group stage followed by a knockout phase. Each group consisted of six teams and Milan were placed with Barletta, Triestina, Ascoli, Sambenedettese and Parma, each team playing one another just once, with the top two moving on. Given the level of opposition, the five games should have been a walk in the park.

The first three were all wins for Milan. It was the fourth game, however, that would prove significant in our story. It saw Parma, a Serie B team, having just been promoted the season before from Serie C1, visit the San Siro in September. Their 40-year-old manager was in his eighth managerial post, having never played professional football, plying his trade as a shoe salesman beforehand for several years. His résumé consisted of a couple of youth-team coaching positions as well as a handful of Serie B and C1 head coach placements. His name was Arrigo Sacchi.

The game was just nine minutes old when Parma took the lead, and that remained the score as they pulled off a shock win. Unsurprisingly Parma and Milan moved on to the knockout stage, but Sacchi's team had earned the attention of new owner Berlusconi.

Ironically, the two were then drawn against each other in the round of 16. It was a two-legged affair, with the first at the San Siro in February 1987. Again Parma shocked the Milanese, scoring the only goal late on. A month later, Milan travelled to Parma for the second leg, where a goalless draw saw them eliminated. Milan had faced the Serie B side three times and had failed to score, Sacchi having completely neutralised them. Berlusconi was impressed, and when something impressed him, he tended to get it.

With Milan's season petering out to another fifth place, Berlusconi pulled the trigger with five games remaining. Nils Liedholm was released from duty and assistant Fabio Capello placed in charge for the remainder of the season. But the appointment was only temporary – Berlusconi had already sealed his preferred full-time candidate for the 1987/88 season. Arrigo Sacchi was about to take his first coaching job in the big league.

The Milanese press were not amused. How could a coach who had never played professional football and never managed a top-flight team be trusted to lead one of Italy's greatest clubs? The accusation led to one of the most famous quotes in football, Sacchi's response being, 'I never realised that in order to become a jockey you have to have been a horse first.' But in a later interview he did confess that in effect 'he [Berlusconi] had given a Ferrari to a complete stranger'.

While Milan had underperformed for several seasons, Sacchi inherited some promising young talent, especially in defence. Back in 1982, a young centre-back named Franco Baresi had been awarded the captaincy, a position he still held. Alongside him were a 19-year-old Paolo Maldini, while 20-year-old Alessandro Costacurta was recalled from his loan spell with Monza. But with his new manager in place, Berlusconi was now ready to shake up world football with some earth-shattering purchases.

The headline change was the sale of the two English players within the team, Ray Wilkins and Mark Hateley, and their replacement with two new foreigners. This time, instead of Englishmen, Berlusconi's eyes coveted two Dutchmen. And not just any old pair of Dutchmen.

* * *

Ruud Gullit grew up in Amsterdam, a product of a Surinamese father and a Dutch mother, playing football in his local streets with another kid named Frank Rijkaard, who will enter our story soon. Gullit made his debut just before the age of 17 at Dutch club HFC Haarlem in 1979, making him the youngest player at the time to play in the Eredivisie, where he helped them during the next three seasons to achieve a fourth-place finish, qualifying for Europe for the only time in their history. His 32 goals across 91 appearances earned him a move to Feyenoord, where his three seasons included a championship won alongside former Ajax legend Johan Cruyff. Gullit was named Dutch Footballer of the Year that season, despite Cruyff's heroics, as he evolved into a box-to-box midfielder. With his distinctive dreadlocks, and his speed and strength, he became a fearsome player, scoring 30 goals in 85 appearances despite not being a true striker.

His success saw him move to PSV Eindhoven, where he became a key member of the team that won back-to-back Eredivisie titles, while earning himself another Dutch Footballer of the Year award. His strike rate increased even further, netting 46 goals in just 68 games, making him one of the most highly rated players within Europe. With the big clubs circling, PSV knew they had a valuable commodity on their books, one that would demand a world record transfer fee should anyone wish to procure his services. Silvio Berlusconi was willing and able and, after tough negotiations, he got his way, breaking the world transfer fee record by signing Gullit for £6m. He had the man that he would later describe as having 'the sun in his heart and dynamite in his muscles'.

Securing Gullit in midfield would be a statement purchase for any owner, but Berlusconi also targeted another Dutchman. While Gullit's attacking style would secure goals, Berlusconi also wanted a pure, deadly striker. And one such striker was also plying his trade in the Eredivisie.

Ajax had unearthed a young striker blessed with incredible talent. Marco van Basten grew up in Utrecht, where he played youth football before being signed by Ajax in 1981 as a 16-year-old. That season saw him make his debut when he came on as a substitute for Johan Cruyff, leaving his mark with his first goal. His early form saw Ajax cash in on current striker Wim Kieft, selling him to Pisa and making Van Basten the main man up front – from that point on, he never looked back.

The next five seasons saw Van Basten destroy Dutch defences. Headers, shots, dribbles, acrobatic finishes – he had them all in his toolbox. He scored from penalties and free kicks too. He was untouchable as he became the top scorer in the Eredivisie for four successive seasons, netting an astonishing 128 goals in 133 league games. His peak came in 1985/86 when he scored 37 times in 26 league matches, including six in one game and five in another, earning him the European Golden Boot. The following season saw him part of the Ajax side that won the Cup Winners' Cup under the managerial leadership of Johan Cruyff, back at his spiritual home after his brief sabbatical at Feyenoord. Van Basten scored the only goal of the final against Lokomotive Leipzig, one of six goals overall in the competition.

Many were unaware that the 'Swan of Utrecht', as Van Basten had been nicknamed, had been brought to Berlusconi's villa in July 1986 for secret talks. Negotiating a deal for Van Basten to join Milan in the summer of 1987, Berlusconi secured his services for a bargain price of £1m, a transfer that CEO Galliani later judged to be Milan's best value-for-money acquisition.

While Sacchi received the two Dutchmen to boost his squad, he also benefitted from the addition that summer of future Milan manager Carlo Ancelotti from Roma, a strong midfielder who could play deeper, allowing Gullit the safety net to play a more attacking role. As the start of 1987/88 approached, Sacchi couldn't complain that he didn't have the goods to challenge reigning champions Napoli – and Berlusconi expected nothing less.

* * *

The opening day saw Milan travel to Pisa, where an excited *Rossoneri* fanbase saw exactly what Berlusconi's money had bought. With 17 minutes remaining, Gullit gave Milan the lead with one of his trademark powerful headers, before Van Basten scored from the penalty spot, was ordered to retake the kick, then calmly scored again to secure victory.

If optimism was flowing after that match, Milan's first home game saw expectations tempered as they were defeated 2-0 by Fiorentina. Their season then incurred another early blow when, in game five away at Sampdoria, Van Basten went down injured, which would see him unable to start again until April. It was a huge loss for Sacchi, losing one of his star purchases for the bulk of his maiden season in charge.

With the spotlight focused on Sacchi and his methods, there were some early grumblings within the camp and fanbase. One of Sacchi's first changes was to implement twice-daily training, as opposed to the four a week they had been used to. The mood then worsened when Milan crashed out of the UEFA Cup in the second round, eliminated by Espanyol, leading to press reports about Sacchi's upcoming demise. But Berlusconi stood by his appointment, declaring that 'between Sacchi and the team, I choose Sacchi', making it clear to the press and squad where his loyalty lay.

It was testament to Sacchi's abilities that Milan then went the rest of the season undefeated, that first home game against Fiorentina being their only genuine defeat in Serie A. There was one other defeat in December as Milan welcomed Roma to the San Siro, but that was due to Roma's keeper being struck by a firecracker. The game was abandoned, and Roma awarded a 2-0 victory. A particularly key period during this unbeaten run came just after the Roma game. Milan faced three successive crunch games – the Milan derby, a home match against champions Napoli and then away at Juventus – three games that could determine their season. The Milan derby was won thanks to an Inter own goal. Then came the big one – at home to Napoli, who were leading Serie A. Milan ran out 4-1 winners, making a statement on their qualifications as challengers to the Neapolitans, who still remained top. Milan then won the third of the tough three games, defeating Juventus in Turin courtesy of a Gullit goal.

As described earlier, Napoli went into meltdown, handing the 1987/88 title to Milan, who sealed the Scudetto on the final day, drawing away at Como. They came back to the San Siro to parade the trophy before a full house of over 70,000 celebrating

Rossoneri, delirious at having won their first Scudetto since 1979. Berlusconi stood on the pitch, grinning in pride at the scenes surrounding him.

Incredibly, Sacchi had won the Scudetto in his first season, and while Berlusconi's spending had obviously helped, it should be noted that Van Basten was missing for the bulk of the campaign. It was Ruud Gullit who drove Milan to the championship, becoming an instant fan favourite, backed up by a strong supporting cast. He scored 13 Serie A goals in the season, second-best scorer for Milan, while putting in some dazzling and commanding performances. Sacchi said later:

> Gullit was the leader. He had a very strong character. For me, he was number one and he helped me a lot to change the team's mentality. In Italy, you score a goal and everyone defends the lead and I would say no, when we score a goal we keep on attacking.

With Van Basten out, Pietro Paolo Virdis stepped up, leading the attack, and finishing with 15 Serie A goals, following on from his strong prior season. The jockey had truly shown that you do not, indeed, need to have been a horse first. Sacchi and Milan were now set for an assault on Europe's top prize, the European Cup.

* * *

With the 1988 Scudetto locked away in the trophy cabinet, players' thoughts turned towards the 1988 European Championship, to be played in Germany during June. Italy had been handed a tough group stage, alongside hosts West Germany, Spain and Denmark, with just the top two moving on to the knockout stages. West Germany had reached the 1986 World Cup Final in Mexico, while Denmark were hoping for a final flourish from their 'Danish Dynamite' generation, who had promised so much in 1986 before being thrashed 5-1 by Spain. Italy's opening game against West Germany saw four Milan players line up: Baresi, Maldini, Donadoni and Ancelotti. A draw was followed by a narrow win over Spain and a more comfortable win over Denmark, placing Italy second behind West Germany, with only one goal conceded.

The other group saw Van Basten and Gullit line up for the Netherlands against England, USSR and the Republic of Ireland. The Netherlands suffered a 1-0 loss to the Soviets, meaning the next match against England, who had surprisingly lost their opener too, was a must-win for both. Van Basten scored a hat-trick as the Netherlands won 3-1. They still needed to beat the Republic of Ireland to qualify, which they duly did.

The semi-finals pitted the Netherlands against host and old enemy West Germany, while Italy faced the impressive USSR. First up were the Dutch where, with the score 1-1, Van Basten scored the winner, a rare win over the Germans on their own home turf. Unfortunately, Gullit and Van Basten wouldn't be meeting their four team-mates in the final, as USSR proved too strong for the *Azzurri*, winning through two second-half goals.

The final would prove that Berlusconi had acquired two of the best players in Europe. While USSR had beaten the Netherlands in the group stage, this time the Dutch were victorious, lifting their first international trophy. Their 2-0 win was produced in Milan. Firstly, captain Gullit scored with a header so powerful that it almost broke the netting. And then came one of the greatest goals to ever grace a final when, early in the second half, Van Basten hit a stupendous volley from a tight angle into the top corner – a strike so physically amazing that even the Dutch coach, Michels, who had seen almost everything, held his face in shock.

As Gullit lifted the trophy in front of the adoring *Oranje* fans, Berlusconi, Sacchi and Milan's fans watched on in glee. The *Rossoneri* had possession of two great talents. But even better news came from Italian authorities – from this point forward, Italian teams were now allowed to start three foreign players, which immediately got Berlusconi thinking – the Dutch were European champions, so why just have two when they could have three?

* * *

Gullit had grown up playing football on the streets of Amsterdam, alongside another child of Surinamese descent, Frank Rijkaard. Rijkaard joined the Ajax youth team before making his first-team debut at the age of just 17 on the opening day of the 1980/81 season. A defender, he made an immediate impression, scoring on his debut. From then on, he was an Ajax regular, playing for seven and a half years in a team that won the Eredivisie three times and the Cup Winners' Cup. Sadly, his time in Amsterdam ended acrimoniously when he fell out with coach Johan Cruyff and swore he would never play under him again. A move to Sporting Lisbon, who loaned him to Real Zaragoza, followed, before he played in every one of the Netherlands' Euro 88 games. Rijkaard was open to a further move, and that was all Berlusconi needed to know. Out came the trusty chequebook, despite the wailing of Lisbon fans who surrounded the hotel during the transfer negotiations, begging Rijkaard to remain.

Traditionally a central defender, Sacchi decided to deploy Rijkaard as a central holding midfielder, a decision he wouldn't regret: 'Rijkaard was a phenomenal midfielder … a truly formidable player.' Franco Baresi was also later effusive in his praise of the Dutchman: 'He had everything, he knew how to defend, he knew how to attack, score goals. Rijkaard's arrival completed a great squad.'

With three foreign starters now permitted, it was obvious who those three would be when all fit, and they became known in the Italian press as 'I Tre Tulipani' (the three tulips). While Serie A remained important to Milan, there was no doubt that Berlusconi's priority was to see his team enjoy a successful run in Europe, Gullit echoing those sentiments, stating that 'the Scudetto is not enough'.

The season started for Sacchi's team with European Cup action, where Milan received a tame first-round draw, pitting them against Bulgarian champions Levski Sofia. A first-leg trip behind the Iron Curtain saw Milan come away with a 2-0 victory, which they enhanced back at the San Siro with a 5-2 win. The good news for Milan fans was that, after missing much of the previous season, Van Basten was back and, if there were any concerns regarding his early season fitness, he blew those away by thumping in four of the five goals.

Back in Serie A, Milan showed that they weren't over-reliant on Van Basten as they opened the season by thrashing Fiorentina 4-0, with Virdis grabbing a hat-trick. The opening five games of the season saw them undefeated as they made a confident start towards retaining their championship, before the European odyssey continued with another trip to Eastern Europe, this time to face more dangerous opposition in Red Star Belgrade. At this time, a new generation of talent was developing at the Yugoslavian club – a generation that would culminate in a team that would lift the European Cup just two seasons later. They would prove extremely tough opponents for the Italian champions and nearly cause Berlusconi's dream to die in this second round.

The first leg took place at the San Siro, where Red Star showed their skill by holding Milan goalless for the first 45 minutes. Just two minutes into the second half, the Yugoslavs shocked the Milan faithful by taking the lead. But in one of those classic TV coverage moments, the replay of the goal was suddenly halted to reveal that Milan had immediately equalised through Virdis, with only his celebration caught for posterity. It ended 1-1, meaning Red Star could go back to their intimidating Marakana stadium level, with an away goal.

In the second half of the second leg, Red Star took the lead. However, those watching on TV could only hear the celebrations as fog was descending, making camera coverage almost impossible. It was this fog that saved Milan, as after 65 minutes it became impossible to continue. The match was rescheduled for the following day but, with Virdis having been sent off and Ancelotti booked, both would miss the game due to suspension. Milan would have to go again in front of 65,000 hostile Red Star fans without two key players.

Thirty-five minutes into the match, Van Basten rose at the far post to put Milan into the lead but, like the first leg, the lead was fleeting, Stojković equalising just four minutes later, following a beautiful through ball from Savićević. It remained level through the rest of the 90 minutes and extra time, meaning the dreaded penalty shoot-out. Milan's European hopes now rested on the lottery of who could best keep their cool from 12 yards.

Red Star had the advantage of going first. They converted their first two penalties, Milan matching them. Next up for the Yugoslavs was the reliable boot of Savićević, who struck it straight down the middle, only to see it saved by the foot of Milan keeper Galli. Alberico Evani converted for Milan and suddenly all the pressure fell on Red Star. With their three best players having all stepped up, it fell next to Serbian midfielder Mitar Mrkela, who could only watch as his effort was turned around the post by Galli. Suddenly Milan were just one kick from escaping Belgrade with a place in the quarter-finals.

It was new boy Rijkaard to take the fourth penalty for the *Rossoneri*. He struck it down the middle to repay his transfer and silence the Marakana. It had been a close shave, helped by the Yugoslavian fog, but Berlusconi's biggest fear had been averted. Milan could now enjoy four months of league action, safe in the knowledge that, come March, they would be involved in Europe again.

Maybe the Red Star experience took its toll because, for some reason, on returning to league action, Milan hit their first real slump under Sacchi, incurring four defeats in their next seven games, including a 4-1 thrashing in Naples. After matchday 12, Milan had fallen to seventh, ten points behind rivals Inter. Barring a miracle, it looked like defending their Scudetto was now an impossibility, and so it proved. Milan did recover from the slump to go the rest of the season unbeaten, pulling them up to an eventual third place behind Napoli and champions Inter. If glory was to come, it would have to be in the European Cup.

The end of 1988 saw the annual award of the Ballon d'Or and an astonishing sweep for the *Tre Tulipani*, the first three places going to Marco van Basten, Ruud Gullit and Frank Rijkaard, respectively. But the Italians in the team weren't forgotten either, as Franco Baresi came joint eighth.

German champions Werder Bremen were Milan's quarter-final opponents. Having finished second in the Bundesliga three times in five seasons, Bremen had finally managed to break Bayern Munich's stranglehold in 1988. The first leg was played in Germany and proved to be a tight affair, the main incidents being a Rijkaard header that led to a crazy scramble in which Milan claimed the ball had crossed the line, followed by what appeared to be a good goal for Bremen disallowed for an apparent foul on the keeper, before a late goal-line clearance denied Van Basten.

The return leg at the San Siro was just as tight, and it took a first-half penalty from Van Basten to separate the two sides. It wasn't pretty but Milan had once again scraped by to book a place in the semi-finals. Their opponents would be European royalty: six-times European Cup champions Real Madrid. This was a Real

Madrid that had won three successive La Liga titles, and their last four seasons had also seen them win the UEFA Cup twice before reaching successive European Cup semi-finals. They were once again running away with La Liga, on their way to the fourth successive title.

The first leg was played in Madrid in front of a packed house and, inevitably, Mexican superstar Hugo Sánchez opened the scoring in the first half and celebrated with his trademark somersault. But after Gullit had a goal dubiously disallowed for a narrow offside, Van Basten snatched a vital equaliser; 1-1 was the final score and Milan had shown they could hold their own with a top European team.

However, while Berlusconi had funded a formidable team, and Sacchi was coaching them superbly, they were still new to most European viewers. Their European Cup run to date had not been particularly dazzling but this would all change on 19 April 1989 when Milan hosted Real Madrid for the return leg. One of the most famous and iconic games in European Cup history would place Milan on everyone's radar. Everything transformed on this evening for Berlusconi, Sacchi and the *Rossoneri* in the space of a magical 90 minutes in front of 73,000 delirious fans. This night, maybe more than any other night, showed that the centre of footballing power was now moving to the Italian peninsula.

* * *

That night saw the classic Milan line-up of this era. In goal was Galli, protected by the fearsome defensive quartet of Tassotti, Costacurta, Baresi and Maldini. The centre of the midfield contained Rijkaard and Ancelotti, while out wide were Colombo and Donadoni. And, of course, up front you had the frightening duo of Gullit and Van Basten. Right from the start, Milan were on the front foot, and it took just 17 minutes to break through, as Gullit collected the ball tight against the touchline, before squaring it to Ancelotti. He brought the ball forward, cut right across two tackles and slammed the ball into the roof of the net from outside the penalty area. In over 100 appearances for the *Rossoneri*, Ancelotti would only score ten times. This would be by far his most famous goal, and its rarity was reflected by the wild celebrations of his team-mates and the San Siro, red flares burning around the terracing.

Milan were in the mood and there was no stopping them. Just seven minutes later, a short-corner routine saw Tassotti swing the ball into the area, where Rijkaard outjumped everyone to send a powerful header past keeper Buyo. Madrid looked stunned, desperately needing to get into the changing rooms to regroup. It looked as if they might reach the half-time break without further damage until, right on 45 minutes, Donadoni exchanged a one-two with Gullit and swung in a cross. Gullit had continued his run into the area and applied his trademark finish, bulleting his header into the corner. The Italian commentator could only marvel at 'grande, grande Milan' as the whistle blew on a statement first half.

With a three-goal aggregate advantage, Milan could afford to sit back in the second half, avoid any injuries and let their watertight defence see out the game. But they didn't. Just four minutes in came the best goal of the night – involving all *Tre Tulipani* in its execution. The ball fell to Rijkaard in midfield. Weighing up his options, he chipped it forward to Gullit at the edge of the Madrid area, who nodded it down to Van Basten. Two touches to settle himself in the middle of the box and then straight into the roof of the net. In a matter of seconds, the three Dutchmen had combined to show that Milan had no intention of taking their foot off the gas. It was a glorious goal from start to finish.

Another Milan short corner 13 minutes later saw Donadoni flick the ball inside to Tassotti, who returned it to the winger. Donadoni let fly a low shot past Buyo at the near post. With an hour gone, Milan were destroying one of the strongest teams in Europe 5-0. Finally, Milan did start to let up, allowing the game to drift to its conclusion with no further scoring. As the final whistle sounded, the San Siro erupted in applause at what it had witnessed.

The attention of the whole of European football turned towards the *Rossoneri*. This team, managed by a coach with no previous big-time experience, had just humiliated the great Real Madrid in a European Cup semi-final. Everything that Sacchi had been preaching to his players for the last two years fell into place that night. Even the Spanish press were effusive in their praise, with journalist Chema Bravo stating: 'With Sacchi, football began to have four main references; the ball, the opponent, the team-mate and space.' Sacchi himself summed it up in a later interview:

We were a bit daunted, but the true satisfaction is that we did something epic. That Real Madrid team was a great one. It was a fantastic occasion for us. For me, it was the moment when Milan astonished the world of football.

* * *

So, what were the tactical innovations that Sacchi had implemented since taking over the reins that helped produce such a historic performance? As we saw earlier, while evolving away from *catenaccio*, Italian football still had a defensive mindset in the 1980s, the overall principle being that if you don't concede, you can't lose, and that a compact defence was the base of a solid side. Sacchi's view of how football should be played differed – he favoured attacking verve but without sacrificing a strong defence.

He generally lined Milan up in a 4-4-2 formation, blessed as he was with one of the greatest back fours in footballing history. But his innovation was to have the whole team play as a tight unit, moving forwards together, or as he once stated, 'All my players have to learn how to play in defence and up front, and they must attack space.' Sacchi's unwritten rule was that, wherever possible, the attack and defence shouldn't be separated by more than around 25 metres, so that pressing wouldn't be so physically exhausting. That often meant Milan played with a high defensive line, leaving space for the opposition to run into, which was countered by good communication between the back four to always ensure a perfect offside trap. When a midfielder tried to break through Milan's lines, the defence would usually rush forwards, often ordered by Baresi, crowding the player while leaving attackers stranded offside, provided the back four were in perfect sync.

Sacchi described it as 'attacking the opponent's attack', a risky approach that also required keeper Galli to be able to play with his feet outside his area when needed in an early sweeper-keeper iteration, but one with which Milan enjoyed success, lifting that back four to mythical status. Sacchi also demanded that his defenders were comfortable bringing the ball forward to force opponents out of any defensive shell, while encouraging Maldini and Tassotti to push on in attacks, allowing the likes of Donadoni to join Gullit and Van Basten up front. As Sacchi once commented,

'If you want to go down in history, you don't just need to win. You have to entertain.'

Another area in which Sacchi was ahead of his time was the press. It's almost mandatory nowadays that teams aggressively press opponents high up the pitch, but in 1989 this was a rare concept. The attack and midfield would pressurise defenders, forcing mistakes by cutting off passing lanes. Once they won the ball back, they would usually look to spring a fast, first-time forward pass to the attack.

Sacchi loved teamwork and argued that his system was so perfect that anyone could be dropped into it and perform. His training programme included sessions without a ball, where players would just practise flow and positioning while Sacchi barked feedback from the stands through a megaphone. It all added up to a new experience for an Italian side. Again, in his own words, 'I saw that all the great teams, in order to be great, had something in common. They all looked to dominate on the pitch, dominate play and control the game at all times. This was my aim, but my greatest objective was to make people enjoy themselves.'

Of course, there were the inevitable counterclaims that, with the players he had at his disposal, anyone could be successful in charge. But we've seen with other teams that stars do not automatically translate into success. Sacchi was aware of the criticism, but also of his own influence. As he once put it, 'De Niro is a fine actor. But you only see it when he appears in a great Coppola film.' Sacchi never suffered from a lack of confidence in his own abilities.

* * *

While Europe marvelled at this Milan performance against Real Madrid, the team still needed to focus on finishing the job. The sublime win would mean nothing if they subsequently failed to convert a place in the European Cup Final into success. Their opponents were once again from behind the Iron Curtain, a team that had surprised Western Europe by winning the European Cup in 1986 to become the first Eastern European club to do so, Romania's Steaua Bucureşti.

Their 1986 victory had seen them defeat Terry Venables's Barcelona before 70,000 in Seville, a crowd almost entirely made up of Barça faithful. After a dull goalless draw, the hero had been

Steaua keeper Helmuth Duckadam, who saved all four Barcelona spot kicks to send the trophy to Romania. The following season's European Cup had seen them eliminated in the second round by Anderlecht before again enjoying a strong run in 1988, reaching the semi-finals, losing out to Benfica. Their team was experienced at this level, and in the eight games played to reach the final had lost just once, scoring 22 goals. While Milan were favourites, Steaua were no novices and contained one player of true genius who could almost single-handedly win a game, the incomparable Gheorghe Hagi.

Steaua Bucureşti were, therefore, opponents not to be underestimated – a fact even acknowledged by Berlusconi, who stressed ahead of the game that the key was that Milan's development was ahead of schedule and they should be happy with just reaching the final, although whether he really meant it is another matter.

On 24 May 1989, Milan lined up against Steaua in front of 97,000 fans, nearly all Italian, at the famed Camp Nou, Barcelona. Berlusconi had arranged for 26,000 Milan fans to travel, chartering a ship, 25 airplanes and 450 buses to transport the *Rossoneri* faithful. Unsurprisingly, Sacchi stuck with the same 11 who had inflicted the second-leg humiliation on Real Madrid. In their last final, Steaua had managed to strangle Barcelona, taking the game to penalties – would they be able to do something similar against Milan? The answer was a swift and decisive no.

Ahead of kick-off, Sacchi recalled the scene:

> In the dressing room, everyone had their heads down. I went around and touched every player on the head, I told them you should have only one thing to worry about. Play like we can, if you do that, then we won't lose.

Milan lined up in their changed strip of all white and put Steaua under pressure from the start. It took just 18 minutes for Milan to crack the tight Steaua defence, keeper Silviu Lung making a double-save before Gullit slotted home from close range. Ten minutes later, Van Basten headed home a cross from Tassotti. Milan fans celebrated, red flares burning. Steaua were mesmerised, unable to do anything to stem the white tide as attack after attack hit them, and six minutes before half-time the game was as good as done. Donadoni crossed to Gullit on the edge of the penalty area. With one touch, he brought the ball under control before sending a vicious shot past Lung. 3-0 by half-time, Milan in imperious control.

If Steaua even thought they had a modicum of hope remaining, that was dashed just 50 seconds into the second half. A Dutch combination saw Rijkaard play a through ball for Van Basten to hammer in his second, Milan's fourth. It was now officially a rout. Milan comfortably dominated the remainder of the game, unlucky not to add a fifth, until the final whistle finally sounded. AC Milan, managed by Arrigo Sacchi, owned by Silvio Berlusconi, defended through a stellar Italian back four and with four goals, scored by Ruud Gullit and Marco van Basten, were champions of Europe for 1989. As captain Franco Baresi lifted the famous trophy into the Barcelona night sky, the rest of Europe could only look on in awe and admiration – a new standard had been set.

* * *

In an interesting side story, the world was at risk of not witnessing this great performance. Technicians at Spanish state broadcasters TVE, who were filming the event for worldwide consumption, went on strike 24 hours before kick-off after a long-running dispute with management. They would, however, allow foreign broadcasters to cover the game, provided the images weren't transmitted within Spain. An Italian military plane was quickly made available to Italian state broadcaster Rai to get an Italian camera crew over to Barcelona and set up as soon as possible. Thankfully they made it in time.

In the following morning's edition of *La Repubblica*, famed Italian football journalist Gianni Brera was effusive in his praise. Milan were like 'that monster from the classic poems which is coaxed out of the abyss by a friendly goddess in order to smash a hated enemy', while Gullit was 'so full of uranium that he was able to recharge Milan's atomic cell as if by magic'. This is the same Brera who once famously said that a perfect match should finish 0-0 – a disciple of defensive tactics. If he was impressed, then Milan had to be something special.

Van Basten's two goals in the final took his season's tally to 33, ten of which were scored in the European Cup, making him the top scorer in the competition. Come the end of 1989, when the Ballon d'Or was voted upon, it would be Marco van Basten that led the way, his second successive win, followed by team-mates Franco Baresi and Frank Rijkaard. For the second year running, Milan players had swept the top three places. And Ruud Gullit came seventh. It was a Milanese world.

* * *

Once the celebrations had died down across the city, it was time for another season and another assault on the European Cup, while trying to regain the Scudetto. In Serie A, the most likely contenders would again be Milan, Inter and Napoli. But then, early in the season, Milan suffered a major blow when Gullit was sidelined with damage to the ligaments of his right knee. It would lead to him missing the whole of the 1989/90 season, so Milan faced the campaign without their talismanic attacking midfielder, a huge absence. It would be crucial for Daniele Massaro to step up to assist Van Basten with striking duties.

September 1989 saw Milan open their European Cup defence with a straightforward elimination of Finnish champions HJK Helsinki, 5-0 on aggregate, but their early form in Serie A was concerning. Their first eight games saw them victorious just three times, while also suffering three losses, one of which was particularly damaging, 3-0 away at rivals Napoli. It meant eighth position for Milan and already the season was beginning to mirror the previous one in that European success may again have to be the priority.

The second round of the European Cup threw up another of those fixtures that so infuriated Berlusconi. In a repeat of the semi-final from the season before, Milan were drawn against Spanish powerhouse Real Madrid, this time playing first at the San Siro. The Spanish giants were still smarting from their 5-0 humiliation at the hands of the *Rossoneri* – revenge would have been top of their priorities.

At the San Siro, Madrid would have been looking for a solid start, but if that was the plan, the game immediately started as another nightmare outing for the Spanish. After just nine minutes, the Dutch connection again haunted Madrid as a Van Basten cross was headed home by Rijkaard. Then, just five minutes later, Milan doubled their lead when the same pair struck again, this time Rijkaard winning the ball in midfield to play Van Basten clean through, resulting in him being brought down by the Madrid keeper as he tried to go around him. Van Basten calmly rolled the ball into the corner from the resulting penalty. Fifteen minutes gone and Madrid were again reeling.

However, unlike six months ago, Madrid were able to stem the tide and limit Milan to those two early goals, meaning they returned to the Bernabéu with a chance. Over 80,000 cheered them on, desperate to avenge the events of April, and their spirits were lifted when Butragueño scrambled in a header just before half-time. But when Madrid's Manuel Sanchís received a red card with 16 minutes left, Milan's famed defence wasn't going to allow ten men to breach them again. For the second time in succession, Real Madrid saw their European dreams ended by the *Rossoneri*. Once again, Milan could now focus on domestic issues until March.

* * *

In December 1989, Milan travelled to Tokyo to play in the Intercontinental Cup. The game, played between the European and South American champions, was a one-off match that would technically decide who was the best team in the world. The 1989 Copa Libertadores (the South American equivalent of the European Cup) had been won for the first time by Atlético Nacional of Colombia, whose best-known player was eccentric goalkeeper René Higuita, the free-kick and penalty specialist who scored 41 goals across his career. A tight game was decided by a goal from Milan's Alberico Evani just one minute from the end of extra time, adding another piece of silverware to Milan's growing trophy cabinet.

The period from November to February also saw Milan imperious in Serie A as they notched up 14 wins in 16 league fixtures, drawing the other two. Despite the absence of Gullit, Milan registered vital wins against Juventus at home, Inter away and Napoli at home. As February ended, Milan had finally wrestled the top spot in Serie A from Napoli with eight games remaining. It had been a superb run of form that they now hoped to carry forward as the European Cup restarted.

Milan's quarter-final opponents were a somewhat surprise package, KV Mechelen of Belgium, and 33,000 of their fans packed the Heysel Stadium in Brussels to witness a respectable goalless draw against the European Cup holders. They proved just as tough back at the San Siro, again holding Milan goalless over 90 minutes to head to extra time. It would take a moment of luck to finally crack the Belgians, when a Rijkaard free kick deflected to Tassotti to cross for an easy Van Basten tap-in, before Marco Simone put the tie to bed with a stunning solo effort just before the final whistle. It had been a struggle, but in the end Milan were again into the semi-finals.

Unfortunately for Milan, March would be a tough month in Serie A. Two back-to-back losses, against first Juventus and then city rivals Inter, saw their lead over Napoli down to just one point. Serie A looked like going down to the wire, but firstly there was a European Cup semi-final to worry about. The last four were all proven winners: Milan, Bayern Munich, Marseille and Benfica – take your pick, whoever you drew would be tough. As it was, Milan would face the German champions, with the first leg at the San Siro.

For 77 minutes, Milan camped in the Bayern half. Chances fell to Van Basten, but Bayern keeper Raimond Aumann was equal to each attempt. Massaro had two penalty claims turned down, while Bayern didn't register a single shot on goal. And then a third penalty shout was awarded – maybe the referee felt it best this time for his own personal safety – and Van Basten finally beat Aumann. Milan continued to dominate but, when the final whistle sounded, Bayern seemed relieved to come away with a narrow 1-0 defeat, considering they had been battered by the *Rossoneri*. It set up a mouthwatering second leg that would not disappoint.

A completely different Bayern emerged two weeks later back in the Munich rain. From the start they went on the offensive, having an early goal ruled out for offside. But after weathering the early storm, Milan began to threaten, with Massaro missing a glorious chance to grab the all-important away goal thanks to a last-ditch tackle from Bayern captain Klaus Augenthaler. Early in the second half, both sides were creating chances, but neither could open the scoring. Finally, with half an hour remaining, Bayern made the breakthrough, sending the Bayern faithful into ecstasy: 1-1 on aggregate.

Milan went on the attack but the match went to extra time. Ten minutes in, a hopeful punt forward saw Milan substitute Stefano Borgonovo ahead of the Bayern offside trap. It was a rare opportunity for Borgonovo to make a name for himself – his playing time was restricted as a back-up to Van Basten, and he only played 13 times for Milan, scoring twice. One of those two would be now, as he calmly lobbed Aumann to give Milan the vital away goal, drawing a hushed silence around the Olympiastadion. It would be a moment Borgonovo, and Milan fans, would never forget.

Bayern now needed two goals, and their substitute, Scotsman Alan McInally, got them back into the tie with a scruffy goal. It was lucky, but Bayern had a chance now, with 15 minutes remaining. Bayern prodded and probed but then Augenthaler played a simple pass back to Aumann but hadn't noticed Borgonovo, who, intercepting, easily rounded Aumann before shooting towards the open goal, only to fluff his lines as the ball sailed narrowly over. It was a horrible miss, and the substitute could only pray that it wouldn't be costly.

It wasn't – Milan saw out the game to book a place in their second successive European Cup Final. Borgonovo could bask in his moment of glory, his miss forgotten. On the same evening, a late goal in Lisbon saw Benfica advance past Marseille to become Milan's opponents in Vienna on 23 May. But first, Milan returned to their domestic battle with Napoli for the 1990 Serie A title.

As outlined earlier, Milan were to fall short, finishing two points behind Maradona and company, smarting from the 'Montina di Alemão' decision in awarding Napoli the result away at Atalanta. Van Basten at least had the honour of lifting the *Capocannoniere* with his 19 Serie A goals. It left the Milan squad a month to contemplate their clash with Benfica and stay focused. Finally, the time came to fly off to Austria.

* * *

Sacchi surprised many, including his own players, when he named Ruud Gullit in the starting line-up for the final after an absence of ten months. It was a risky move, with questions marks over his fitness after such a long break, but for the first time in ages Sacchi started all three Dutchmen, dropping Massaro to the bench.

Managed by future England manager Sven-Göran Eriksson, Benfica decided upon a game plan where they would closely mark Gullit and Van Basten, while playing an offside trap. And for the first 45 minutes, it was extremely successful, Milan making the running but unable to craft any real chances of note. It didn't make for classic viewing, but Benfica were nullifying the *Rossoneri*.

The second half saw Benfica grow in confidence, starting to journey more into the Milan danger area, but with just over 20 minutes to go, the game desperately called out for a goal – it would be a tactical tweak by Sacchi that would break the deadlock. With Van Basten and Gullit so closely marked, it made sense for them to try to drag their markers out of position to allow Milan's midfielders to charge into the vacated space. As Costacurta brought the ball forward into midfield, he spotted Van Basten coming back towards him, dragging his marker along. Costacurta hit a quick pass to Van Basten, who instantly flicked the ball forward into the space he had left, into which Rijkaard was running from midfield. Clean through, he settled himself before poking the ball past the outrushing Benfica keeper. It was Sacchi tactics at their best – a change in tempo and a quick, direct move forward through the heart of the opponents' defence.

That goal would prove enough for Milan to lift the European Cup again as Benfica could offer no real response, allowing the champions to see out the match comfortably. Sacchi had done the incredible – the relatively inexperienced manager had led his team to two European Cup titles and one Serie A title in the space of just three seasons, aided by Berlusconi's ambition and financial backing. It was safe to say that this Milan team had revolutionised football through their pressing and high defensive line, placing them at the pinnacle of Europe. The rest of the continent could only look on in admiration – if you wanted to see innovative football played by the best players in the world, Italy was indisputably the place to be. Napoli and Milan had led the way – other Italian teams were to continue the dominance.

The question now for Milan was whether they could follow in the footsteps of Real Madrid, Ajax and Bayern Munich and win a hat-trick of successive European Cups. They had an early advantage in this respect in that, while 1990/91 would be the first season that English clubs were allowed back into the competition since their Heysel ban, that did not yet apply to Liverpool, who had won the English league, so England would still have no entrant. Also, Dutch champions Ajax were barred from this year's tournament after a fan threw an iron bar that struck Austria Wien's keeper in the prior season's UEFA Cup, resulting in a one-year ban. Therefore, with 31 teams present, one team would get a first-round bye, which was awarded to Milan as champions.

The second round saw Milan less than convincing as they narrowly beat Club Brugge 1-0 on aggregate, but once again, they were into the quarter-finals, with four months to focus on domestic issues. But that win included a straight red card for Van Basten near the end of the second leg for throwing an elbow, making him ineligible for the next round.

December again saw Milan fly to Tokyo, to attempt to retain the Intercontinental Cup, where they faced Paraguayan outfit Olimpia. This time they wouldn't struggle to win, scoring three unanswered goals, two from Rijkaard, to again crown themselves champions of the world. The silverware collection just kept growing.

Having failed to win Serie A during the last two seasons, Berlusconi could be forgiven for wanting to correct that, and as Milan's European Cup quarter-final approached, the *Rossoneri* were sitting in third position, just one point behind Inter and Sampdoria. The European Cup quarter-final would see them play a strong Marseille team, also funded by a rich media mogul in Bernard Tapie, who shared many of the same personality traits as Berlusconi. He had funded a squad that could challenge the likes of Milan, including Dragan Stojković and the fearsome striking talents of Jean-Pierre Papin. It would be a tough tie for the Italians.

Milan got off to the perfect start in the first leg at the San Siro when Mozer tried a disastrous back pass to keeper Pascal Olmeta that Gullit intercepted to slot home. But just before the half-hour mark, Marseille equalised, Papin scoring his sixth goal of the tournament. Marseille continued to match Milan, hitting the post in the second half, to come away with a precious draw and an away goal to take back to the south of France two weeks later.

With Milan needing to score at least once, the second leg seemed to be drifting away from them, goalless with just 15 minutes left. Then came one of the great European Cup goals of all time. Abedi Pele picked up the ball on the wing, crossing it to Papin on the edge of the Milan area. The Frenchman had the vision to know Chris Waddle was behind him, so he flicked his header out towards him. Just inside the area, Waddle hit the ball with a first-time volley, arrowing it past keeper Rossi into the corner of the net. It was a fabulous strike, one that would endear the Englishman deeper into Marseille hearts. Milan were staring at elimination unless they could find an equaliser.

As the game moved into injury time, Marseille still held their one-goal lead. A huge cheer went up as the referee appeared to blow for full time, Marseille players celebrating a famous victory. Except that he wasn't blowing for full time, and he suddenly indicated to play on. With seconds remaining, the pitch was suddenly enveloped in semi-darkness as one set of the four floodlights failed. Waddle, who had the ball at the time, didn't seem bothered as he went on an incredible solo run that almost resulted in a Maradona-esque goal. Confusion then reigned as players assumed that the game must now be over. Shirts were starting to be swapped but the referee seemed to be insisting that play again continue.

Everyone milled around the pitch, bewildered, while the damaged floodlight was half restored, providing enough light to play by. It was at this moment that Milan director Adriano Galliani decided to take matters into his own hands, coming onto the pitch and directing the Milan players to leave. The referee retaliated by making a big show of putting the ball in position for a goal kick, but Milan refused to continue, despite adequate light. Having no choice, the referee called the end of the game, eliminating Milan and allowing Marseille celebrations to begin long into the night.

Galliani attempted to defend his stance after the match, stating: 'When some of the lights came on again, we were asked to continue, but I didn't think there was enough light, and the players told me that they didn't feel in the right spirit to begin playing again.' UEFA took a dim view (pun intended) of Milan's histrionics. While awarding the match 3-0 to Marseille, which mattered not a jot to the Italians, they also banned Milan for a year from European competition as well as banning Galliani from official club functions for two years.

Not only was Milan's run of European glory over for this season but also for the subsequent one – a huge blow for Berlusconi.

March 1991 proved to be a terrible month for the Milanese. Not only were they eliminated from the European Cup, but they also lost to Roma in the semi-finals of the Coppa Italia and lost two vital Serie A games, against Sampdoria and Atalanta. Rumours surfaced of discontent within the squad, now in their fourth year of working under Sacchi's demanding training regimes, with Gullit and Van Basten allegedly fed up. *La Repubblica* reported a leaked ultimatum from Berlusconi to Sacchi stating that if he failed to win Serie A or the European Cup, he would be sacked. As the season came to an end, Berlusconi was faced with no trophies to add to the cabinet, Milan ending second in Serie A. It was the first season for him without domestic or European success and would signal in a new era at the San Siro, as the summer saw Berlusconi part ways with Sacchi, who moved on to become the national coach of the *Azzurri*.

It was a harsh end for a coach who had achieved so much but reflected the tough world of Italian football and the demanding aspirations of Berlusconi. Sacchi could leave Milan with his head held high, having transformed the fortunes of the *Rossoneri*. Under his leadership, Milan had lifted their tenth Scudetto, their first for nine seasons, earning them a star above their badge. They had enjoyed back-to-back European Cup success, including the iconic 5-0 thrashing of Real Madrid and 4-0 win in the final against Steaua Bucureşti. Their dominance was also demonstrated by twice winning the European Super Cup (1989 and 1990) as well as twice winning the Intercontinental Cup. Milan players had led the Ballon d'Or awards and Marco van Basten twice won the *Capocannoniere* award for Serie A's top scorer. They were without doubt the top side in Europe during Sacchi's reign – a team that would go down in footballing history as one of the greatest club sides of all time. Not too bad for a former shoe salesman.

MILAN (1987–1991)
European Cup winners – 1988/89, 1989/90
Intercontinental Cup winners – 1989, 1990
Serie A champions – 1987/88
European Super Cup winners – 1989, 1990

Chapter 8

The Greatest Serie A
Game of the Era?

*In years to come, people will be saying I was here
... I was at that game. So much that will live
long in the memory.*

Martin Tyler during the famous Inter/Sampdoria clash

IT WAS shortly following the end of the Second World War that
two sports clubs decided to merge. Up to that point, Sampierdarenese
and Andrea Doria had been competitors, based in the Ligurian
capital of Genoa. Both were playing in the Northern Italian Serie
A, but Sampierdarenese had finished bottom of the standings, with
Andrea Doria not doing much better. Perhaps it would be better
to pool their resources? So with that in mind, they merged, slicing
their names up to form a new club, and designing a new kit that
would take the blue shirts of Andrea Doria and the white, red and
black midsection of Sampierdarenese. From now on, they would
play under the name Unione Calcio Sampdoria.

From then until 1977, Sampdoria played almost entirely in
Serie A, only suffering one season below that, in 1966/67. However,
they never set the league alight, their highest achievement being
one fourth-place finish. At the end of 1976/77, they dropped for a
second time to Serie B but, unlike before, they wouldn't immediately
bounce back. Instead, they settled into what looked like their new
ranking – mid-table in Serie B.

But, like Milan later, a businessman saw the opportunity to
buy the club and try to restore it to the top flight. While Berlusconi
made his wealth in media, Paolo Mantovani made his in oil, and

in 1979 moved to invest in Sampdoria. Again, like Berlusconi, it would herald a period of ownership that would completely change the trajectory of the club.

Although raised in Rome, where he supported Lazio as a boy, Mantovani moved to Liguria in his 20s. Initially he followed Sampdoria's city rivals, Genoa, but became disillusioned when they sold star player Gigi Meroni, despite asking supporters to commit to buying season tickets to help fund his stay. Switching his allegiance to Sampdoria, Mantovani started to make a name for himself, founding his own oil business while also acting as Sampdoria's press secretary. As Sampdoria suffered the ignominy of relegation to Serie B, Mantovani watched as the long-time club president Glauco Lolli Ghetti resigned, leaving the club in desperate need of funding.

The 1979 energy crisis was kind to Mantovani as profits soared at his oil company, allowing him to make his move and buy Sampdoria. Like Berlusconi, he was ambitious, stating his aim of not just getting Sampdoria back into Serie A but also to eventually win the Scudetto, brave words considering they had never been close to doing so throughout their history.

The project started slowly, with Sampdoria finishing ninth in Serie B in the year of Mantovani's purchase, followed by a seventh-place and a fifth-place finish, movement upward but still stuck in the lower division. Finally, promotion was achieved in 1981/82 when Sampdoria finished third under coach Renzo Ulivieri. Back in the promised land, Mantovani started to release some serious funding into the club to help them compete at the top level.

The summer of 1982 saw some top-class signings join the *Blucerchiati*. First, having been cruelly pushed out of Juventus to make way for Michel Platini and Zbigniew Boniek, came Liam Brady to strengthen the midfield, along with Francesco Casagrande from Fiorentina. But the real excitement centred around the attacking signings. Trevor Francis, who had been the first £1m transfer in England when he moved from Birmingham City to Nottingham Forest, where he scored the winning goal in the 1979 European Cup Final, was bought from Manchester City for £700,000. But the signing that would have most impact on Sampdoria in the long run would be a 17-year-old from Bologna who had netted nine goals the previous season – one Roberto Mancini.

Even as a youngster, Mancini had been on many top teams' radars, including Milan, before signing for Bologna at the age of 13. At 16, he made his debut for the *Rossoblù*, playing in the 1981/82 season and scoring nine goals, an impressive start at such a tender age. It earned him a £2.2m transfer to Sampdoria (it was rumoured that Milan tried to buy him first, but sent his contract to the wrong address). Naturally an attacking midfielder, playing behind a central striker, he was what the Italian media liked to term a *'fantasista'*, or a classic No.10, blessed with silky skills and a great volley. He would go on to be a sturdy presence during his Sampdoria career, showing strong leadership both on and off the pitch across an amazing 15 seasons. In fact, even as a teenager, he had a reputation for not being afraid of authority or seniority, including picking fights with senior players, including Trevor Francis and Liam Brady, during training sessions, as well as challenging Juan Sebastián Verón after a match, causing the Argentine to describe him as 'not an easy person, [with a] complicated personality'.

Such was the excitement among the Sampdoria faithful that over 50,000 came along for the opening home game of the season, delighting in a 1-0 victory over Juventus, after which Sampdoria beat Inter and then Roma in their next two fixtures. That early burst couldn't be maintained all season, though, with both Francis and Mancini spending time on the injury list, but it still ended in a credible seventh-place finish. Sampdoria repeated this the next season too, cementing their place in the top flight, young Mancini ending as top scorer with ten goals, and a centre-back named Pietro Vierchowod added to the squad. But then Mantovani again made crucial signings over the summer of 1984.

Liam Brady moved on to Inter, while the squad was strengthened with the signing of Graeme Souness, the Scottish captain of serial winners Liverpool, for a fee of £650,000, bringing top-level experience into the heart of the team. The youth development, meanwhile, continued with the purchase of a young striker from Serie B's Cremonese, who had scored ten league goals the previous season. That 20-year-old was named Gianluca Vialli.

Unlike many a footballer that had been raised in the mean streets of Buenos Aires or Messina, Gianluca Vialli had been born into privilege, growing up in a 60-room castello in Lombardy. A traditional striker, he was the perfect player to place in front of Mancini, and the two of them would form an incredible partnership during their time at Sampdoria, becoming known as the *I Gemelli del Gol* (the goal twins), with Vialli scoring many vital goals, often assisted by Mancini. It was Mancini who, as an Italian U-21 colleague of Vialli, convinced the young striker to join Sampdoria, despite the interest of bigger clubs.

Sampdoria now had a team capable of challenging for major honours. Their football was praised as aggressive and exciting, and their league form saw them earn a fourth-place finish. But it was in the Coppa Italia that Sampdoria first won silverware, reaching the final by overcoming Torino and then Fiorentina to set up a final against the Milan of Hateley and Wilkins, managed by Liedholm. The first leg at the San Siro saw Sampdoria leave with a one-goal advantage, courtesy of Souness, bringing them back for a glorious night at the Stadio Luigi Ferraris, where a Mancini penalty and a Vialli goal gave them a 2-1 victory on the night. For the first time in their history, Sampdoria players and fans could celebrate a trophy, via a competition that they would dominate over the next few years.

With fan expectations now so high, the next season was a disappointment, Sampdoria unable to build on the prior season's success. They dropped to 12th, just four points above relegation, while their Cup Winners' Cup campaign ended in the second round against Benfica. The only light was in the Coppa Italia, where they once more reached the final, this time losing out to Roma. It was a frustrating campaign after so many seasons of continual improvement, and its conclusion saw manager Eugenio Bersellini accept a position at Fiorentina. The question was, who would Mantovani bring in as his replacement?

* * *

In 1961, Sampdoria signed a 30-year-old Yugoslav defender from Vojvodina, where he had enjoyed 14 seasons behind the Iron Curtain but was now, due to his age, allowed to move west. Vujadin Boškov played just 13 games for the *Blucerchiati* over one season – making no significant impression on Sampdoria's history. Almost immediately afterwards, he moved into management, becoming quite the nomad as he took positions in Switzerland, Yugoslavia, the Netherlands and finally Spain, where he led Real Madrid to the European Cup Final against Liverpool, before moving to Italy and Ascoli in 1984.

At the time, Ascoli were a lower-half Serie A team with limited resources. A difficult campaign saw Boškov unable to save them from relegation but, despite that, his Ascoli team had impressed with their style of football. Although it placed him on the radar of other Italian clubs, he chose to stick with them and help them in their fight to return to Serie A, which is exactly what he achieved. He not only brought them back up to the top flight, but they also won the Serie B championship, losing just five times in a 38-game season within a division that at the time included the likes of Lazio, Bologna and Genoa.

Having done the honourable thing at Ascoli and once again demonstrated his managerial talent, it was time for a bigger move, and it was Sampdoria that offered Boškov a position. With Bersellini out, Mantovani was on the lookout for a replacement and, in his quest to build a family structure at Sampdoria, Boškov fitted the bill, having shown loyalty at Ascoli in remaining during the tough times. And for Boškov, he was taking the reins of a team that had just won its first silverware. It would turn out to be a successful partnership.

The 1986/87 campaign began with the two British stars leaving the *Blucerchiati*. Graeme Souness took the position of player-manager at Scottish giants Rangers, where he would enjoy success as the club would go on to a nine-in-a-row title surge, the first three under his watch. Trevor Francis, meanwhile, stayed in the country, moving across to Atalanta for one season before joining Souness's revolution over at Ibrox. Replacing them were two more foreign signings: German Hans-Peter Briegel and Brazilian Toninho Cerezo. Briegel was a defender who had been part of the miraculous Hellas Verona title-winning side of 1985, becoming Germany Footballer of the Year despite being based outside the country. Midfielder Cerezo had been a member of the Roma team that had lost the European Cup Final in 1984 but had lifted the Coppa Italia in 1984 and 1986. Together, two very useful additions whose experience would help to balance the youth of Mancini and Vialli.

The start of the season saw Sampdoria stutter in the league, losing four of their first six games, until Boškov started to form a team that gelled. From then on they only lost four more times all season in Serie A, finishing a respectable sixth, narrowly missing out on a UEFA Cup place in a play-off against Milan. Vialli finished the campaign with 12 goals, while Mancini grabbed six, making it a good start for the new Yugoslav manager, providing a base to build upon.

The 1987/88 season saw further improvement. This time Sampdoria finished fourth, above both Inter and Juventus, losing just six Serie A games all season. But the real success came in the Coppa Italia. Having topped the initial group stage with a 100 per cent record, Sampdoria progressed through the knockout stages to reach their second final in four seasons, eliminating Pisa, Ascoli and Inter en route to setting up the deciding match against Torino. It was a two-legged affair, with the first played at Sampdoria's Stadio Luigi Ferraris, where early goals from Briegel and Vialli meant advantage Sampdoria. Two weeks later, however, in a packed Stadio Comunale, Sampdoria gifted Torino two early own goals from Vierchowod and Antonio Paganin to take the game into extra time. With just eight minutes remaining, midfield substitute Fausto Salsano scored to bring the Coppa Italia trophy back to Genoa. Having never previously won silverware, Mantovani's Sampdoria now had two trophies in four seasons, along with their fourth-place finish. They were becoming a force to be reckoned with within Italy.

* * *

Sampdoria's Coppa Italia win gained them entry to European competition in the form of the 1988/89 Cup Winners' Cup. Briegel retired, to be replaced by the experienced midfielder Giuseppe Dossena from Udinese as Boškov continued to tweak his squad, looking to build on the prior season's achievements. From the start of the season in October until early March, Sampdoria were on fire. Their Serie A campaign saw them lose only twice during their first 21 matches, to Inter and Roma, placing them third, behind only Inter and Napoli. Vialli scored 13 goals across this period, establishing himself as the young striking talent within Italy, while Mancini contributed five of his own, the two of them forming a deadly partnership.

At the same time, Sampdoria were again enjoying a strong run in the Coppa Italia, while their European adventure was proving more successful than their last outing, as Swedish side IFK Norrköping, East Germany's Carl Zeiss Jena and Romania's Dinamo Bucureşti were all eliminated, helped by four goals from Vialli, taking them to a semi-final against holders Mechelen of Belgium, to be played in April. Boškov's leadership had Sampdoria competing strongly on all three fronts.

Unfortunately, April and May saw Sampdoria run out of steam in Serie A. Their eight games saw them beaten six times while drawing the other two, dropping them down to sixth place. It could have represented a depressing end to a season that started so brightly, except that salvation came in the cup competitions.

April saw Sampdoria's visit to Belgium and the small Achter de Kazerne stadium, holding around 13,000 fans for the first leg of the Cup Winners' Cup semi-final. Two headed goals saw the Italians face an uphill battle before, inevitably, Vialli grabbed a precious away goal just 15 minutes from time. The second leg was played at the Stadio Giovanni Zini in Cremona (temporarily used by Sampdoria as work was done on Stadio Luigi Ferraris ahead of the 1990 World Cup), holding just over 18,000 fans, and again Sampdoria struggled in front of goal. It was goalless after 68 minutes with the *Blucerchiati* facing elimination. But then Boskov's team turned it around. First Mancini threaded a beautiful ball through for Cerezo to put Sampdoria ahead, before Dossena was put clean through from his own half as Mechelen threw caution to the wind. He took the ball around the keeper before making the tie safe. Finally, Salsano put the icing on the cake with two minutes remaining to send Sampdoria into their first-ever European final.

And so it was, on 10 May 1989, that Sampdoria travelled to the Wankdorf Stadium in Bern, Switzerland to face Johan Cruyff's Barcelona – a team that would evolve into the 'Dream Team', winning the European Cup in 1992. Playing in their change kit of all white, Sampdoria got off to the worst possible start when, after just four minutes, Gary Lineker crossed for Julio Salinas to head Barcelona in front. From that point on, Barcelona continued to dominate, until with just 11 minutes remaining, Luis Rekarte broke the Sampdoria offside trap to seal the cup for the Spaniards. It had been one step too far for the evolving Sampdoria team, who just couldn't match Barcelona on the day, but it had been a great achievement just to reach their first European final.

The season ended with yet another Coppa Italia Final for Sampdoria – this time a two-legged affair against Maradona's Napoli. The first leg saw Napoli seal a 1-0 win in Naples before the tie returned to Cremona. It would prove to be one of the greatest nights in Sampdoria history.

It should be remembered that Sampdoria were facing a Napoli that had won the UEFA Cup a month earlier, while also finishing second in Serie A. A Napoli that included in its starting line-up the Brazilians Alemão and Careca, and, of course, captain Diego Armando Maradona. But Sampdoria showed no fear, starting at breakneck pace, resplendent in their iconic blue shirts, almost scoring early on from a Vierchowod free kick, before Vialli gave them the lead with a trademark bullet header. Sampdoria were flying and Mancini almost immediately added a second, shooting narrowly over after a flowing break. It would prove to only be a temporary respite, as six minutes after Vialli's opener, Mancini floated in a cross for Cerezo to head home at the far post, giving Sampdoria the aggregate lead. With the stadium in delirium, Napoli did well to reach half-time only two down.

Sampdoria came out intent on continuing where they left off and, just two minutes into the half, Vierchowod brought the ball forward, played a delightful one-two involving a Mancini backheel, before placing the ball into the corner for Sampdoria's third. Things got even worse for Napoli as Maradona lost the ball to Dossena, who played Mancini through on goal. Faced by Napoli's Alessandro Renica, Mancini nutmegged him to burst into the area, where a floundering Renica tripped him from behind – Mancini gratefully converted the penalty.

Napoli were 4-0 down after just 60 minutes and there was no way back. Sampdoria had successfully defended their Coppa Italia title, winning their third in five seasons, the trophy handed to a beaming Mantovani. More importantly, they had secured another berth in the Cup Winners' Cup, while fast evolving into one of the strongest teams in Italy and Europe. The question was, after coming so close only to lose out to Barcelona, could Sampdoria go all the way this time?

* * *

Heading into the new season, Sampdoria made one further key addition to their squad. They had been keeping an eye on a 23-year-old winger making a name for himself at Serie B Cremonese, where he had scored 17 goals, while creating many more. Even at this age, he was starting to go bald on top, making him look older than he was. In terms of the Sampdoria attack, he would be the third crucial piece alongside Gianluca Vialli and Roberto Mancini. Attilio Lombardo would write his name into Sampdoria folklore along with his two compadres.

Kicking off their 1989/90 Cup Winners' Cup campaign in Bergen, Sampdoria progressed through the first two rounds and the quarter-finals with relative ease, eliminating Norwegian club Brann, German giants Borussia Dortmund and Swiss club Grasshopper to set up a semi-final clash against France's AS Monaco. This was the Monaco side managed by Arsène Wenger that included the overseas striking talents of a young George Weah (who had just won African Footballer of the Year for 1989), Ramón Díaz and Mark Hateley.

The first leg in France saw Monaco take the lead when Weah powered in a header from a corner. With 15 minutes remaining, Vialli went down rather theatrically in the penalty area, but it was convincing enough for the referee – Vialli then having the cheek to 'Panenka' keeper Jean-Luc Ettori. Just three minutes later, Vialli struck again, this time heading home a Mancini cross, only to then see Díaz equalise shortly after with a deflected shot. It meant Sampdoria left Monaco with a draw and two away goals – not a bad night's work.

Returning to Genoa, it took just nine minutes for Vierchowod to open the scoring from close range before Lombardo finished off a lightning-fast second-half break to seal Sampdoria's second successive appearance in a Cup Winners' Cup Final. Their opponents this time would be Anderlecht, who had eliminated champions Barcelona in the second round, with the final to be held on 9 May 1990 in Gothenburg. This time Sampdoria were determined to come home with the trophy in hand.

The game was tight, with the better chances falling Sampdoria's way, Vierchowod and Mancini going especially close but unable to breach the Belgian defence. As the game moved into extra time,

Sampdoria continued to press and finally, just before the break, the Anderlecht defence broke. Lombardo did exactly what he was bought for, breaking down the wing before setting up a shot that rebounded off the post and straight into Anderlecht keeper Filip De Wilde's arms; only he couldn't hold it, allowing Vialli to steal in and poke home. Straight after the second half kick-off, the Mancini-Vialli partnership struck again to send the Sampdoria fans into ecstasy – Mancini crossing for Vialli to head home his second.

And with that, Sampdoria were the 1990 Cup Winners' Cup winners. The team that Mantovani had built and that Boškov had coached, the team that eight years before had been playing in Serie B, had won their fourth trophy of their reign. They became only the fourth Italian team to lift the trophy, and part of an Italian treble sweep of European trophies during the season as AC Milan and Juventus won the European Cup and UEFA Cup, respectively. There was little doubt throughout Europe as to who the dominant country was now.

* * *

Sampdoria had proved themselves to be a strong cup side with their four trophies, but could they finally develop the consistency over 34 matches to make a run for the Scudetto? Vialli and Mancini had grown into a fantastic partnership, Lombardo had enjoyed a strong first season, Vierchowod was a rock at the back, while the midfield saw Cerezo pulling the strings. The last two seasons had also seen the development of their young goalkeeper, Gianluca Pagliuca, meaning the spine of the team was now firmly in place. As usual, Mantovani was determined to keep improving and the summer of 1990 saw Sampdoria add midfielder Oleksiy Mykhaylychenko from Dynamo Kyiv, where he had been a part of the hugely impressive squad that had won the 1986 Cup Winners' Cup under the leadership of legendary coach Valeriy Lobanovskyi.

The first three months of the 1990/91 Serie A season saw a strong start from the *Blucerchiati* as they went unbeaten until the end of November, sitting atop of the standings. That included a superb 4-1 win away at champions Napoli, a statement result powered by two goals each for Vialli and Mancini. Infuriatingly, the unbeaten run came to an end via a home defeat to their city rivals, Genoa (the *Derby della Lanterna*), at the start of a shaky December and January, where two further defeats left them in third place, just a point behind leaders Inter.

March 1991 would prove to be a huge month in Sampdoria's history. Going into it, they had won six Serie A games in succession, putting them back on top – one point above Inter and two ahead of Milan. They had once again advanced to the quarter-finals of the Cup Winners' Cup, defeating German side FC Kaiserslautern and Greece's Olympiacos to set up a meeting with Legia Warsaw, their love affair with the competition continuing. And they were set to meet Napoli over two legs in the semi-finals of the Coppa Italia. An incredible treble hung tantalizingly in sight, but to succeed would require winning the Scudetto for the first time in their history. Much would depend upon their next two Serie A home matches, against third-placed Milan and Maradona's Napoli. Five Serie A, two Cup Winners' Cup and two Coppa Italia games to be played over the space of just 31 days. Crunch time.

First up was a trip to Atalanta, where a late equaliser from Argentina's Claudio Caniggia deprived Sampdoria of a vital win. Three days later, Sampdoria flew behind the Iron Curtain for their first leg in Warsaw, where a rare mistake by Pagliuca gifted the Poles a one-goal advantage to take to Genoa. It was not the perfect start ahead of the critical home game against Milan at the weekend.

A packed Stadio Luigi Ferraris eagerly awaited the clash against Arrigo Sacchi's European Cup winners – a game that would cement whether Sampdoria really were title contenders. Sampdoria made all the early running, pinning Milan back, but were unable to breach the famous back four – Milan seemingly happy to play on the break or leave Genoa with a draw if need be. The second half saw Mancini continue to torment the Milan defence until, finally, he forced them into an error, bringing him down in the area. It was the breakthrough Sampdoria had been pushing for, Vialli calmly slotting the penalty home to send *Blucerchiati* fans crazy. Gullit threatened to spoil the party but his goal was disallowed for a foul on Pagliuca, after which Mancini wrapped up a famous 2-0 statement win for Sampdoria, keeping them level with Inter at the top but starting to pull away from Milan – in effect setting up a two-horse race for the title.

There was hardly time to celebrate as just two days later Sampdoria travelled to Napoli for the first leg of their Coppa Italia semi-final, where only a Maradona goal separated the two teams after 90 minutes. In both the Coppa Italia and the Cup Winners' Cup, Sampdoria had suffered narrow away losses – not ideal but not fatal either. Their punishing schedule would continue as they next travelled to Pisa, where they were held goalless until the last 25 minutes, after which three goals kept their Serie A challenge on track. It was the perfect tune-up for the return leg against Legia Warsaw.

A disastrous first 55 minutes saw Warsaw score two aways goals, both from the boot of Wojciech Kowalczyk, leaving Sampdoria with the unenviable task of needing three goals in 35 minutes to progress to the final. But hopes rose when Mancini pulled one back with 23 minutes remaining, after which Vialli fired home an equaliser with just two minutes left. With the crowd baying for a third, it proved just too much for the exhausted Sampdoria side, meaning any hope of a historic treble was gone, focus now fully back onto Serie A and the Coppa Italia.

If the players were disappointed, they had little time to process it as the weekend meant their second huge home game in succession – this time facing Maradona's Napoli for the second time in 12 days. Sampdoria had stunned Napoli earlier in the season by thrashing them 4-1 at the San Paolo but this game fell within a heavy schedule of fixtures for the *Blucerchiati*. Still, they got off to the perfect start when Cerezo thumped home a header after just 12 minutes. Seven minutes later, the deadly duo struck again as some lovely skill by Mancini set up Vialli to double their lead. Vialli struck again after 64 minutes, this time with his head, before Maradona pulled one back from the penalty spot. Finally, Lombardo got on the scoresheet to duplicate the result earlier in the season, 4-1. Combined with the win over Milan two weeks before, Sampdoria fans could start to dare to believe, three points ahead of Inter at the top of the standings.

Ten days later Sampdoria again welcomed Napoli to the Stadio Luigi Ferraris, this time for the renewal of their Coppa Italia clash, although Napoli would be without their Argentine superstar. As mentioned earlier, a failed drug test saw Maradona flee the country and, although no one knew it at the time, the 4-1 defeat to Sampdoria was to be Maradona's last game for Napoli. Unsurprisingly, the Napoli organisation and team were still shell-shocked by the speed of events – which Sampdoria took advantage of, beating them 2-0 through a late winner from Giovanni Invernizzi to seal yet another Coppa Italia Final berth, this time against Ottavio Bianchi's Roma.

That final was scheduled after the season's end, but before that Sampdoria faced one last hurdle to winning Serie A. With just four games remaining, they sat three points ahead of Inter, in an era of two points for a win, but with a visit to the San Siro up next to face the *Nerazzurri*. It was the game that would likely decide the championship – an Inter win would place them within touching distance of Sampdoria, a win for Sampdoria would open a five-point gap with just three games left. It would prove to be one of the greatest games in Serie A history.

* * *

A Saturday afternoon kick-off – 4 May 1991. All eyes were upon this game as Sampdoria travelled to the imposing San Siro to face the mighty Inter. The Inter starting line-up included Walter Zenga in goal, Giuseppe Bergomi and Andreas Brehme in defence, Nicola Berti and Lothar Matthäus in midfield, and a fearsome attack of Jürgen Klinsmann and Aldo Serena, all managed by the legendary Giovanni Trapattoni. They had already booked themselves a place in the UEFA Cup Final, where they would be facing fellow Italians Roma. This was a must-win game for them – Sampdoria could expect to face a tidal wave of attacking football. The question on everyone's lips was could they weather the storm and come through the other side with a result?

No team outside of Milan had faced Inter at the San Siro and come away with a victory since February 1988, over three years before, when Torino had emerged with a 1-0 win. That was the level of difficulty facing Sampdoria on this spring afternoon, so unsurprisingly the early part of the game saw Inter do all the probing, while Sampdoria stuck to a sound defensive shape. After all, should the game end in a draw, it would suit Sampdoria more than Inter.

The first chance of note involved Klinsmann bravely throwing himself into a diving header at the far post, ending up sprawled in the net as the ball went narrowly wide. Shortly after, tensions surfaced when a foul by Cerezo on Berti led to a yellow card and a shoving match involving several players. Matthäus then fired in a trademark screamer that Pagliuca did well to tip around the post. Sampdoria were struggling to get the ball out of their own half, Vialli cutting a lone figure up front. The intensity didn't drop as Inter fans roared their team on, Berti producing another sharp save from Pagliuca, until, five minutes before half-time, it was finally all too much for the Sampdoria defence, Klinsmann breaking clear to poke the ball into the corner – only to see the linesman's flag raised. What made it more galling for the Inter faithful was the replay, which seemed to clearly show Klinsmann onside. Sampdoria were riding their luck.

Just before the half-time whistle, Sampdoria broke out of their half, setting Lombardo free on the right. Getting to the byline, he cut the ball into the area, where Mancini was lurking, before going down rather theatrically following a brush with Paganin. It seemed Mancini was the sole person in the stadium who felt it was a foul, as he sprang to his feet and chased the referee in protest. Bergomi, for one, was less than amused and seemed to kick out at Mancini as he passed by, causing Mancini immediately to spin around as the two faced off without too much malice. But to the shock of both, the referee produced a straight red to each, leaving them to trudge off, still arguing but also consoling each other, until Bergomi appeared to be erroneously struck by a thrown coin, probably aimed at Mancini. Thankfully, the referee immediately blew for half-time, allowing tempers to cool. The game was living up to the hype.

The second half commenced with Inter straight back on the front foot, pressuring Sampdoria and keeping Pagliuca busy, Matthäus looking dangerous at every set-piece opportunity. Ten minutes in, Inter had a strong penalty appeal ignored as Vierchowod appeared to sweep Stringara's leg from under him, greeted by whistles reverberating around the stadium as the game continued, Inter fans furious. Their fury turned to frustration as Berti played a smart one-two with Serena to get through on goal, only to see his shot parried by Pagliuca straight to Bianchi, who somehow contrived to blast it over the bar with the goal gaping.

You felt Sampdoria couldn't survive much more of this battering. As Martin Tyler stated in his commentary: 'Nowhere in the world will you see club football played at this intensity.' Inter were attacking in waves, cranking up the force, while Sampdoria defended with their backs to the wall. Some 80,000 fans were screaming for a goal – and finally one came with 30 minutes remaining. Matthäus played the ball back to Stringara in midfield, who let it run by, thinking a colleague was behind him. Unfortunately, he was mistaken and Vialli charged after the loose ball, narrowly beating Paganin to it, holding the play up and then finding Dossena. Just outside the area, Dossena looked up, picked out the corner of the goal and fired home.

Tyler takes up the tale again: 'Would you believe it! Fifteen minutes into the second half. The first shot in anger.' It was Dossena's first goal of the season, resulting in him being submerged by celebrating team-mates, including substitutes. Inter looked stunned.

Suddenly the momentum of the game changed. From hardly entering Inter's half, Sampdoria attacked again, Lombardo breaking away from Brehme before narrowly shooting wide. But the game quickly swung back into the Sampdoria penalty area as a goalmouth scramble resulted in Berti going over easily after a bump from Cerezo. While looking much less a penalty than the earlier incident, this time the referee pointed to the spot, causing tensions to surface once more, Pagliuca furiously following Berti, while Lombardo gave him some sarcastic applause. Responsibility to bring Inter level would fall to the European Footballer of the Year, Lothar Matthäus, a player with a fearsome reputation from the spot. The San Siro held its breath.

Matthäus blasted it hard and low – and too near Pagliuca, whose save left the ball tangled by his legs as Matthäus rushed in to convert the rebound. As they both went for the ball, it flew narrowly wide. Incredibly, Sampdoria were still ahead with 23 minutes left. Inter lifted themselves from the canvas and threw themselves forward yet again, with seemingly unending levels of energy. Matthäus powered a vicious header at goal, which Pagliuca again saved, leaving the German to kick the post in frustration. A looping overhead kick from Klinsmann was tipped over the bar. It was crazy, frantic stuff – the game being played entirely in the Sampdoria penalty area at times – but leaving opportunities for the breakaway counter-attack, which occurred when Lombardo broke free. Rounding Zenga, his flick hit the post, bouncing back to him. He immediately set up Vialli – and his shot was cleared off the line by Brehme, flying back to help.

Martin Tyler could take no more: 'Lombardo … he's round the goalkeeper … it's hit the post! Vialli's still waiting in the middle … here he is … and it's off the line! In years to come, people will be saying I was here … I was at that game. So much that will live long in the memory.' And there were still 15 minutes to go!

While the crowd were recovering their breath, Pagliuca collected the ball and threw it out wide to Mannini. Looking up, he fired a long ball to Vialli, who found himself one-on-one with Ferri in the penalty area. A beautiful first touch left a bamboozled Ferri on the floor before Vialli calmly took the ball past Zenga and fired home into an empty net. Martin Tyler somehow prevented himself from fainting as he exclaimed: 'Grown men, hardened football watchers … are scarcely able to turn their eyes to this … and surely it's two this time … it is!'

Zenga ran to the linesman pleading for offside, but to no avail, while Vialli threw a celebratory somersault. Sampdoria were edging towards the Scudetto. With defeat staring them in the face, the Inter faithful behind Pagliuca's goal started to get restless. Flares flew down onto the edge of the pitch, smoke swirling. Objects appeared to be thrown as fans tried to move to the sides of the stand. Suddenly, Pagliuca was down, requesting assistance, team-mates trying to help him while also looking out for flying missiles. Matthäus and Zenga pleaded with the support for calm as fans could be clearly seen trying to tear up the seats in rage. It was a genuinely scary scene, Pagliuca's goal strewn with thrown flagpoles.

Eventually the game restarted, although the urgency seemed to have been dampened by the violence. Thankfully, the match ended shortly after, a pocket of brave Sampdoria fans wildly celebrating in one corner. Inter had 24 shots to Sampdoria's six, and 13 corners to Sampdoria's one. Pagliuca made 14 saves, while Zenga made none. Yet Sampdoria were leaving with a 2-0 win, on the brink of winning their first-ever Scudetto. It was a classic smash-and-grab – and one of the greatest games in Serie A history. Just ask Martin Tyler.

* * *

With the win over Inter, the route to Sampdoria's first Scudetto was smooth. A draw in Turin the following weekend meant they could clinch the title in front of their own fans against Lecce. If there were any pre-game nerves among the faithful, they were quickly calmed as Sampdoria rushed into a three-goal lead within half an hour. Mantovani was sitting in the stands, a smile glued upon his face as he watched his dream come true. He had saved the team in their dark days, Sampdoria mired in Serie B, and while he had invested money to help secure a better squad, he had in no way spent the sums that other Serie A clubs had. Yet the team he had funded were now Serie A champions, ahead of some of the finest the Italian league would ever see. No one could begrudge this kind, paternal owner his joy.

As the final whistle sounded and flares lit up around the stadium, the fans saluted the players who had achieved so much, as they did a lap of honour, surrounded by journalists and TV cameras. Genoa turned blue for days, flags draped from apartment blocks, washing lines, every surface imaginable. It showed that even in this time of riches, there was still the possibility of a Cinderella story in Italy. Their seemingly annual appearance in the Coppa Italia Final came two weeks later, but this time Sampdoria lost out to a Rudi Völler-led Roma.

Reflecting on Sampdoria's historic title-winning season, it's easy to focus on Vialli and Mancini. After all, they had scored 31 Serie A goals between them – over half of Sampdoria's total. But Sampdoria only conceded 24 goals across 34 league games, demonstrating that the defence was just as important in securing the championship. Gianluca Pagliuca had impressed all season, especially during that Inter game, where he pulled off a string of important saves, including the penalty, causing Matthäus to say of him, 'The penalty didn't cost us the match. We missed so many chances. I've never seen a goalkeeper like Gianluca Pagliuca. He played like he had ten hands today.'

In front of Pagliuca was a well-drilled defence, including the rock that was Pietro Vierchowod, full of experience, including being in the 1982 World Cup-winning squad and a title with Roma – an old-school, powerful centre-back, also comfortable with the ball at his feet. A mark of his impact was Maradona's summary of him: 'An animal with muscles on his eyelashes. It was easy to pass by him, but when I raised my head, he was in front of me again. I would have to pass him two or three times more and then I would pass the ball because I couldn't stand him anymore.' High praise indeed.

The midfield included Giuseppe Dossena, the only player to participate in every game of that title-winning season and one of the two wingers along with Attilio Lombardo. Vialli and Mancini could thank the winger Lombardo for setting up many of their strikes, with his lightning pace and exceptional work rate, allowing Sampdoria to be such a successful side playing on the fast break. His looks and speed would earn him two nicknames over his career – 'Popeye' on account of his baldness and physique, and 'the ostrich' due to his electrifying pace.

The last word on the title win should fall to their manager, Boškov, who summed it up perfectly:

> In my life I've won but the Scudetto won with Sampdoria was the most beautiful; the sweetest. Because I won it in the most difficult and most balanced league in the world and because it was the first for a club that had yet to celebrate half a century of existence. It is a bit like when your first child is born. The joy is greater.

Gaining access to the European Cup, Sampdoria had conquered Italy and now had the chance to take on the best of Europe. They had already shown the rest of the continent their abilities by reaching two Cup Winners' Cup finals – Europe had been warned.

* * *

The celebrations continued throughout the summer, until it was time for the inevitable hangover to set in. Maybe the players had also overindulged, because they made a terrible start to 1991/92, losing six of their first 11 games, leaving them 13th in the standings and closer to a relegation battle than championship retention. Luckily, the early rounds of the European Cup weren't unduly difficult, meaning that, despite their funk, Sampdoria got through the initial knockout rounds without too much trouble – easily overcoming

Norway's Rosenborg before making slightly harder work of Hungary's Budapest Honvéd, after which they faced a new wrinkle in Europe's premier club competition.

Ever since Berlusconi's public musings about the fairness of a straight knockout competition, plans were being put in place to rebrand the tournament and include a group stage, allowing more games, more opportunity for the bigger clubs to avoid an early exit and, of course, more TV revenue. The UEFA Champions League would be launched the following season, 1992/93, but in between a group stage was introduced to the 1991/92 version for the first time. Instead of playing quarter-finals, the last eight were split into two groups, where the top team in each group would meet in the final. When the group draw was done, Sampdoria found themselves opposite current European champions Red Star Belgrade, Anderlecht and Panathinaikos.

Thankfully, Sampdoria's form improved massively just as the group stage commenced. In Serie A, the *Blucerchiati* went on a 15-match unbeaten run, lifting them to fifth place by the end of March. The European Cup group games were tighter, Sampdoria starting with an impressive 2-1 home win over Red Star Belgrade, followed by a goalless draw in Athens before throwing away a 2-1 lead in Brussels to lose 3-2, leaving the Italians tied in second with Anderlecht, one point behind Red Star. Revenge was gained two weeks later when Sampdoria beat Anderlecht 2-0 in Genoa, only to hear that Red Star had also beaten Panathinaikos. The group was going to come down to the final game between Sampdoria and Red Star, where thankfully for Sampdoria they wouldn't have to travel to the fearsome Marakana for the match. Sadly, the worsening ethnic incidents occurring across Yugoslavia as the country slipped towards civil war necessitated a move to Sofia.

In a must-win game for the *Blucerchiati*, they got off to the worst possible start when Siniša Mihajlović fired in one of his trademark free kicks from outside the area, a skillset that would see him secure a move to Roma next season. Sampdoria needed a quick response and just 15 minutes later they got it – Srečko Katanec converting his saved shot to level the game. Then a moment of luck as, just before half-time, Vialli broke into the penalty area where Red Star defender Goran Vasilijević attempted a desperate tackle, unfortunately hooking the ball into his own net. The game had turned around, with Sampdoria taking a valuable lead into the half-time break.

With 14 minutes left, Sampdoria wrapped up a crucial win as the Mancini-Vialli combination struck yet again, Vialli setting Mancini up to score the third. It was a huge victory – one that took Sampdoria a point ahead of Red Star. Now Sampdoria just needed one point from their final match at home to Panathinaikos to book a place in the final. They got the draw they needed, so a date at Wembley Stadium beckoned, where the opposition would be their nemesis from the 1989 Cup Winners' Cup Final – Johan Cruyff's Barcelona – now fully in their Dream Team phase.

As their Serie A season ended, Sampdoria improved to finish in sixth position, unfortunately just outside of the European qualification places. The Coppa Italia offered Sampdoria their usual deep run, but this time they fell just short, losing to an emerging Parma in the semi-finals. Their only route back into Europe next season would be to win the big one, and with that in mind, fans of the *Blucerchiati* mixed with the Catalan hordes to descend upon London on 20 May 1992. One of the two was about to win their first-ever European Cup.

Barça were on their way to winning their second successive La Liga. The team included the talents of Andoni Zubizarreta in goal, Ronald Koeman and Pep Guardiola in defence, Michael Laudrup in midfield and the striking partnership of Hristo Stoichkov and Julio Salinas. They were favourites in many experts' opinions.

The final was a cagey affair, with few chances during regular time. Lombardo went close with a shot that was well saved by Zubizarreta, while a mazy run by Salinas needed Pagliuca to be on his toes. Pagliuca then pulled off a good double save from Stoichkov and Eusebio Sacristán before the best chances of the 90 minutes fell first to Vialli, who hit Lombardo's cross over from close range, and then Stoichkov, whose shot rebounded off the post. Vialli had one more chance towards the end, his chip falling narrowly wide. The match moved into extra time.

Early in the second period, Invernizzi was penalised for a foul on Sacristán just outside the Sampdoria penalty area. It was a questionable call but allowed the fearsome Ronald Koeman to line up, faced by a seven-man Sampdoria wall. A couple of touches to set up the shot, after which Koeman fired a rocket into the bottom corner before wheeling away to celebrate with the Catalan masses. It was a beautiful strike, giving Pagliuca no chance, and with just eight minutes remaining, Sampdoria had nothing more left to give. Barcelona had won their first European Cup, led by Cruyff.

* * *

While Sampdoria had narrowly fallen short of the ultimate prize, it was yet another testament to the strength of Italian football at this time. For a team that had been mired in Serie B in 1982 to be playing in the final of Europe's top club competition just ten years later was an incredible achievement. And while Mantovani had helped to fund that success, they had built the team wisely, investing in young talent such as Vialli and Mancini. Pagliuca had joined at the age of 20, Sampdoria being his first professional club. Vierchowod joined at the age of 24, Lombardo at 23. Even coach Boškov had been a left-field choice, brought in from Ascoli.

Sadly, the European Cup Final was the height of Sampdoria's success. Having taken them that far, Boškov moved on to join Roma, to be replaced by Sven-Göran Eriksson, who had enjoyed success at Benfica. The bigger blow was the loss of Gianluca Vialli, whose form inevitably led to a move to one of Italy's more established clubs, Juventus, for a world record fee of £12.5m, bringing the goal twins era to a close.

Sadly, Mantovani passed away in October 1993, losing a long battle with lung cancer. A warm man, who preferred to work in the background rather than being in the spotlight, he was loved by the fans, viewed as one of their own, who just happened to make money to invest in the club he adored. A plaque still exists at the Sampdoria training ground, dedicated to him, showing the celebrating players with four words inscribed beneath:

A Paolo … Anni Indimenticabili (To Paolo …
Unforgettable Years)

SAMPDORIA (1984–1992)

Cup Winners' Cup winners – 1989/90

European Cup runners-up – 1991/92

Cup Winners' Cup runners-up – 1988/89

Serie A champions – 1990/91

Coppa Italia winners – 1984/85, 1987/88, 1988/89

Chapter 9

Il Divin Codino

Roberto Baggio was the best Italian fantasista; he
was better than Meazza and Boniperti, and he
was amongst the greatest of all time, right behind
Maradona, Pelé, and maybe Cruyff. Without the
injury problems, and the difficulties with his knees,
he would have been the very best player in history.

Carlo Mazzone, former Brescia coach

The angels sing in his legs.

Aldo Agroppi, former Fiorentina coach

WHEN ONE looks back on these golden times for Italian football, thoughts often turn to those glamorous foreign players who lit up Serie A. Maradona at the peak of his powers leading Napoli to its first Scudetto. The three Dutchmen of Milan and the three Germans of Inter. Gabriel Batistuta smashing in goals for Fiorentina. That's because Serie A at this time attracted all the top players from around the world – anyone who was anyone wanted to play in Italy. But that shouldn't diminish the high Italian talent available at that time. There were players such as Baresi, Vialli, Mancini – all who helped make the *Azzurri* a fearsome side. And then there was Roberto Baggio.

The story of Baggio is one filled with heartache, triumph, pain and adversity. One of the greatest Italian players of all time, he excelled during this era of foreign stars, leaving his mark on all those who witnessed his genius. His tale begins in the small town of Caldogno, where Baggio was raised in a strict Catholic family. From an early age, he was enraptured by football, playing indoors, outdoors, whenever and wherever he could. As a nine-year-old, he entered Caldogno's youth set-up, playing as a striker, and immediately all who saw him recognised the potential within. Over the next two years, he made 26 appearances, scoring 45 goals, including six in one game, while setting up many more. Coaches regularly threw him in against older kids but still he shone, the word 'prodigy' frequently bandied around.

As word spread, it was inevitable that scouts would appear. The first to make a serious move was Antonio Mora from Vicenza, who wisely invested a paltry £300 of the club's money to secure the 13-year-old. Entering the youth team, Baggio was a skinny teenager but made up for lack of strength with speed and impressive dribbling. Such was his talent that, even at 14, he was thrown into training with the first team – and it didn't faze him one bit.

On the last day of 1982/83, Roberto Baggio stepped out for the first time for the Vicenza senior team in a Serie C1 game against Piacenza. There was no immediate fairy-tale start – Vicenza lost 1-0 – but he was now a full professional. It would take Baggio almost a year to score his first senior goal, a penalty in a 3-0 win over Brescia. The 1984/85 season saw Baggio cement himself as an emerging star, scoring 14 times in league and cup games as he helped Vicenza win promotion to Serie B. Already at that young age, he was playing with a style that would become his trademark. A disciplined role was never his forte – Baggio liked to be given freedom to roam around the final third. He loved to dribble, he loved to round the keeper and he loved to do the unpredictable. Shirt out, socks around his ankles, he was fluid rather than strong. A shy individual, he wasn't a natural leader on the pitch, not a shouter.

Unsurprisingly, the roving eye of giants Juventus swiftly turned its focus on to the youngster, but they weren't the only interested party. Fiorentina had a new owner and managed to snatch him away from the Old Lady's clutches, agreeing to pay £1.5m for the 18-year-old (the world record at the time was £5m for Maradona, which shows how significant this transfer fee was). Everything looked set for a move upwards and the continuation of an exceptional career as Baggio lined up for Vicenza's next game, against Rimini on 5 May 1985, just two days before officially signing the Fiorentina deal.

It took Baggio just four minutes to score his 12th goal of the season, which must have caused smiles across watching Fiorentina officials. But four minutes after that, Baggio's whole world would be turned upside-down. The snap was audible within the stadium – a breakaway into the Rimini half saw Baggio collapse in a crumpled heap. As Baggio described it: 'I put my leg down badly and left my meniscus and cruciate ligament on that pitch.' He had not yet officially signed for Fiorentina and his career was suddenly on a knife edge.

The initial diagnosis wasn't good, doctors informing Baggio that he may never play again. As treatment began, there was another complication – Baggio had an allergy to painkillers, which meant any pain had to be faced full-on. Not good news when repairing the anterior cruciate ligament, which would require 220 internal stitches. According to Baggio:

> The surgery in France was the worst. They had to drill a hole in my tibia to anchor the tendon, which had been lacerated. I couldn't take anti-inflammatories because I was allergic … I was in agony. I even told my mother if you love me, then kill me.

Given the extent of his injuries, it would have been no surprise if Fiorentina had pulled out of their obligation to purchase Baggio. But, behaving with honour, they stuck by their deal, funding his surgeries and recuperation, even though it would take 18 months before he could return to first-team action. Baggio would never forget the faith shown to him by *La Viola*, stating:

> I had my first knee injury and I never played with people who cared about me and were as close to me as Fiorentina. They showed affection, urged me not to give up and told me they would wait for me. That's something I will never forget.

It was a gamble that would pay Fiorentina back in spades. Up to this point in time, they had enjoyed minimal success. They had won Serie A in 1956 and 1969 and been runners-up in four successive seasons from 1957 to 1960 – a golden period for them when they also reached the 1957 European Cup Final, losing to Real Madrid, before winning the 1961 Cup Winners' Cup, beating Rangers, and losing the following final to Atlético Madrid. But since the 1950s and 60s, trophies had been rare.

The 1980s commenced with the purchase of Fiorentina by Flavio Pontello, of a rich house-building dynasty. Already blessed with the young talent of Giancarlo Antognoni, Pontello funded the acquisition of further gifted youths such as Francesco Graziani, Daniel Bertoni, Daniele Massaro and Pietro Vierchowod, and in 1982 they made a serious challenge for the Serie A title, losing out on the final day to Juventus, who were awarded a dubious penalty in their match. It would start a hatred of Juventus by Fiorentina fans – a hatred that would be further fuelled by later events.

Sadly, Fiorentina failed to build on that near miss, although still finishing in the top ten over each of the subsequent six seasons. There were some interesting additions to the squad – most notably Brazilian superstar Sócrates, who joined at the start of 1984/85, having been part of the magnificent 1982 Brazilian World Cup side that fell to the Italians and Paolo Rossi. Unfortunately, Sócrates failed to settle into Florentine life and headed back to Brazil after just one season. Given that experience, Fiorentina's management again decided to bet on youth.

The 1985/86 season would see Baggio continue his tough recovery process, which would cause him to lose 12kg due to an inability to eat properly. He felt isolated from his new team-mates, only able to start in five matches during the campaign – all in the Coppa Italia. The following season saw him recover enough to start the campaign for *La Viola*, where, under a new manager, Eugenio Bersellini, he was joined by another significant signing – Argentine striker Ramón Díaz. There was genuine excitement to see Díaz and Baggio in action up front, and their first pairing in front of the Fiorentina faithful saw them run out 2-0 winners against Sampdoria – Díaz scoring both goals. And then fate dealt Baggio yet another cruel blow – in training that week his knee broke down again, requiring another major operation on the meniscus. Baggio was still just 19 and had now gone under the surgeon's knife for a second time. One struggles to imagine what he must have been going through at the time, questioning: why me?

It was probably that kind of question that started steering Baggio away from his childhood Catholicism towards other forms of faith, namely Buddhism. It would remain a crutch from this time forward – a controversial move in a country as rooted in Catholicism as Italy.

> I had lost faith in myself, went out very little and was feeling very melancholy. I started to read about Buddhism, then one day, on 1 January 1988, I knocked on Maurizio's [a Buddhist friend] door at half past seven in the morning and said, 'I have to start my journey now.' I understood that I had to react. I had to find the courage to live. The road of faith was like a form of training in spiritual courage. Sometimes, during training, the pain in my knee was like a hammer in my brain but I never stopped. Others would have quit, I wouldn't.

Happily, Baggio was helped through these dark times by the continued support of the Florentine fanbase, who continued to chant his name even during his long absence. It led to his pledge, made somewhat unwisely in hindsight, that 'I will never leave Florence. Nobody is going to take me away from here.'

* * *

As the 1986/87 season approached its end, Fiorentina found themselves at risk of being relegated. The second-to-last game saw them travel down to Naples to face Maradona and company, with Baggio finally able to start again for *La Viola*, but he could only watch as Andrea Carnevale put Napoli ahead after half an hour. Then, ten minutes later, Baggio demonstrated what Fiorentina had been missing, curling a free kick around the wall from just outside the penalty area to earn his team a vital point that ensured their safety, while also giving Napoli their first-ever Scudetto. It was Baggio's first Serie A goal – the first of many free-kick goals to follow – earning him the man-of-the-match award, ahead of Maradona, despite the Argentine having just helped to clinch the league title.

One week later, Fiorentina finished in tenth spot, Díaz having contributed ten goals to the campaign. It wouldn't be enough for

Bersellini to keep his position, replaced by former IFK Göteborg, Benfica and Roma manager Sven-Göran Eriksson. His two seasons in charge saw the team develop but remain trophyless. Now able to play a fully fit Baggio, Eriksson initially suggested sending him out on loan to Cesena to gain experience, except Baggio was having none of it, flatly refusing to go. Shortly afterwards, at an away game against Milan, he proved just what an impact he would make for *La Viola*.

This was the Milan that had just hired Arrigo Sacchi, sporting their new high-profile signings of Marco van Basten and Ruud Gullit for the first time in the San Siro. Unsurprisingly, anticipation was at fever pitch to see the Dutch stars in action. Instead, frustration built as Milan couldn't break down Fiorentina, prior to Díaz giving *La Viola* the lead with 14 minutes remaining. Before the crowd could fully absorb what had happened, Baggio announced himself to the world. Picking up the ball in midfield, he moved forward before slowing slightly as two Milan defenders moved across his line of sight. Then, spotting a gap between them, he accelerated through to put him one-on-one against the keeper. Without slowing, he dummied past keeper Galli, leaving him stranded on the ground, before sliding the ball into an empty net. It was a magical goal, showing no fear regarding the occasion or the opposition, and his celebration, falling to his knees, seemed to represent his relief after so much pain. This was why Fiorentina had stuck by him.

Both Eriksson seasons saw Baggio able to make a full contribution to the team, playing 74 times over the two years and scoring an impressive 33 goals. The second season was particularly remarkable, with Baggio ending as the team's leading scorer with 15 Serie A goals, one ahead of fellow striker Stefano Borgonovo. It was a season that also saw one of the greatest games ever at the Stadio Comunale when Inter, who would go on to win Serie A, rolled into town. An early Inter lead was cancelled out by Baggio before Fiorentina went on to post a famous 4-3 victory, coming back from 3-2 down late on through a brace by Borgonovo, the two earning themselves the nickname 'B2' from Italian media.

That season ended with Fiorentina playing Roma in a one-off game in Perugia, where the winner would gain entrance to the following year's UEFA Cup. A single goal was enough for Fiorentina to achieve European football, ironically scored by Roberto Pruzzo in his final Serie A game. He had joined Fiorentina just for that single season, having played 240 times and scoring 106 goals for – Roma.

Eriksson wouldn't oversee Fiorentina's European campaign. Over the summer, he left to return to Benfica, who he would lead to the 1990 European Cup Final. In his place came the coach who had first developed a young Baggio at Vicenza – Bruno Giorgi. Baggio's strike partner from the previous season, Borgonovo, moved on to Milan to be replaced by Argentine Oscar Dertycia, who unfortunately would pick up a knee injury in January following a clash with Maradona, curtailing the rest of his season. Fiorentina's early league form was unimpressive, placing them only just above the relegation zone, so fans turned to the UEFA Cup for hope.

* * *

Fiorentina were handed a nasty first-round draw, having to play a skilful Atlético Madrid managed by Javier Clemente and containing the Brazilians Donato and Baltazar, along with Portuguese talent Paulo Futre, who had recently placed second in the Ballon d'Or in 1987 behind Ruud Gullit. A single-goal defeat in Madrid was overturned by a goal in Perugia (Fiorentina played many games this season away from their Stadio Artemio Franchi due to improvements being made ahead of the 1990 World Cup), meaning the tie moved into extra time and then penalties. With Atlético players missing three of their first four penalties, including Futre, it was left to Baggio to convert the fifth and ensure Fiorentina moved on to the round of 32.

Next up for the Florentines were French side FC Sochaux. Once again, the two legs were low-scoring affairs, starting with a goalless draw in Perugia. Back at Sochaux's home in Montbéliard, Fiorentina took the lead after just over half an hour through Renato Buso, set up by Baggio. That lead would last a mere three minutes before Sochaux equalised, but Fiorentina did have the vital away goal and were able to see out the game without conceding again to book a place in the round of 16 – and a trip behind the Iron Curtain.

Dynamo Kyiv were a force to be reckoned with during this period. The team was managed by the legendary Valeriy Lobanovskyi and contained some outstanding talent, including

Volodymyr Bessonov, Oleh Kuznetsov, Oleksiy Mykhaylychenko, Ivan Yaremchuk, Vasyl Rats, Oleg Salenko, Igor Belanov and Oleh Protasov. Under Lobanovskyi's leadership, the USSR had reached the European Championship Final of 1988 with a squad of 20 players, 11 of whom came from Dynamo Kyiv. Facing them would be a major test for Giorgi's Fiorentina.

The first leg was once again in Perugia with the Soviets proving extremely difficult to break down, until finally they made an error with 12 minutes remaining, giving away a penalty. Up stepped Baggio to send the keeper the wrong way and score his first European goal. It was a slender advantage to take back to the Ukraine in winter, always a tough proposition, where freezing conditions saw the Fiorentina players lined up in gloves and tights against a backdrop of shovelled snow. They survived a first-half scare when a deflection almost resulted in an own goal, but apart from that, Kyiv didn't really threaten, despite dominating possession. Another goalless draw saw Fiorentina take a notable scalp – the kind of result that would get them noticed around Europe.

The quarter-finals saw Fiorentina again face French opposition, this time in the form of AJ Auxerre, and 1-0 wins for *La Viola* both home and away saw them through to the semi-finals and more sizeable opposition in German side Werder Bremen, managed by Otto Rehhagel, with an attack led by the prolific Karl-Heinz Riedle. While Fiorentina were besting Dynamo Kyiv, Bremen had gone to Napoli and beaten them 3-2 in Naples, before thrashing them 5-1 back in Germany, an impressive 8-3 aggregate, with Riedle plundering six goals. If Fiorentina were to reach the UEFA Cup Final, this would prove a significant hurdle.

Ahead of the Bremen tie, Fiorentina's league struggles saw the departure of coach Bruno Giorgi, who was replaced by Torino striking legend Francesco Graziani in his first managerial post. The first leg in Bremen saw Marco Nappi give *La Viola* the lead with just 12 minutes remaining. As stoppage time approached, it appeared that Fiorentina were once again going to get a valuable 1-0 win to take back to Perugia, until, with virtually the last kick of the game, a corner was swung into the Fiorentina area, which keeper Marco Landucci mishandled into his own goal. It was a horrible howler that he could only hope wouldn't prove costly.

Luckily for Landucci, it didn't. A goalless second leg meant Fiorentina had reached the UEFA Cup Final. It hadn't been a run full of thrills and excitement – over ten matches Fiorentina had scored just six goals but conceded only three. However, one of Italy's smaller teams had given Italian football yet another European final appearance. And if that wasn't enough for Italian pride, their opponents would be Juventus – the team who had controversially pipped them to the Serie A title so recently. The rivalry between the two would be further heightened by this match-up.

Juventus had reached the final through a very Germanic route. The third round, quarter-final and semi-final had seen the Italians eliminate FC Karl-Marx-Stadt, Hamburg SV and Köln, respectively. Their season had been powered by the goals from a new striker picked up from Serie B team Messina – a Sicilian named Salvatore 'Toto' Schillaci – with talk that his form might even get him selected for Italy's 1990 World Cup squad.

The first leg was played in Turin, with 45,000 packing the stadium to see whether their home team could lift its first European silverware since that fateful night back in Heysel. They didn't have long to wait as a cross from Schillaci was fired home by midfielder Roberto Galia after just three minutes. But then, just seven minutes later, Fiorentina scored an almost identical goal, Alberto Di Chiara weaving his way to the byline before crossing for midfielder Renato Buso to level the game. It remained level until 15 minutes into the second half when Pierluigi Casiraghi was in the right place to put Juventus back in front, although, before scoring, it appeared as if he had pushed Fiorentina's Celeste Pin, which was overlooked by the referee. Then, 13 minutes later, Juventus extended their lead courtesy of another mistake by Fiorentina keeper Marco Landucci, allowing a shot from Luigi De Agostini to bounce over him. *La Viola* faced an uphill battle back in the second leg. The second goal would rankle with the Fiorentina players, Pin yelling *'ladri'* (thieves) at Juve coach Dino Zoff after the match.

While it had been hoped that the second leg would be once again played in Perugia, close to Florence, crowd trouble during the home tie against Werder Bremen meant that the match was moved to Avellino as punishment. This meant staging the game east of Naples – a considerable distance from Florence – in an area with sizeable Juventus support, given their widespread following in Italy, obviously something that angered Fiorentina management.

The stadium was lit by orange flares all around as the teams emerged for the match. Despite Fiorentina's best efforts, the Juventus defence held strong to earn a goalless draw and lift the UEFA Cup in a smoke-filled atmosphere. It had been a valiant run by *La Viola*, especially given their league struggles over the season, which had seen them end in 12th place, just one point above the relegation zone. The most encouraging sign for the fans was seeing Roberto Baggio emerge as a potent force, scoring 17 goals in Serie A to place him second behind Marco van Basten in the scoring charts, ahead of Maradona, and earning him eighth place in the Ballon d'Or, while still only 23 years old.

After his 15 Serie A goals the previous season, it was apparent that any injury woes were finally behind Baggio. Fiorentina fans had also been treated to another classic Baggio goal to add to his growing pantheon early in the season when Fiorentina travelled to Napoli. Scoreless after 22 minutes, with Maradona watching from the bench, a Napoli attack broke down as Baggio received the ball deep in his own half. Running into the space ahead, he accelerated into the Napoli half, calmly waltzed around defender Alessandro Renica without breaking stride, cut between two more Napoli defenders, before sitting keeper Giuliano Giuliani down with a beautiful feint, taking the ball around him and finishing into an empty net. Or, in the words of the English commentator, 'Dunga finding Baggio ... now, what can he do here ... a very impressive run by Baggio ... and he's threatening to go all the way ... and he has! Magnificent individual goal by Roberto Baggio.' Put that goal and his one against Milan on a loop and enjoy!

Fans of *La Viola* could look forward to 1990/91, safe in the knowledge that they had reached a European final and had a player of incredible talent – if only Juventus hadn't spoilt the party. And let's not forget that Fiorentina fans still had a huge grudge against Juve for the final-day events of the 1982 Serie A season, when they felt they had been robbed of the title by biased officiating. Now they had the Casiraghi push to add to their list of injustices. But their hatred for the Torinese was about to go into overdrive.

* * *

Given the two seasons that Baggio had just enjoyed, there were of course constant rumours that one of the Italian giants would try to secure his services. Baggio had grown up an Inter fan, so Milan always seemed the most likely destination, should the unthinkable happen. Fiorentina's financial situation had worsened, with the rebuilding costs for the Artemio Franchi coming in way over budget and making bankruptcy a real risk, meaning owner Flavio Pontello knew he had to cash in on their star asset. Baggio's agent was making similar statements and probably every Fiorentina fan knew, in their heart of hearts, that it was only a matter of time. After all, his transfer could probably earn a record fee, given his age. But who would pay such a sum?

Then came the news that shocked *La Viola* fans to the core. On 18 May 1990, it was finally confirmed that Roberto Baggio would be exiting Fiorentina for a world record fee of £8m – to Juventus! This just two days after Juventus had beaten Fiorentina to the UEFA Cup Final. It was too much for Fiorentina fans to stomach and they poured out to the stadium to make their feelings clear. Bricks and Molotov cocktails were hurled at the club headquarters as Pontello sheltered within the stadium, petrified by the mob outside. Rioting ran for two days, so bad that it took 350 riot police to restore order, eventually making nine arrests, while 50 people were injured. British journalist James Horncastle recalled scenes of old women throwing potted plants and lemons from their balconies at the police to distract them.

Baggio claimed that he hadn't been party to the move but that he was just caught in the middle:

A profound bond was created with the Fiorentina fans and I tried so hard to remain with La Viola but everything had been decided for me. I just wish they'd been clearer.

Not all Fiorentina fans were convinced, the words 'Judas' and 'traitor' being bandied around. At his signing, Baggio stated that he was still going to the 1990 World Cup as a Fiorentina player. Except he wasn't. But with the World Cup upcoming, Baggio had to join the squad at Italy's Coverciano training camp, which unfortunately lies just outside Florence, meaning he had to be smuggled in while training sessions were held behind closed doors.

It was a devastating loss to the fans and squad. For teams like Fiorentina, it's not often that they get a player of such mercurial skills. And even more rewarding to the fanbase was that Baggio had risen to fame with them – he hadn't just been bought as a famous name. They had watched him suffer through injury hell and come out the other side as an extraordinary talent. He had scored the vital goal against Napoli that saved them from possible relegation and played as a free spirit within a league full of extremely regimented teams – with a type of style and panache that fans probably dreamed they would flaunt if they had the same skills. Baggio scored enough goals to almost win the *Capocannoniere*, yet he wasn't a dedicated striker – he was more of a No.10, an attacking midfielder. In fact, the great Michel Platini once described Baggio as a number nine and a half, just because of this blend of roles. As Maradona's flame started to dim in Italy, Baggio stepped in as the new torch bearer of greatness.

* * *

The date 6 April 1991 was marked on Italian press calendars – the date when Baggio would return to Tuscany to represent his new employers against his beloved Fiorentina. From the start, every Baggio touch of the ball was greeted by loud whistles, with all eyes upon the No.10. Fiorentina scored just before half-time to add salt to the wounds before the drama increased further when early in the second half Baggio earned his new Juve team a penalty – a penalty that should have fallen to him to take. But he didn't take it, according to Juve because the Fiorentina keeper may know his preferences too well. Instead, Juventus team-mate Luigi De Agostini took charge, only to see Gianmatteo Mareggini save his effort.

Baggio was substituted off soon after and, as he walked from the pitch, objects began to be thrown. Deciding to skip the bench and instead head off down the tunnel, a Fiorentina scarf was tossed to him. He couldn't help himself, picking up the scarf and clutching it in front of the *Curva Fiesole*, still perhaps yearning for their love. However, that behaviour, combined with the eventual Fiorentina victory, didn't exactly endear him to his new fanbase, causing hundreds of Juve fans to protest at his actions at the next training session. It also didn't help that on his Juventus unveiling he had been given their club scarf, but instead of donning it he had merely placed it on the chair beside him. The juxtaposition was clear to all – it summed up Baggio's complicated relationship with both the Fiorentina and Juve faithful.

Of course, there was much more to Fiorentina than just Roberto Baggio. A team doesn't reach the UEFA Cup Final relying on just one exceptional young talent. For example, future World Cup-winning Brazilian captain Dunga was in midfield, ahead of a defence including recent Milan manager Stefano Pioli. So, while Baggio's loss was a huge blow to the club, it shouldn't have been fatal. Unfortunately, it was – Fiorentina finishing 12th the next two seasons before being relegated to Serie B the season after. Luckily, they would immediately return to the top flight, powered by a new hero in Gabriel Batistuta, but it would be a long time until they again progressed significantly in European competition.

The fact that one of the traditional non-powerhouse teams of Italy had reached a European final in 1990 spoke to the depth of talent within Serie A during this time. And while his time at Fiorentina was brief, Baggio is still revered by those fans in purple who saw him in his pomp, time healing the pain of the Juventus move. The words 'Fiorentina' and 'Roberto Baggio' will always be intertwined.

FIORENTINA (1986–1990)
UEFA Cup runners-up – 1989/90

Chapter 10

Trap and the Tre Tedeschi

Lothar Matthaus. Definitely the German. There were good defenders, and they were all tough in Italy – you had no chance to walk away without pain. But he was different. Clever, quick and very powerful. I would say definitely he is the best player I played against in Italy. And a real champion. I always wanted Napoli to get him.

Diego Maradona

THE EARLY 1970s were a frustrating time for the Old Lady. Three Serie A titles in the first five years of the decade was all well and good but what Juventus really wanted was European glory. And they had come close – except that a Johnny Rep goal after just five minutes had been enough for Ajax to lift their third successive European Cup. A semi-final place in the UEFA Cup two years later was no improvement, so Juve decided to hire a new, young manager to shake things up. That man was Giovanni Trapattoni – and shake them up he most certainly did.

Joining in 1976 with almost no managerial experience, he inherited a strong side, including the likes of Dino Zoff in goal, a fearsome defence of Claudio Gentile, Gaetano Scirea, Antonello Cuccureddu and Antonio Cabrini, a midfield with Franco Causio and Marco Tardelli and a prolific strike partnership of Roberto Bettega and newcomer Roberto Boninsegna. His first season in charge saw Juventus win their fourth Serie A title over the past six seasons, but that wasn't the reason for his hire – that was to bring European success – and that came much quicker than chairman Giampiero Boniperti could possibly have imagined.

Having finished second in the league the previous year, Juventus were in the UEFA Cup, where the first and second rounds saw them visit Manchester twice – first eliminating Manchester City 2-1 on aggregate before then disposing of Manchester United 3-1 on aggregate, despite losing 1-0 each time in the rainy city. From Manchester, they then travelled behind the Iron Curtain, first-beating Ukraine's Shakhtar Donetsk and then East Germany's Magdeburg to set up a semi-final against AEK Athens. A 4-1 first leg victory at home saw them comfortably into the final, where once again they stood on the precipice of winning a first European trophy. All they had to do was overcome Athletic Bilbao over two legs.

After a 1-0 first-leg home win, courtesy of Marco Tardelli, Juventus survived a nervy second leg when Bilbao took a 2-1 lead with 12 minutes remaining. Their European hoodoo had finally been broken – and Trapattoni had delivered the holy grail in his first season in charge. He may have started with limited managerial experience, but he had learned fast and learned well.

That successful first season with the Old Lady led to a ten-year love affair between Trapattoni and the Juve faithful. As mentioned earlier, an incredibly strong Italian backbone was complemented by foreign talents such as Liam Brady, Zbigniew Boniek and Michel Platini, resulting in five more Serie A titles, a Cup Winners' Cup title and, on that fateful night in Brussels, a European Cup win, meaning that he had overseen Juventus winning all three European trophies, becoming the first team to ever achieve such a feat. In ten years, he had established himself as one of the greatest footballing managers, respected by fans and press alike. He had achieved everything one could possibly hope for during that period – but all with the one club. Trapattoni felt it was time for a fresh challenge.

* * *

While Juventus had been enjoying huge success over those ten years, the same could not be said for Inter. One Serie A title in 1980 under the leadership of Eugenio Bersellini was all the Milan giants could muster during that time, unable to even reach any European finals. After Bersellini left in the summer of 1982, Inter went through three managers over the next four seasons with no success, apart from two frustrating UEFA Cup campaigns where they were eliminated in the semi-finals, both times by Real Madrid and both after holding a comfortable home first-leg advantage, letting 2-0 and 3-1 home wins be overturned at the Bernabéu. They needed to make a successful managerial change after years of turmoil, so chairman Ernesto Pellegrini turned his attention to the best there was in Italy at that time. He wanted Trapattoni – and Trapattoni wanted a fresh challenge. The timing was perfect for both.

The summer of 1986 saw Trapattoni take the reins over at the *Nerazzurri*, inheriting a team that had been massively reliant on the goalscoring of one man for the past nine seasons – Alessandro Altobelli. Having joined Inter in 1977, he had been their leading goalscorer for the next eight seasons, making himself a club legend with 174 goals over 379 games, playing almost every match across that time. But age was starting to catch up with him and Trapattoni knew that eventually he would need someone else to shoulder the burden. Luckily for him, in 1984, Pellegrini had invested in another striker of renown – the German forward Karl-Heinz Rummenigge.

The Bayern legend had taken the fresh challenge of Serie A after ten seasons with *Die Roten*, during which time he had earned two European Cup winners' medals as well as two Bundesliga titles, scoring 217 goals. His first season with the *Nerazzurri* saw him bag a respectable 18 goals across all competitions. He repeated the feat the following season, again scoring 18. With him and Altobelli, Trapattoni had strike power, but also two strikers who were getting on in age.

The first significant squad change that took place under the new regime was allowing Liam Brady to move to Ascoli. The Irish midfielder had enjoyed two seasons at Inter, following his stints at Juventus and Sampdoria. The move was probably not a surprise – Trapattoni had after all been manager of Juventus when Brady was moved on from there to make way for Michel Platini, which probably led to a breakdown in their relationship. The defence was strengthened with the arrival of 1978 Argentina World Cup-winning captain Daniel Passarella from Fiorentina. It was with this squad that Trapattoni began his mission to bring Inter the same level of success that he had achieved at Juventus.

* * *

The 1986/87 season proved frustrating. A blistering start to the league campaign saw Inter lose just two of their opening 18 games, but also lose the services of Rummenigge towards the end of that run to injury. Three successive defeats, including a home loss to rivals Milan, caused their title charge to fade, eventually finishing third after taking just one point from their final three matches. In March, Inter met IFK Göteborg in the UEFA Cup quarter-finals, where, after a goalless draw in Sweden, Inter took a home lead through an own goal, only to suffer elimination when Stefan Pettersson equalised with just 12 minutes remaining. It meant a trophyless start for Trapattoni, who still had to address his ageing attack as Altobelli again ended as Inter's leading goalscorer at 31 years old. Given Rummenigge's injury, he was moved on to finish his career in Switzerland with Servette, with his place as a foreigner in the Inter squad taken by the signing of emerging Belgian midfield star Enzo Scifo from Anderlecht – sadly, Scifo would not settle at the *Nerazzurri*, lasting just one season before heading to France.

The following season saw Inter again suffer a disappointing time, finishing fifth in Serie A while once more being eliminated in the UEFA Cup, this time to Spanish side Espanyol in the third round. Concern started to be felt around the San Siro. Pellegrini had gone out and hired the hottest young manager in the game and had nothing to show for it after two seasons. The pain was accentuated by watching Milan's revolution under Berlusconi and Sacchi as they won the Scudetto ahead of Napoli. Trapattoni's relationship with Altobelli was also worsening, leading to his transfer to rivals Juventus. All eyes turned to Pellegrini to see whether he would stick with Trapattoni or make yet another managerial change. He decided to stick.

Not only did Pellegrini support Trapattoni as manager, but he also opened his wallet to fund a significant rebuild of the team during the summer of 1988. The European Championship was taking place in Germany, where the host nation reached the semi-finals before falling to the Netherlands, powered by Ruud Gullit and Marco van Basten of Milan. If the best Dutch players were being assembled by Milan, then Inter would shop nearby too – only they cast their net into Germany, and in particular their young captain, who was emerging as a world-class talent: Lothar Matthäus.

* * *

Matthäus began his professional career in 1979 as a midfielder with Borussia Mönchengladbach, before the mighty Bayern Munich prised him away. Four successful seasons saw him win three Bundesliga titles and play in a European Cup Final, while continuing his impressive scoring record with 69 goals from 150 appearances – a remarkable strike rate for his position. Noted for his box-to-box running and goalscoring abilities, with an uncanny ability to surge late into the penalty area and score, he could play equally well as both an attacking midfielder and holding midfielder, which he paired with strong leadership qualities on the pitch. Still only 27 years old, he was one of the hottest properties in world football – and now he was heading to the San Siro, not to join Milan but Inter. It was a statement signing for the club.

But why buy one German international when you could have two? West Germany's Euro 1988 campaign had started with a match against Italy, in which Roberto Mancini gave the *Azzurri* an early second-half lead. Italian viewers, including presumably Pellegrini, then watched as West Germany won a free kick just outside the area. Matthäus rolled the ball sideways and in thundered the left-back to blast the ball past Walter Zenga and level the game. The scorer was Andreas Brehme – a companion of Matthäus at Bayern. A player ahead of his time in terms of attacking ability, he was a full-back who loved to push forward, while also being a dead-ball specialist – and two-footed. Franz Beckenbauer once said of Brehme: 'I have known Andy for 20 years and I still don't know if he is right or left-footed.' Matthäus was also a huge fan, so Brehme joined the German revolution at Inter that same summer. But Pellegrini still wasn't done.

With Rummenigge and Altobelli out of the picture, strike power was needed. The previous season had seen striker Aldo Serena return to Inter after two years at Juventus, scoring just six Serie A goals as he played second fiddle to Altobelli. A new partner was needed for him, so Inter went out and signed the Argentine marksman Ramón Díaz, from Fiorentina. While pillaging Fiorentina, Inter also decided to pick up Nicola Berti to play in midfield alongside Matthäus. Trapattoni had no excuses for failure – he had been given a strong squad and now it was up to him to deliver, as another season of disappointment would surely push even Pellegrini's loyalty to breaking point.

Suddenly it all clicked. Starting the season with three wins and a draw, the *Nerazzurri* found themselves top of Serie A after just four matches, and from that point onward they never looked back. Once again, the UEFA Cup proved a disappointment, with Bayern getting some revenge for the removal of Matthäus and Brehme by eliminating Inter in the third round. But elimination allowed Inter to focus on Serie A, where they remained unbeaten until the 4-3 thriller at Fiorentina in February finally saw them undone. Even then, they got straight back into the groove, not losing again until the penultimate fixture at Torino, when they already had the title sealed. Effectively, this came on 28 May when Inter welcomed title rivals Napoli to the San Siro, with just three points the difference. Level with seven minutes remaining, Inter won a free kick, which Matthäus rifled into the corner of the goal to secure the victory, almost guaranteeing Inter would finish champions. As ever, Matthäus had a knack for delivering when needed most with that lethal thunderbolt of his.

To go from fifth place the previous season to winning the title ahead of Napoli by 11 points was an incredible achievement – testament to an Inter side that connected under Trapattoni's leadership. In fact, their 58 points still stands as a Serie A record for the period of an 18-team league with two points for a win – and during a time of intense competition within Serie A. Matthäus remembered it thus in an interview with *FourFourTwo* magazine:

> It was an amazing time. Italian football was probably at its peak, with some magnificent players: Diego Maradona, Ruud Gullit, Roberto Baggio, Marco van Basten … and that was just our rivals! Every weekend was a battle, and at Inter we were willing to die on the field for one another.

While Díaz chipped in with 12 Serie A goals, it was Serena who rolled back the years, banging in 22, while Matthäus contributed nine. Inter finished with a goal differential of plus 48, conceding just 19 times across 34 league games, a demonstration of the defensive abilities of Zenga, Bergomi, Brehme and Giuseppe Baresi – including

20 clean sheets. Such was their defensive power that Brehme was Serie A player of the year, despite all the attacking power in the league. And as the San Siro welcomed the Scudetto, Milan brought home the European Cup. It was a great year to be Milanese.

The two Germans had enjoyed a great season with Inter, standing out as stars within the team, so Pellegrini decided to continue to mine that rich seam. While Aldo Serena had been red hot, Díaz had been mediocre at best, and with a European Cup campaign looming, mediocre wasn't going to cut it for Trapattoni. After Inter had suffered UEFA Cup elimination to Bayern, the Germans had lost the semi-final against Napoli, who would then face another German side in the final – VfB Stuttgart. Napoli narrowly emerged victorious, but Stuttgart had attracted attention, especially the young striker who had scored four goals during the tournament, taking his output to 94 goals over five seasons. The 24-year-old German Footballer of the Year, Jürgen Klinsmann, might just be the ideal partner for Serena, so Díaz was moved on to Monaco, to be replaced by the blond hitman. Hopes were running high for a defence of their Serie A title and a tilt at Europe's premier competition.

Inter's European Cup dream died instantly. Drawn in the first round against Swedish champions Malmö, Inter were defeated by a solitary goal in Sweden. It still seemed incomprehensible that the Serie A champions, who had lost just two league matches the previous season, would fail to go through – they would surely swat the Swedes aside back at a packed San Siro. But they struggled, until finally Serena gave them the lead with 20 minutes remaining. Then, with just ten minutes left, Inter's world fell apart. Malmö won a corner and the ball was swung in, where a poorly marked Leif Engqvist headed home. A deathly silence fell over the San Siro, broken only by a chorus of whistles as the game ended. Inter were out of the competition, which would eventually be won again by Milan, adding salt to the wound.

Returning to league action, Inter failed to replicate the form of the previous season. The good news was that Klinsmann bedded in swiftly, taken to Inter fans' hearts with 13 Serie A goals, just ahead of his countryman Matthäus, who contributed another 11. But the Serena/Klinsmann partnership didn't blossom as hoped, so Inter had to settle for third place and a UEFA Cup slot, behind champions Napoli and rivals Milan. As Inter faced the 1990/91 season, they did so knowing that it would be the final season of Trapattoni's contract, with the real risk that he may refuse a new one and move on to a new challenge.

* * *

That summer, the 1990 World Cup came to Italy. While by no means a classic tournament, it did see a strong West Germany emerge as champions, including Matthäus, Klinsmann and Brehme. It had been an outstanding tournament for the three Inter players, all named in FIFA's 1990 World Cup All-Star Team, while scoring ten of West Germany's 15 goals between them. Further recognition would come later in the year as Matthäus swept the 1990 Ballon d'Or, the 1990 IFFHS World's Best Player and the 1990 *World Soccer* magazine's World Player of the Year award, while Brehme came third in the 1990 Ballon d'Or. Inter had three of the world's greatest players in their possession, and with Matthäus especially at the peak of his powers, their fans had a lot to be excited about as 1990/91 kicked off.

Management continued to strengthen the squad, as defenders Sergio Battistini and Antonio Paganin joined from Fiorentina and Udinese, respectively. Midfielder Davide Fontolan was brought in from Genoa, while Trapattoni would again look to Klinsmann, Serena and Matthäus for goals.

The 1990/91 season has already been covered in detail in the chapter on Sampdoria, in particular their epic encounter against Inter on matchday 31 when they came away from the San Siro with a two-goal smash-and-grab and, effectively, the league title, ending Inter's dreams on that fateful afternoon. Inter once again had to settle for third place but it was a season in which they finally quelled their recent European competition blues, 26 years after having lifted their last European trophy.

It was Inter's form at fortress San Siro that saw them go on a UEFA Cup run. The first round saw them lose 2-1 to Rapid Wien in Austria before a 3-1 win at home after extra time, with two goals from Berti and one from Klinsmann, saw them through. It was a similar story in the next round as Aston Villa defeated them 2-0 in

Birmingham before a stirring comeback saw Inter win 3-0 at home, Berti again on the scoresheet along with Klinsmann. The third round saw them play at home first, where they crushed Partizan Belgrade 3-0, before an away draw put them into the quarter-finals.

Their quarter-final was an all-Italian affair, as Inter were drawn against Atalanta. Coming away from Bergamo with a goalless draw, two second-half goals in quick succession from Serena and Matthäus put Inter into a semi-final meeting with Sporting Lisbon. This followed the same pattern as the quarter-final – a goalless draw in Lisbon followed by a 2-0 win at the San Siro, courtesy of Matthäus and Klinsmann, putting Inter through to their first European final since their 1972 European Cup defeat at the hands of Cruyff's Ajax. After watching Milan win two successive European Cups, it would finally be Inter's turn to enter the European spotlight.

The previous season had highlighted Italy's complete domination of European football when all three tournaments were won by Italian clubs – Milan claiming the European Cup, Sampdoria the Cup Winners' Cup and Juventus the UEFA Cup. Juventus's UEFA Cup Final win had seen them beat Fiorentina, and now, for the second successive time, the UEFA Cup Final would be contested by two Italian clubs. Inter's opponents over two legs would be Roma, who could boast two German starters of their own in defender Thomas Berthold and striker Rudi Völler. The first leg, just four days after that fateful loss to Sampdoria, would be played at the San Siro, with almost 70,000 fans baying for their heroes to overcome the southerners.

The first half was a relatively mild affair, with Inter applying most of the pressure but without creating any dangerous chances, while Roma appeared content to leave Milan with a goalless draw. However, whatever Trapattoni said to his team during the break had an effect, as ten minutes into the second half a cross from Serena towards Berti saw the midfielder go down in the area. With the home crowd baying, the Russian referee had no hesitation in pointing to the spot, despite Roma protests. The replay showed it was probably the correct call, and Matthäus duly lashed the ball into the net.

The goal at least provoked a reaction from Roma, with midfielder Manuel Gerolin coming close to immediately equalising with a deflected shot. But then, just 12 minutes after the penalty, a piece of Klinsmann magic saw him turn his marker, break into the area and provide Berti with a near-post tap-in to double Inter's lead. It was then straightforward for Inter to see the game out, the only scare coming when Antonio Paganin got himself into a defensive mess, earning himself an earful from an unimpressed Brehme. It was job done at home – now Inter just had to survive the trip to the Stadio Olimpico.

A huge tifo of orange and yellow greeted Inter into the Roman cauldron, accompanied by balloons and orange flares burning at both ends of the ground, smoke enveloping the players as they kicked off. The first significant chance fell to Roma striker Ruggiero Rizzitelli, who saw his vicious effort strike the outside of the post. Next, Völler went down in the area, but the referee waved play on, to Roma protests and howls of anger from the 70,000 in attendance. Spurred on by the crowd, the *Giallorossi* were pressurising Inter, who just needed to weather the storm. Roma attacks came in waves but the Inter defence held strong, enabling them to get to half-time goalless and still in pole position.

The players re-emerged to another wall of orange fire as the Roma faithful cheered their gladiators on. Roma continued to carve out chances, but Zenga was resolute between the posts and, as the clock wound down, it appeared that Inter were comfortably heading for their first European trophy for 26 years, their two-goal advantage intact. But with nine minutes remaining, Roman hopes were raised when Rizzitelli got free to score at the back post. Suddenly the noise was deafening, Roma fans bouncing in the stands as their side pushed for the vital second. Rizzitelli nearly made himself a Roma legend, his header flying narrowly over the bar, but, try as they might, Roma couldn't break the Inter defence again. Minutes later, the final whistle blew and Inter players dropped to their knees. They were UEFA Cup champions.

* * *

Lothar Matthäus finished the season as Inter's leading goalscorer, despite being a midfielder, with 23 goals across all competitions, including six in the UEFA Cup, making him the second-highest scorer in Serie A behind Gianluca Vialli over at Sampdoria. Having won the Ballon d'Or the season before, the German now added 1991 FIFA World Player of the Year to his résumé, cementing himself as one of the leading players of the era. Jürgen Klinsmann contributed 17 goals – the two Germans responsible for over half of Inter's Serie A tally for the season.

Unsurprisingly, Inter fans had taken Matthäus, Klinsmann and Brehme to their hearts giving them the nickname of *Tre Tedeschi* (three Germans) in response to Milan's *Tre Tulipani*. Pellegrini's financing and Trapattoni's leadership had built a superb Inter side, which was not solely about the three Germans. In goal, Walter Zenga was emerging as a world-class talent, which would result in a 12-year career with Inter, 58 caps for Italy and the IFFHS World's Best Goalkeeper award in 1989, 1990 and 1991. Alongside Brehme in defence were the Italian stalwarts Sergio Battistini, Riccardo Ferri, Antonio Paganin and Inter legend Giuseppe Bergomi, who would spend his whole 20-year career with the *Nerazzurri*, making over 750 appearances. Midfielder Nicola Berti would spend ten years with Inter, forming a great partnership with Matthäus during the early 1990s, while striker Aldo Serena was enjoying an Indian summer.

Pellegrini's faith in Trapattoni had paid off. His leadership had delivered a first Serie A title for nine years and their first European silverware since the summer of 1965. He had taken them from the shadow of rivals Milan, bringing a third consecutive European trophy to the city. Trapattoni's reputation, built so strongly with Juventus, continued to soar, so it was no surprise when, once again, Juventus came calling. Since Trapattoni's departure, the Turin club had failed to win a Serie A title and had even endured spending four of the five seasons outside of the top three – an unthinkable position for the Agnelli family to stomach. They had succeeded in lifting the UEFA Cup in 1990 under Dino Zoff's stewardship, but with Roberto Baggio recently added, they wanted more. So, following the UEFA Cup success, Trapattoni bid farewell to the Inter faithful and moved back to his first love, Juventus – a place assured in the hearts of the *Nerazzurri* for bringing them back from the wilderness.

INTER MILAN (1986–1991)
UEFA Cup winners – 1990/91
Serie A champions – 1988/89

Chapter 11

Mondonico's Chair

There is only one club in the world that could lose a final like this. This is Torino. We are cursed.

Torino captain Roberto Cravero

IT HAD only been a friendly game. There were four matches remaining in the season and, looking set to win a fifth consecutive title, the team decided to fly to Lisbon to play a testimonial for the Portuguese captain, Francisco Ferreira. It would be an enormous honour for the player and the Benfica crowd, the chance to see the great all-conquering Italian team in the flesh. Grande Torino.

As the Second World War widened to engulf Europe, the 1942/43 Italian season would be the last before games were suspended. The winners that year, by just one point, were Torino, and once the war ended they would continue to enjoy domestic success, earning the nickname Grande Torino. They won the first three post-war titles and a fourth was on its way before the game in Lisbon. They had become feted as the greatest team around and were so dominant that, when Italy defeated Hungary 3-2 in May 1947, ten of the team were members of Torino. But disaster would strike on the return journey from Portugal – and sadly it wouldn't be the only tragedy in Torino's history.

As the plane approached Turin, the pilot was informed that the skies were thick with cloud, accompanied by heavy rain and poor visibility. For an unknown reason, possibly altimeter malfunction, the plane's descent lined up with the Basilica of Superga, situated on a hill at 2,195ft above sea level, instead of to its left. Flying through the cloud, the pilot was suddenly faced by the monastery while travelling at 110mph. There was no time for him to react – the plane disintegrated on impact, with only the tail area left intact. All 31 passengers died, including 18 Torino players, three club officials and three coaching staff, one of which was manager Egri Erbstein. In a matter of seconds, the Grande Torino were no more – the date was 4 May 1949.

* * *

Unsurprisingly, Torino went into a slump during the following years. Performances improved when Nereo Rocco, the legendary Milan coach, was appointed in 1963, along with the signing of Gigi Meroni, who became a cult figure in Turin. A fantastic dribbler, positioned out on the wing, he earned the nickname *La Farfalla Granata* (the maroon butterfly), while gaining notoriety for his dress and lifestyle, embracing the mid-1960s counter-culture. In fact, in hindsight, he was an early prototype for the upcoming George Best, beloved by the Torino faithful.

On 15 October 1967, Meroni played for Torino in a home match against Sampdoria, which saw his team record a 4-2 win but also saw Meroni sent off. Out later that night with his friend and team-mate Fabrizio Poletti, Meroni crossed the busy Corso Re Umberto, only to be hit by a motorist, who happened to be a Torino fan by the name of Attilio Romero. The accident cost Meroni his life, at just 24 – tragedy had once again struck the *Granata*.

Despite this second heartbreak, Torino enjoyed a period of success in the early 1970s. After finishing in the top six for four seasons in a row, they finally lifted their first title since the Superga disaster in 1976, narrowly pipping Juventus to the prize. The second half of the 1970s saw continued strengthening until they faded again into Serie A mediocrity, except for a second-place finish behind surprise champions Hellas Verona in 1985. However, even that period was tinged with bad luck as Torino lost the Coppa Italia for three years in a row, twice against Roma on penalties. Eventually the humiliation of relegation struck in 1989 for just the second time in their history. While other Italian teams were going from strength to strength, it appeared that Torino were heading in reverse.

A change in manager saw Eugenio Fascetti arrive to secure immediate promotion back to Serie A as champions, powered by the goals of a young Brazilian, Müller, within a strong squad that also included Roberto Mussi, Dino Baggio, Benito Carbone and an emerging striker, Gianluigi Lentini. Despite their success, however, club president Gian Mauro Borsano felt fit to relieve Fascetti of his services, replacing him with Emiliano Mondonico (known to his players as 'Il Mondo'), who had just guided Atalanta to the semi-finals of the Cup Winners' Cup. He also continued to invest in the squad, most notably signing midfielder Rafael Martín Vázquez from Real Madrid and bringing striker Giorgio Bresciani back from a loan spell at Atalanta. Bresciani repaid the faith placed in him by scoring 13 goals as Torino finished an impressive fifth, ahead of city rivals Juventus, earning them a place in the following season's UEFA Cup.

While Vázquez represented the silk in Torino's team, they also signed steel that summer. Pasquale Bruno bravely came over from city rivals Juventus, where initial displeasure would soon change to admiration from the *Granata* faithful. Earning the nickname 'O' Animale', Bruno was a no-nonsense defender who would set an Italian record by receiving over 50 days of suspension during his career, as well as allegedly threatening to shoot Brescia striker Florin Răducioiu at the end of a game. Not a man to mess with then.

Gian Mauro Borsano was one of the most intriguing owners within Italian football during the 1990s. Never one to be overly concerned by such trivialities as accounting rules and financial regulations, he helped to fund Torino's future success until his shenanigans finally caught up with him, resulting in two future jail sentences and over ten counts of money laundering and bankruptcy. But that was all for the future – for now he brought in Mondonico and gave him funds.

Further reinforcements followed during the summer of 1991. While Dino Baggio went off to Inter on loan for the season, in came Belgian midfielder Enzo Scifo and Brazilian striker Walter Casagrande. Scifo, an elegant midfielder, could pull the strings in Mondonico's team, dictating the rhythm of the game. Casagrande, meanwhile, had made a name for himself at Ascoli, becoming a cult hero when, after his third season, they suffered relegation to Serie B, only for Casagrande to stand by them and help get them immediately promoted. His 38 goals across 96 appearances helped his reputation, leading to the move by Torino to secure his services.

La Grande Inter – *Sandro Mazzola strikes in the 1964 European Cup Final*

Red Sky at Night – *Liverpool lift their fourth European Cup in eight seasons in Rome*

Le Roi – *Michel Platini during his Juventus pomp*

Heartbreak – *the 1985 European Cup Final turns tragic*

Let the Party Commence – *Maradona brings joy to the Neapolitans*

Money Can Buy You Love – *Berlusconi's Milan celebrate the 1989 European Cup*

Big in North Korea – *Sampdoria's class of 1991 gets a stamp of approval*

Parting is Such Sweet Sorrow – *Baggio still holds a soft spot for La Viola*

Un Tedesco – Trapattoni and Matthaus plot another Inter success

Chairs Beware – *Mondonico contemplates the whereabouts of nearby furniture*

Vola Tedesco Vola– *Voller endears himself to the Roma faithful*

The first £13m man – Lentini battles for Milan before his accident

Derby della Capitale Hero – Gascoigne's finest Lazio moment

They also had a young striker on their books who, although born in Bologna, had been raised in Australia, where he developed a love of both football and cricket. He was still too raw to play much for the first team, limited to seven appearances during 1992, but he scored his first senior goal in a cup tie against Lazio. Christian Vieri was making his first steps on a successful career path.

Ironically, the transfers once again involved a character who we saw at Napoli in Chapter 3, and who would continue to haunt Italian football – Luciano Moggi – who had moved back to Torino after his spell at Napoli.

The season started well for the new-look side, and by the start of December they sat eighth in Serie A, while also moving through the first three rounds of the UEFA Cup comfortably, eliminating KR Rejkjavik, Boavista and AEK Athens. However, their first 12 Serie A games saw them score just eight goals, but only concede five – with five goalless draws to date. It was efficient but hardly stirring stuff. What was more stirring was the revelation in 1993 from the former Torino accountant Giovanni Matta that Moggi and his assistant had funded call girls for the referee and his assistants ahead of the home legs against both Boavista and AEK Athens from a secret slush fund. As ever, Italian football never ceases to amaze.

The stern defence was a product of Mondonico's footballing philosophy. From early in his managerial career, he had embraced organisation and a strong defensive shape, earning its own nickname, 'Pane e Salame' (bread and salami) – meaning a simple approach, a moniker that Mondonico enjoyed, stating that he found bread and salami delicious, having always enjoyed it as a child. But while defence was his trademark, he also had talent up front, which he was more than happy to allow to express itself, especially with the talented wing play of Lentini and midfield skills of Vázquez.

As March started, Torino had moved up to fourth place, their goal difference still showing tight games, with 23 goals scored but only 12 goals conceded. A return to UEFA Cup action saw them face Danish side Boldklubben 1903 in the quarter-finals – a team that had shocked Europe by earlier eliminating Bayern Munich 6-3 on aggregate, including a 6-2 victory in Copenhagen. The trip there saw Casagrande scramble in an opener before Roberto Policano doubled Torino's lead late on with a thumping free kick.

Taking a two-goal advantage back to Turin, they finished the job when Casagrande drew a tackle that saw an unfortunate own goal, meaning that Torino had reached their first European competition semi-final since 1965. But if their run had been straightforward to date, they now faced a formidable last four, alongside Ajax, Real Madrid and close neighbours Genoa. The draw paired them with Real Madrid and a trip to the Bernabéu for the first leg. It was time to see what the *Granata* were really made of.

Torino travelled to face Real Madrid on 1 April 1992, a side containing the likes of Butragueño, Míchel and the incomparable Gheorghe Hagi. The Bernabéu reserved a special hostile welcome for Vázquez, whistling him throughout the match. In true Torino form, they kept the game extremely tight through the first half, going into the break goalless against the Spanish giants. Then, after 59 minutes, a rare foray into the Madrid half saw Policano fire in a low cross, which took a deflection off a defender, causing keeper Buyo to make a smart save at his near post. He could only deflect the ball out to Casagrande to tap home. It was a valuable away goal, and if the Torino defence could be as miserly as usual, it would mean an away win.

Sadly for Torino, the goal only served to anger Real Madrid. Almost immediately, Hagi lashed a long-distance attempt narrowly over the bar. Then Míchel threaded a through ball to the Romanian wizard, who didn't need a second invitation, thrashing the ball in from close range. Madrid had levelled just two minutes after Casagrande's opener. And they weren't finished yet – just four minutes later Fernando Hierro headed home a Hagi free kick to give Madrid a goal advantage. To make matters even worse, Politano then received a red card with 17 minutes remaining, but Torino managed to limit the damage to the two goals. The tie was nicely balanced – a one-goal advantage to Madrid but an away goal for Torino. The prospect of a European final remained within reach.

The return leg took place two weeks later in front of almost 60,000 fans packed into the Stadio delle Alpi, the stadium draped in maroon. Torino got off to the perfect start when Madrid's Brazilian defender Ricardo Rocha tried to prevent Casagrande getting on the end of a dangerous cross, only to put the ball into his own net after just seven minutes. An already excited crowd took the volume up a few notches as Madrid tried to settle back into the game against a Torino defence that had already shown how tight it could be this season.

Torino saw out the first half professionally, packing the midfield, while defending deep, limiting Madrid's chances, and even coming close to a second when Buyo saved a Casagrande effort with his feet. The second half continued in the same vein – a well-disciplined Torino limiting Madrid to long-range shots, mainly from Hagi, while Casagrande continued to threaten, supplied by Lentini, who was on fire that night, tormenting the Spanish defence. As the half progressed, Madrid threw more players forward, leaving themselves open to the counter-attack and, with 16 minutes remaining, Luca Fusi slid in at the far post to double Torino's lead. A Madrid goal would still send the tie to extra time but could they find a way through the resolute Italian defence?

They couldn't, as Torino continued to smother their attack. The final whistle allowed the Torino players, staff and fans to celebrate a UEFA Cup Final appearance. After everything that had occurred in their history, it was an emotional moment, proving they could still compete at the highest level. Their opponents over two legs would be Ajax, with the first leg to be played in Turin.

* * *

At the start of the season, Ajax had replaced Leo Beenhakker with his assistant in what would be his first high-profile managerial post of many – Louis van Gaal. He inherited a strong squad, but the jewel in the crown was their attacking midfielder, Dennis Bergkamp, who led their goalscoring and had already netted six goals in taking Ajax to the final. It was a team that three years later would evolve into the one that won the Champions League – one of the greatest Ajax sides of all time. If Real Madrid had been a tough challenge, facing Ajax was going to be monumental.

The first leg took place on 29 April 1992, as Torino still sat a commendable fourth in Serie A with just four games remaining. Van Gaal, never a man afraid to speak his mind, cranked up the pre-match atmosphere by declaring the final to be a battle between Dutch Total Football and Italian *catenaccio*. The two teams emerged to a sea of red flares as over 65,000 fans roared the *Granata* on. If the atmosphere was supposed to be intimidating, it didn't faze the Dutch as Wim Jonk fired a 35-yard thunderbolt into the top corner after just 14 minutes, sending a pocket of Dutch fans into delirium. Ajax continued to fly at Torino, but gradually Torino got back into the game, inevitably Casagrande creating the most threat, but they went into the half-time break a goal down.

Casagrande finally made the breakthrough for Torino when Ajax keeper Menzo couldn't hold a stinging Scifo shot, giving the Brazilian an easy tap-in. Suddenly Torino had the bit between their teeth, Lentini creating problems for the Ajax defence with his skill and running. But then a loose pass from Scifo allowed Bergkamp to break into the Torino area before being brought down by Silvano Benedetti. A clear penalty, and Pettersson calmly stroked the ball past Marchegiani to give the advantage once again to the Dutch with just 17 minutes remaining.

Torino refused to lie down, and with eight minutes remaining Casagrande struck again, finishing off a neat move by poking the ball past Menzo to draw matters level. The seesaw game finished that way, two goals apiece, sending Ajax back to Amsterdam with a distinct advantage, although Torino had shown great spirit by clawing their way back into the game twice. The Italian dream was not yet dead.

Two weeks later, the two sides once again emerged to a cauldron of red flares, only this time at the Olympisch Stadion in Amsterdam. The first significant chance fell to the Dutch as Pettersson saw his thundering header from a corner cleared off the line. The noise was intense as Ajax continued to press, Brian Roy bringing a good save out of Marchegiani. But Torino looked threatening on the break, Lentini producing a great piece of wing play before seeing his cross headed against the post by Casagrande. Torino continued to break with speed, captain Roberto Cravero seeing a dubious penalty shout denied by the Yugoslavian referee although the replay seemed to indicate a dive. It was at this moment that manager Mondonico expressed his frustration. However, rather than ranting at the nearest official or thumping the bench, he instead picked up his pitch side chair and waved it above his head, holding it aloft for several seconds as if lifting the UEFA Cup itself. The action was later described by the Italian journalist, Massimo Gramellini, as a demonstration of 'rebellion; the Granata defiance in the face of destiny's injustice.' It became an enduring image in Torino folklore.

As the tempo of the game increased, it was Ajax's turn to have a penalty shout denied when Marchegiani dived at Winter's feet to thwart him. This time the replay showed that Torino may have got lucky, Marchegiani getting no contact on the ball when bringing down Winter. And with that, an exciting, eventful first half came to an end. Torino hadn't yet scored the goal they needed but they had weathered the early Dutch storm to keep the final on a knife edge.

The second half commenced at the same high pace, Pettersson coming close almost from the kick-off. Again, the play swung back to Torino, as Mussi saw his deflected shot rebound off the post – the woodwork denying the Italians for a second time. It was thrilling and tense, finally leading to the first flashpoint when Ajax substitute John van Loen clashed with Torino substitute Gianluca Sordo. The game continued at a frantic pace, Van Loen missing a clear-cut chance for Ajax. He was then involved again, appearing to elbow Policano in the side of the head, which the Italian not surprisingly took offence to. Torino flew forward and, with just one minute remaining, Sordo saw his fantastic swivel and shot cannon off the Ajax crossbar, before Policano flew in on Van Loen to continue their feud, although the referee still deemed neither player worthy of a yellow card. As the fans awaited the final whistle, Policano continued his one-man mission to assault the entire Ajax team, flying into the back of Pettersson as he held the ball near the corner flag, leaving him in agony on top of the fallen flag. As medics rushed to his aid, a glowering Van Gaal paced the sideline while his striker was stretchered off. Incredibly, Policano once again avoided punishment.

And finally it was all over. The young Ajax side had triumphed, with celebrations breaking out around the stadium as their players lifted the trophy before the glum-faced Italians. But it had been a great performance by Torino. Having eliminated Real Madrid in the semi-final, they had taken Ajax to the wire, lady luck deserting them as they struck the woodwork three times in Amsterdam. They hadn't lost either game – instead suffering defeat by away goals. Their feelings were summarised post-match by captain Cravero when he tearfully gave his famous quote about Torino's curse.

They could return home with their heads held high, flying the flag once again for Italian domination of Europe. Casagrande especially impressed, ending the tournament with six goals, equal with Ajax's Dennis Bergkamp, two of which had been scored in the final. Lentini had also proved himself to be an exciting winger, leading to his involvement in Chapter 11's Sixty-one Days of Madness.

The season ended with Torino a commendable third in Serie A, behind only city rivals Juventus and champions Milan. Their defence proved to be the most effective in the league, conceding just 20 goals over 34 games, to earn Torino another UEFA Cup place. The following season would see them finally lift a trophy when they eliminated rivals Juventus in the Coppa Italia semi-finals before overcoming Roma in the final. It would prove to be the last prize to date.

* * *

Sadly, Torino would never hit such heights again, suffering financial problems that saw them relegated in 1996 and spend the next 16 years yo-yoing between Serie A and Serie B. They would never again finish in the top three or progress beyond a European quarter-final. But for one time in their history they showed that even a non-powerhouse Italian team in the early 1990s could reach the heights of European competition. Mondonico had produced a team capable of returning a smile to *Granata* fans. The Torino faithful loved him. After defeating cancer later in life, he lived another seven years, until finally sadly passing away in 2018.

TORINO (1990–1993)
UEFA Cup runner-up – 1991/92
Coppa Italia winners – 1992/93

Chapter 12

Roma and Il Tedesco Volante

*Vola Tedesco vola, sotto la Curva vola, la Curva
si innamora, tedesco vola.*

*(Fly German fly, under the Curva fly, the Curva
falls in love, the German flies.)*

Roma's Curva Sud

EVER SINCE the early 1980s, AS Roma had suffered frustration.
As they watched teams such as Napoli and Sampdoria enjoy success,
the giants from the capital had spent seasons in the shade. It was
1983 that saw the *Giallorossi* lift the Serie A championship – a team
managed by Nils Liedholm and led by the goals of the great Roberto
Pruzzo, Roma's top goalscorer for eight successive seasons. The same
team then went on the following season to reach the European Cup
Final, only to lose to Liverpool in their own stadium, before adding
the Coppa Italia to their trophy cabinet. At that time, all looked rosy
at the Stadio Olimpico, but sadly that would prove to be the calm
before the storm. From 1984 onwards, the decline set in.

With Nils Liedholm moving back to his spiritual home of
Milan, a young Sven-Göran Eriksson moved over from Benfica,
who he had taken to the 1982/83 UEFA Cup Final. His first season
proved a bedding-in period, Roma finishing seventh in Serie A
and no silverware even close to being won. But then his methods
began to take root in 1985/86 as Roma came narrowly second behind
Juventus but claimed the Coppa Italia by defeating Sampdoria.
Sadly for Eriksson, that would prove to be a false dawn, and with
Roma drifting towards another seventh-place finish the following
year, he was relieved of his role just before the season's end, following
a particularly painful 4-1 defeat away at Milan.

The 1987/88 season saw Roma trying to rekindle the old days by bringing Nils Liedholm back for another managerial stint. They also bought themselves a new overseas star to strengthen their squad. Rudi Völler had been making a name for himself over five seasons at Werder Bremen, banging in 119 goals across 174 games, including being the leading goalscorer in the Bundesliga in his first season there and helping his team to finish second in the Bundesliga three times – a remarkable achievement for a club that was in the league below in 1980. His first season for Roma saw Völler struggle with injuries, only scoring three goals, while Roma managed a third-place finish. Sadly, once again the next season saw regression back to a seventh-place finish, although Völler was now up to speed with ten Serie A goals, including his trademark diving headers. Liedholm again moved on, this time to take a sabbatical from the game.

The 1989/90 season therefore saw another new manager installed, Luigi Radice, coming over from Torino. Völler welcomed an international team-mate into the Roma fold as defender Thomas Berthold arrived from Verona, both players having been involved for West Germany in their 1986 World Cup Final against Argentina. But even with new management, Roma continued to stagnate, finishing sixth in Serie A. The *Giallorossi* had now gone seven seasons since winning the Scudetto – it was time for chairman Dino Viola to install someone who was a proven winner.

* * *

Ottavio Bianchi had suffered enough politics at Napoli, with the wrath of Maradona aimed at him for their infamous 1989 title challenge meltdown. That dispute meant a manager who had taken Napoli to their first-ever Scudetto and a UEFA Cup success was now available, and Viola needed no second invitation. The chequebook was produced, and Bianchi came over to the capital – his remit, to bring success back to stagnant Roma. Taking the reins, Bianchi saw his squad strengthened with the purchase of Brazilian defender Aldair from Benfica – a player who would go on to become a Roma legend, playing for 13 seasons, eventually earning him a place in the AS Roma Hall of Fame. It was time to wake the sleeping giant.

The 1990/91 season started superbly as Roma crushed Fiorentina at the Stadio Olimpico 4-0, and then the wheels swiftly started to come off. They lost five of their next eight Serie A games, including a 5-0 hammering at the hands of Juventus, containing a Schillaci hat-trick, putting them down to tenth place. This had certainly not been the expectation when hiring Bianchi, causing nervous glances within the Roma boardroom. But on the plus side, they had reached the quarter-finals of the Coppa Italia, eliminating Foggia and Genoa, while also negotiating the first two rounds of the UEFA Cup at the expense of Benfica and Valencia. Given their league standing, the focus would now switch to those two cup competitions.

The third round of the UEFA Cup paired Roma against Bordeaux, a team that included Patrick Battiston (of 1982 World Cup infamy), Didier Deschamps (on loan from Marseille), Wim Kieft and a young Bixente Lizarazu. It should have been a team that would give Roma a run for their money, but it was all over after 74 minutes – Roma 5-0 up in front of almost 49,000 fans in the Olimpico. Völler scored a hat-trick in the first 50 minutes, before Manuel Gerolin added the icing with a brace.

The second leg in France was a formality, Roma again running out winners, this time 2-0, Völler on the scoresheet again. That comprehensive thrashing saw Roma advance to the UEFA Cup quarter-finals, one of four Italian teams to reach the stage, along with Inter, Atalanta and Bologna. The draw saw Roma avoid their countrymen, instead pitting them against Anderlecht, with the first leg scheduled for 6 March in Rome.

Roma's league form continued to disappoint as they became the kings of drawing matches. Following on from the Juventus debacle, Roma drew ten of their next 16 matches, drifting along in mid-table. However, February saw them exact some revenge over Juve by eliminating them in the Coppa Italia quarter-finals, thanks to a 2-0 away win in Turin, including a rare goal from Berthold, setting up a semi-final against Sacchi's Milan.

Before that, though, it was back into Europe and Roma's quarter-final match-up against Anderlecht. Roma again came out all guns blazing in front of their fans. This time, goals from Stefano Desideri, Giuseppe Giannini and, inevitably, Völler, saw the *Giallorossi* once more face a second leg with a degree of comfort. Two weeks later, any faint hopes Anderlecht fans may still have harboured were swiftly dashed as Völler went on another scoring spree, grabbing his second hat-trick of the tournament. With Roma 6-0 up on aggregate, they took their foot off the gas, allowing Anderlecht to score two late goals, but it was academic. Roma had now scored a combined 13 goals against both Bordeaux and Anderlecht over four matches, with Völler responsible for eight of them. Their league campaign may have been marked by a glut of draws, but in the UEFA Cup they were looking the most exciting team in the competition.

Returning to the Coppa Italia, Roma travelled to the San Siro to face Sacchi's fearsome back-to-back European Cup winners, coming away with a creditable draw. One game away from the final, the return leg saw Van Basten open the scoring, except for once at the wrong end, as his deflection gave Roma a 24th-minute lead. And that was all they needed, as they survived a veritable Milan onslaught to emerge winners, booking a place in the final against a Sampdoria side that looked like winning Serie A.

With the Coppa Italia Final not scheduled until early June, Roma could refocus on their UEFA Cup mission. Their league form saw them to a ninth-place finish, while Sampdoria secured their first-ever Scudetto, meaning the possibility of a double if they could overcome Roma in the Coppa Italia Final. But before all that, Roma had a UEFA Cup semi-final to negotiate.

While Inter had also reached the same stage, Roma avoided them, instead drawing Danish side Brøndby, who had surprised many with their run to this point. Having hired former national team coach Morten Olsen, it was a team packed full of Danish talent that would go on to be the backbone of the successful 1992 European Championship squad – Peter Schmeichel in goal, Lars Olsen and Kim Christofte in defence, John Jensen and Kim Wilfort in midfield and Bent Christensen up front. Travelling to the small Brøndby Stadium, in front of 17,000 screaming Danes, Roma emerged relatively unscathed, calmly securing a goalless draw to take back to Italy. Just secure a home win and a trip to the final would be in the bag.

If only the second leg could have been that simple. In front of 58,000, everything seemed to be going smoothly when Ruggiero Rizzitelli headed Roma ahead after just 33 minutes. But then a

Brøndby breakaway after 62 minutes saw a dangerous cross fired low into the Roma area. Stretching to intercept, Sebastiano Nela could only watch in horror as his toe poke sent the ball into the Roma net. It was 1-1, but Brøndby had the all-important away goal, so Roma had 28 minutes to try to find a winner or face elimination.

A Desideri free kick flew narrowly wide, before another free kick, this time struck by Nela, was well saved by Schmeichel. From the resulting corner, Berthold powered his header goalward, only to see it cleared off the line. Roma players surrounded the referee, appealing that the ball had crossed the line, but their protestations fell on deaf ears. Roma continued to pile on the pressure, but Schmeichel was equal to everything, consistently denying the *Giallorossi*. With just two minutes remaining, Roma fans were beginning to give up hope. But Roma still had Rudi Völler.

The ball fell to Desideri just outside the area, whose low shot was saved by Schmeichel. Völler and Rizzitelli were both lurking and smashed home the loose ball, seemingly simultaneously, sending the Olimpico into ecstatic celebrations. The official records would give it to Völler but at the time no one really cared – all that mattered was that they had saved the game at the death. Roma would be going to two cup finals to finish their season.

* * *

First up was the UEFA Cup Final, played over two legs in May – an all-Italian affair against Trapattoni's Inter. As discussed previously, this would prove one step too far for Roma, losing 2-0 in Milan before an 81st-minute goal from Rizzitelli in Rome gave them hope. But in the end it was Giuseppe Bergomi who lifted the trophy into the Rome night sky – Brehme, Matthäus and Klinsmann overcoming Völler and Berthold. Once again, Serie A had demonstrated its strength as a Roma team, who could only finish ninth, had reached a European final, and an all-Italian European final at that.

The 1990/91 season would finish on a high note for the *Giallorossi*, though. A 3-1 home win over Sampdoria, aided by goals from Berthold and Völler, was followed by a 1-1 draw in Genoa to secure Roma's first trophy for five years. And who scored Roma's final goal of the season in Genoa? Of course, it had to be Rudi Völler.

He ended the season with 25 goals in total – 11 in Serie A, ten in the UEFA Cup and four in the Coppa Italia – in what would prove to be his most prolific season for the *Giallorossi*. Top scorer in the UEFA Cup and joint-top scorer in the Coppa Italia with team-mate Rizzitelli, Völler would play one more season in Rome before moving on to Marseille with 68 Roma goals to his name. But he would always remember his Roma days fondly, telling *FourFourTwo* magazine years later: 'In those days you only had Italy. England was far away and Spain fell behind. All the players who wanted to achieve something, to make it big and to play in the best league in the world, came to Italy.'

Team-mate Berthold described him as 'the complete striker. He had complete skills. Header, right and left foot, keeping the ball very well, very fast. He is one of the best strikers ever in German football history. He was also a fantastic person. We had a fantastic time together at Roma.'

For Roma, the 1990s would go on to be a decade of misery, even flirting with relegation in 1997, until Capello brought back the glory days in 2001. While many other Italian teams were enjoying the limelight in the 1990s, Roma lay in the shadows. But at least they had their 1990/91 season to look back on during those dark days – primarily due to the prowess of a German hero, sporting that distinctive perm and moustache, who they took to their hearts, bestowing him with the nickname '*il Tedesco volante*' (the flying German) and serenading him with 'Fly, German, Fly!'

ROMA (1985–1991)
UEFA Cup runners-up – 1990/91
Coppa Italia winners – 1985/86, 1990/91

Chapter 13

Sixty-one Days of Madness

An offence to the dignity of work.

The Vatican, on Lentini's world record transfer to Milan

IT SEEMED like financial insanity – the world of football had gone money mad. On 26 May 1961, Inter agreed the purchase of Barcelona star Luis Suárez for a world record transfer fee. For the first time in football history, a player would move for over £100,000 – in fact the final fee would be £152,000 – smashing the previous record of £93,000 paid by Juventus to bring Uruguayan Omar Sivori over from River Plate. There was no doubt that Suárez was an outstanding talent, an attacking midfielder who had netted 62 goals for Barcelona in just 122 appearances, but those crazy Italian clubs were surely throwing money around like drunken sailors.

Up until 1952, all but two of the world record transfers in footballing history had been set by English clubs, with the other two being in Scotland and Argentina. Then, for the first time, Italian teams took the lead when Swedish striker Hans Jeppson moved from Atalanta to Napoli for a world record fee of £52,000, leading to his nickname of 'the bank of Naples'. From that point forward, Italian money ruled world football. The record would be raised a further nine times between 1952 and 1980, eight of which would involve Italian clubs as the purchaser. Juventus, Inter, Milan, Roma and Napoli would all hold the record at some point during that time, with the only transfer not involving an Italian team being Barcelona's purchase of Johan Cruyff from Ajax in 1973, a record that lasted for two years before Napoli broke it. As the 1980s began, the record sat with Juventus when they purchased Paolo Rossi from Vicenza for £1.75m.

The 1980s kicked off with the transfer of Diego Maradona from Boca Juniors to Barcelona for an eye-watering £3m at the age of just 21 in the summer of 1982. Just two years later, Maradona would become the first player to be transferred for a world record fee twice when Napoli swooped in with their £5m purchase. To put that fee in context, the British record at the time stood at just £1.5m, shared between Manchester United's signing of Brian Robson from West Bromwich Albion and Ray Wilkins's move from Manchester United to Milan, Italian money yet again. Next came Milan, powered by Berlusconi's wealth, splashing out £6m for Ruud Gullit from PSV Eindhoven. As the 1980s ended, no countries could compete with the power of the Italian lira.

The summer of 1990 saw the record again fall in Italy as Roberto Baggio made his controversial move from Fiorentina to Juventus, taking it up to £8m. It seemed just a matter of time before the psychological £10m would be broken, but who would be the first club to shatter that ceiling? It would finally fall in 1992 during 61 days of transfer madness that summed up the strength of Serie A to a watching world, many of whom shook their heads at what looked like a market out of control. It was the Italian equivalent of the Dutch Tulip Mania – reason appeared to have gone out of the window.

* * *

While Italian clubs were flaunting their wealth across Europe in the late 1980s, there was another European club who, like Milan, had been purchased by an ambitious businessman with deep pockets. Bernard Tapie had earned a fortune in France by acquiring bankrupt companies and restructuring them during the 1970s and 1980s, and decided that he wished to invest his millions into sport. He started with France's national passion – cycling. Having enjoyed success in that arena, he next turned to French football, purchasing Olympique de Marseille in 1986. Over the next six years, he spent huge amounts in building one of Europe's strongest teams – a team that would win Ligue 1 for four successive seasons from 1989 to 1992, while losing a European Cup Final in 1991 to Red Star Belgrade, before finally fulfilling Tapie's dream and lifting the big one in 1993, overcoming Berlusconi's Milan by a single goal.

Among all of Marseille's signings during this period, the most important was probably that of a young striker plying his trade with Club Brugge. That first summer of 1986 under Tapie saw the purchase of a 22-year-old Jean-Pierre Papin. He immediately developed into a world-class finisher, particularly known for his volleys, which even became known after him: a 'Papinade'. He was the leading scorer in Ligue 1 for five successive seasons (1988 to 1992), and his talent was honoured by the award of the Ballon d'Or for 1991, making him one of Europe's hottest properties.

Maybe it was seeing a foreign businessman competing at the same level as himself that drove Berlusconi to raid Marseille in July 1992. With Marco van Basten still suffering injury problems, Milan coach Fabio Capello wanted another striker to spearhead his attack during his absence. Jean-Pierre Papin was the only striker in Europe at the time at Van Basten's level, so a world record of £10m was paid to bring the Frenchman over to Serie A. The £10m ceiling had been broken, and unsurprisingly it was Berlusconi who funded it. The nuclear arms race was on.

Incredibly, Papin's record would last just 24 days. Juventus had watched Milan's rise to the top of Europe with covetous eyes and wanted to get back into the big time. They had broken the bank to get Roberto Baggio just two years before, but that move hadn't quite worked out as strongly as hoped. In the meantime, they had watched Sampdoria come from nowhere to reach two successive Cup Winners' Cup finals, in 1989 and 1990. They then went on to lift the Scudetto in 1991, powered by Vialli's 19 goals, before reaching the 1992 European Cup Final, where they narrowly lost to Cruyff's Barcelona, Vialli scoring six goals across the tournament, only one behind the joint-leading scorer, Jean-Pierre Papin. If Milan were going to get Papin, then Juventus would turn their attention to Vialli.

A transfer fee of £12.5m was agreed, immediately breaking the £10m record. Both clubs had spent huge amounts on getting a star player into their squad for the upcoming 1992/93 season, so surely now their summer business was done. But again, the record stood for only a matter of days. Berlusconi still had another item to check off his shopping list.

As discussed earlier, Torino had put together a strong team that went all the way to the UEFA Cup Final in 1992. A key member of that team had been their young winger, Gianluigi Lentini, who at the age of just 23 had terrorised the Real Madrid defence in the semi-final, especially the second leg when Torino won 2-0 at home. While Torino were keen to retain the services of their young talent, they were also facing financial difficulties, so it was with great reluctance that they entered transfer negotiations, as Juventus and Milan, having both already spent big, once again went head-to-head.

The issue for Juventus was that this time they were dealing with their immediate neighbours and rivals, Torino, rather than Sampdoria. That brought back memories from 25 years earlier when Juve had looked to buy Gigi Meroni, only for Torino fans to bring the city to a standstill through protests. With Juventus owned by the Agnellis, who could count many Torino fans among their Fiat employees, they pulled out of that deal, and now the Juventus management recognised that swooping for Lentini would probably create similar issues. That opened the door for Berlusconi, who invited Lentini to his villa in a helicopter to secure his signature.

If Torino were going to sell Lentini, they at least wanted to get as much for him as possible. But to everyone's surprise, they managed to obtain another world record fee from Berlusconi. After just spending £10m on Papin, just 61 days later they splashed out an eye-watering £13m for a Torino academy product who had played in just one European tournament. There was no doubt Lentini had potential – he had pace, intelligence, worked hard and could play on both wings – but to break the world record for his services looked pretty bold. It would place a huge amount of pressure upon such young shoulders.

Interestingly, neither transfer yielded the success Milan hoped for. Papin struggled to hold down a first-team place, suffering injury problems along with having to compete against other foreign talent in the Milan squad under the three-foreigner rule. He scored 20 times in his first season, equal with Van Basten, but was left on the bench for the Champions League Final against his old team, Marseille, coming on after 58 minutes to replace Roberto Donadoni but unable to help find Milan an equaliser. The following season he appeared just 26 times, contributing nine goals, missing out altogether on the Champions League Final victory over Barcelona. And with that, his Milan career came to an end, moving on in the summer of 1994 to Bayern Munich for just £2.1m.

Sadder than Papin's story was that of Lentini. Initially everything seemed so bright for the youngster. The fee didn't seem to faze him as he played 45 times during 1992/93, an almost ever-present, contributing eight goals on top of his wing play to help Milan lift the Serie A title and narrowly miss out in the Champions League Final, where Lentini played for the whole 90 minutes. He went into the summer break full of optimism for his second season.

As that new season approached, Milan started to warm up with some pre-season friendlies, one of which was in nearby Genoa. At the time, Lentini had entered a romantic relationship with Rita Bonaccorso, who just happened to be the wife of Italia '90 hero Salvatore 'Toto' Schillaci, their marriage crumbling. Based in Turin, Lentini was keen to see her after the Genoa game, so he set off in his yellow Porsche 911. Annoyingly, he suffered a puncture, so had to stop at a service station to have a replacement tyre fitted. Wanting to make up for lost time, he sped away, unaware that the new tyre was the incorrect style and not suitable for speeds above 50mph. Driving at a reported 125mph, he lost control on the A21 motorway and crashed. Luckily for Lentini, a following truck driver pulled him from the wreckage just before the car burst into flames, saving his life, but he still had to be placed into an induced coma, with a fractured skull and damaged eye socket.

Lentini was never the same player thereafter, with some claiming that his balance had been affected by the head injury, along with memory loss. In the summer of 1996, he was sold on to Atalanta before eventually returning to Torino. It was a sad end to what had been a promising career.

* * *

Looking back at that summer of 1992, over the space of just 61 days, Milan and Juventus broke the world record transfer fee three times – a clear demonstration of the absolute power that Serie A now wielded over European football. In terms of setting new records, it had happened 17 times since 1951 – and 15 of those involved Italian clubs as the buyers (the other two being Barcelona). If Italian clubs saw players they coveted, they clearly had the means to go and get them. It was an Italian world, and the rest of Europe could only look on in envy as their talent continued to be cherry-picked.

Chapter 14

A Geordie's Roman Odyssey

He was a lovely boy, lovely, such a heart. But a troubled boy. He ate ice cream for breakfast, he drank beer for lunch ... but a player? Oh, beautiful, beautiful.

Dino Zoff, Lazio manager

STANDING IN the tunnel, waiting to step out onto the hallowed Wembley turf, the player was a bundle of wound-up energy. Unable to stay still for a second, he appreciated that this game against Czechoslovakia could determine whether he boarded the plane to Italy for the World Cup. He had shown great youthful potential to get himself into this position, although his over-exuberance had also caused England manager Bobby Robson to describe him as 'daft as a brush'. This game would be his opportunity to show that he could handle the pressure and maintain his discipline on the big stage. Ninety minutes for Paul Gascoigne to earn Robson's trust.

It turned out to be a night to remember for the young lad from Newcastle. Right from the kick-off, he played exactly as instructed while still peppering in some moments of individual genius. The Czechs took a surprising early lead before Gascoigne set up three goals for England – Steve Bull bagging two of them. The Czechs then pulled the game back to 3-2 before Gascoigne delivered his *coup de grâce*, scoring England's fourth in the final minute to cap off the evening. It was a mature performance that would earn him a place in England's Italia '90 squad. A sliding doors moment for the Geordie, beautifully summed up by David Lacey's quote for *The Guardian*: 'The England manager may still consider Paul Gascoigne to be "as daft as a brush", but last night the brush was in the hand of a man who did not need artistic licence to make his point.'

We've all seen the highlights and the iconic images. Gascoigne turning Ronald Koeman inside out during the group stages. Gascoigne pulling the strings as England put in their best performance of the tournament in the titanic semi-final against West Germany. And, of course, that mistimed tackle on Berthold, leading to the yellow card that would deny Gascoigne a place in the World Cup Final, should England win, and the tears that tugged the heartstrings of a nation. Paul Gascoigne left for Italia '90 a young man with limited international experience – he returned as a household name of enormous potential. Naturally, such a high-profile performance would attract the eyes and wallets of football's biggest clubs. And that meant Italy.

* * *

The 1980s were a time of turmoil for Italian club Lazio. One of the key two clubs based in Rome, along with rivals Roma, they had won Serie A in 1974 before hitting the rocks over the following decade. Caught up in the *Totonero* scandal of 1980, they found themselves dropped to Serie B as punishment, where they remained for three seasons before finally clawing back into Serie A. Even then, the following season would need a last-day performance to ensure avoiding an immediate return. It proved only a stay of execution – 1984/85 saw them relegated, winning just twice all season. Again, they wallowed in Serie B for several years, including another season of punishment due to a further betting scandal, before finally returning to the promised land in 1988. A change was needed if Lazio were going to be able to compete with the likes of Milan in the early 1990s.

Following on from his successful World Cup, Gascoigne was back at his English club, Tottenham Hotspur, under the management of Terry Venables. The 1990/91 season would be notable for Tottenham enjoying a great run in the FA Cup, with Gascoigne shining throughout. The fourth round saw them overcome Oxford United 4-2, with Gascoigne getting the final two goals, before repeating that brace away at Portsmouth in the fifth round to secure a 2-1 victory. The quarter-finals saw Tottenham given a home tie against Notts County, and once again Gascoigne was the hero, scoring the winning goal with just seven minutes remaining, putting them into the draw for the semi-final, along with West Ham, Nottingham Forest and arch-rivals Arsenal. The footballing gods couldn't resist it – Tottenham were handed a tie against Arsenal and for the first time ever, given that it was a North London derby, the FA deigned to have the semi-final played at Wembley Stadium, where over 77,000 fans could enjoy the spectacle.

As the teams came out onto the pitch, Gascoigne already looked like he was hyped for the occasion, mugging at the cameras along the way. Five minutes into the match, Paul Stewart was adjudged to have been fouled around 35 yards from the Arsenal goal, setting up a direct free kick. The commentator Paul Dempsey takes up the story:

> It's a long, long way from goal here, but Paul Gascoigne's already sized it up. It's Gascoigne. IT'S GASCOIGNE! You cannot believe it and you cannot make it up! But it is Boy's Own stuff again.

Gascoigne had thrashed the ball right into the top corner, giving Arsenal keeper David Seaman no chance. It would be an iconic moment in both Gascoigne's and Tottenham's history – a moment no one who witnessed it would ever forget. Two goals from Gary Lineker ensured Tottenham moved on to the final, vanquishing the Gunners 3-1. In hindsight, it was probably the high point of Gascoigne's career.

While Gascoigne was enjoying his fairy-tale run to the FA Cup Final, Lazio were in contact with the Tottenham hierarchy. Tottenham were experiencing financial difficulties at the time under control of a new chairman, Alan Sugar. While loath to do so, they knew they had to sell their prize asset to the Italians, and so began secret negotiations around February 1991. Initially they asked for £10m, which was countered by a £5m offer from Lazio. Meeting halfway, £7.5m was agreed, along with a contract that would see Gascoigne's salary increase tenfold from that at Tottenham. An agreement was made for him to officially sign for Lazio once the 1991 season was finished.

Interestingly, it could have been Juventus that Gascoigne moved to, if an oft-quoted story is to be believed. Italy had played England in the 1990 World Cup third-place play-off and, after the game, Juve president Gianni Agnelli had asked to visit Gascoigne in the England changing rooms. Gascoigne stepped out of the shower, at least clad in a towel, to meet the Italian magnate – deciding that the best greeting would be to place him in a headlock and slap the top of his head repeatedly. Apparently, the classy Italian was not best amused.

With the Lazio agreement in place, there remained the FA Cup Final to be played, Gascoigne's magic having earned Tottenham a chance of glory against Brian Clough's Nottingham Forest. It would be a game that would have enormous repercussions for Tottenham, Lazio and Gascoigne himself.

By his own admission, Gascoigne was a basket case as he awaited entry to the hallowed Wembley turf on 18 May 1991. He recalled: 'I didn't sleep the night before the final and I was too hyped up, maybe.' As the teams warmed up before stepping out, Gascoigne could be seen hammering balls at the tunnel wall furiously. Gascoigne started the game like a man possessed. In fact, his very first tackle would have been a red card in today's game, as he went in studs-up on Garry Parker's chest, leaving Parker stricken on the ground in pain. If Venables hoped that the referee's lecture would calm his star player, he was to be sadly disappointed, as shortly after that 'tackle', Gascoigne again flew in late to a challenge as Gary Charles cut across the field near the Tottenham penalty area. This time, though, it was Gascoigne who was in pain, signalling immediately a problem with his knee. Amazingly, and this says a lot about how different football was back then, when Gascoigne limped over to take his place in the wall, his two offences didn't merit even a yellow card.

To makes matter worse, Stuart Pearce smashed the free kick home, meaning that Gascoigne's foul had cost Tottenham a goal. As Tottenham kicked off, 1-0 down after 16 minutes, Gascoigne collapsed to the turf in obvious distress. His final was done, stretchered off in tears and missing their comeback, winning the FA Cup after extra time. Lazio management would have been watching in horror.

As he lay in the dressing room, Gascoigne received the initial diagnosis of his injury – torn cruciate ligaments and probably nine months of rehabilitation. Obviously, that put the whole transfer to Lazio at risk but, to Lazio's credit, the first thing they did was to send their senior management to visit Gascoigne in hospital and allay his fears. They did, however, also renegotiate the transfer with Tottenham, eventually agreeing on a £5.5m fee.

* * *

Starting the long rehabilitation process, Gascoigne flew out to Rome to get his first taste of the atmosphere surrounding Lazio. He was met with the Italian form of Gazzamania as he let fans know how keen he was to start playing for their beloved club. Returning home excited, he continued to work on his recovery, until a trip back to his native North East threw a spanner into the works. While out in a nightclub, a random man punched him for no apparent reason, sending him to the floor. The fall broke his kneecap on his injured leg, raising fears about both his Lazio move and possibly even his career. It was horrible luck for him, just when his hopes had been rising, and could have sunk him, but instead Gascoigne jumped straight back into his rehabilitation programme, determined to show Lazio management that he was still a worthwhile investment. However, he missed the whole of the 1991/92 season as his healing continued.

An official transfer date of 31 May 1992 was finally agreed, by which time Lazio had changed ownership. Sergio Cragnotti was a businessman who had cut his financial teeth in Brazil, before returning to his birthplace of Rome to become CEO of several grain and sugar companies. In the early 1990s, having earned a substantial fortune, he had started to court Lazio directors, laying the path for him to eventually gain the club presidency in March 1992. Suddenly Lazio had increased leverage in Serie A, able to spend more than before in building a team to compete with the likes of Milan, and Cragnotti wanted to start his reign with a statement.

The summer of 1992 saw the departure of Uruguayan striker Rubén Sosa to rivals Inter – a player who had been the leading goalscorer at Lazio during three past seasons – but Cragnotti's wallet allowed the squad to add Aron Winter from Ajax and

Giuseppe Signori from Foggia to accompany the return to fitness of Gascoigne. A sense of optimism filled the air.

Gascoigne finally flew back to Rome on 7 July 1992, to be greeted by cheering Lazio fans at the airport, eager to finally see their English superstar in the flesh. With Gazzamania again in full swing, Gascoigne had to be rushed with a security escort through arrivals as the fans exploded into pandemonium. Driving to the stadium, the car windows were pounded by supporters eager to get a glimpse of the mercurial Geordie. One person expressed the occasion as 'when we got him, my god, it seemed like Jesus Christ was arriving'. No pressure then.

It would be the fourth game of the season when Lazio management finally decided that the time was right for Gascoigne to make his debut, with Genoa the visitors to the Olimpico. They had supplied Gascoigne with the No.10 shirt, a great honour within any Italian team, and the same as worn by Maradona and Baggio. Incredibly, it was 498 days between that FA Cup Final for Tottenham to this Lazio debut – a debut televised to an English audience by Channel 4. Zoff later complained that he felt pressure: 'I had to get him on to the pitch … lots of people were waiting to see him.' Inevitably, there was a moment in the game when Gascoigne received a hard tackle across his rebuilt knee. As the stadium held its breath, Gascoigne rose gingerly before continuing to play – it would be enough to have him substituted at half-time and miss a few more weeks, but at least the knee had held. He was back playing first-team football, setting up chances for his new team-mates in a fresh environment.

Lazio had a disappointing start to the season, sitting just tenth after ten matches with only two league victories. From the start of the season, however, all eyes had been on one fixture: matchday 11 when Lazio would face Roma in the *Derby della Capitale*. The frustrations of the first ten weeks could be erased if that game went their way. It would be Gascoigne's first taste of the intense rivalry.

Around 74,000 filled the Olimpico, awash with flares and smoke, giant tifos at either end, to greet the two teams. From the start, Roma fans showed their disdain for the Englishman, mocking him by holding up wheelchairs and throwing Mars bars onto the pitch, which merely backfired when Gascoigne unwrapped one and bit into it there and then. Early in the second half, Roma made the breakthrough when Giuseppe Giannini was on hand to prod home a rebound before removing his shirt as he rushed to the Roma fans, vaulting the advertising boards surrounding the pitch. A concerned Zoff looked on, smoking outside the dugout. With just four minutes remaining, things were looking bleak for the Eagles until Signori floated a free kick into the Roma penalty area. Outjumping his marker, Gascoigne's powerful header nestled in the corner before he too set off over the advertising hoardings to take the acclaim of the Lazio faithful. At that moment, Lazio's *curva nord* took Gazza into their hearts, embracing his bubbly character.

If that goal helped to convince Lazio fans that Gascoigne had been worth the wait, that view was heightened in their next game away at Pescara. On 23 minutes, Gascoigne picked up the ball in midfield and went on a forward run, bursting first between two Pescara players before shimmying past two more, beating another on the edge of the box and slotting the ball home. It was typical of that dribbling ability he had, whereby he would run pretty much in a straight line, but somehow ride through attempted tackles, ball glued to his feet.

However, soon after, the rest of Italy would take issue with the Englishman's behaviour. After being asked by a reporter about being dropped for a game against Juventus, his response was to burp into the microphone. Moral outrage ensued, whipped up by the press, leading Cragnotti himself to go on television, saying, 'It was absolutely not a nice thing to do and I didn't take it well at all. I expect my players to behave in a most serious manner,' before also stating that he would never again buy English players. But while the press and management may have been up in arms, the fans still loved Gascoigne, as he continued to shine on the pitch.

* * *

Tales of Gascoigne's high jinks at Lazio are legendary, as were their capacity to drive Lazio management to distraction. There's the story of Gascoigne lying on the roadside, covered in blood by a stricken motorcycle, only to lick the tomato sauce when team-mates rushed to help him. There's the tale of Gascoigne standing stark naked in front of Zoff as the team bus left a dark tunnel. There's the description of Gascoigne pretending to his bodyguards to have jumped from his apartment balcony.

Cracks were beginning to appear, though. Gascoigne was feeling hemmed in by the continuous attention from a rabid Italian press regarding his every movement. England manager Graham Taylor observed that he felt Gascoigne was unhappy with Lazio trying to rein in his natural exuberance. Then, at the end of February 1993, Gascoigne was sent off in a game away at Genoa, where he received praise from the Italian press because of how he accepted the decision, not wildly remonstrating with the officials or opposing players. It was a reprieve that relaxed the Englishman, demonstrated by his performance two weeks later against the mighty Milan, in which he scored Lazio's opener while playing one of his best games to date in Italy, before then scoring again in the following game against Atalanta.

The season ended with Lazio pushing their way to fifth place in Serie A – their best finish since 1977, earning a place in the following season's UEFA Cup. Gascoigne had played in 22 Serie A matches, scoring just four goals, while the star of the season was undoubtedly striker Signori, who ended with an incredible 26 league goals, winning him the *Capocannoniere*.

The next season, 1993/94, started angrily for Gascoigne when the Lazio doctor told Italian press that he felt the Englishman had returned from the summer overweight – an accusation he denied. For the first three months, Gascoigne didn't complete 90 minutes for Lazio, which only built on his insecurities about his weight. His confidence was clearly impacted, leading to a drop in form, although he wasn't the only player guilty in that respect, as demonstrated by Lazio's elimination from the Coppa Italia at the hands of third division Avellino, and elimination from the UEFA Cup in just the second round by Portuguese club Boavista. Gascoigne continued to incur niggling injuries, which again led some to speculate that his weight was the cause. Rumours of a transfer swirled, but Lazio management swore they were sticking by him, waiting for him to come back from injury and grace their side.

Finally returning in December, Gascoigne was on form once more, scoring against Juventus, while playing well overall – the joy obvious on his face for all to see. A beautiful free-kick goal against Cagliari in February continued the comeback, earning him praise from the fickle Italian press. But just as things seemed to be back on track, a skirmish with a journalist led to criticism once again. And then another *Derby della Capitale* came up on 6 March 1994.

An aggressive tackle by Gascoigne, followed by his run involving a loose elbow, led to a retaliatory tackle on him from behind. After such a good couple of months, Gascoigne's face was contorted in anguish as he limped off, injured once again. This latest setback seemed to break the already strained relationship between Lazio management and the Englishman. There were allegations that Gascoigne was missing training sessions, that he was emotionally unstable. And then, to cap it all, he suffered a serious injury during a five-a-side training match in an innocuous tackle against a young Alessandro Nesta. It was soon announced that he had suffered a double fracture on the same leg that he had damaged in the 1991 FA Cup Final.

As a long programme of recuperation began, Gascoigne's life underwent more turmoil as his relationship with his partner fell apart. He later confessed to having physically abused her during this period, driven by the depression and pressures of his latest injury. Lazio, meanwhile, recovered from their shaky start to finish one place higher than the previous season, ending in fourth place, with Signori once again the *Capocannoniere* with 23 Serie A goals.

The summer saw Cragnotti change manager, moving Dino Zoff up to the position of club president, while handing the managerial reins to the Czech, Zdeněk Zeman, who had taken Foggia from Serie C to Serie A, where they more than held their own. A disciplinarian, his appointment was always likely to make life at Lazio even tougher for Gascoigne. Zeman immediately increased the training regime, while also complaining about Gascoigne's weight as he tried hard to return to fitness.

But even as his fitness returned, Gascoigne could sense that his time at Lazio was coming to an end. They had signed another foreign star during the summer of 1993, Croatian striker Alen Bokšić from Marseille, and that signalled less playing time for the Englishman. Once back to fitness, Gascoigne made only four appearances during 1994/95, watching from the sidelines as Zeman's team ended the season strongly to finish second, although still ten points behind champions Juventus. Rumours surfaced that Chelsea, Aston Villa and Glasgow Rangers were all interested in bringing Gascoigne back to the UK, and each met with Gascoigne for talks, after which it was Glasgow Rangers that sealed a deal in July 1995. A transfer fee of £4.3m was agreed, not much less than Lazio had paid for Gascoigne's services, meaning little loss for them. After just 43 Serie A appearances, a host of injuries and six goals over three seasons, the Geordie's Roman odyssey was over, with Italian journalist Gianni Mura cruelly sticking the knife in: 'Paul Gascoigne has finally gone home. He has been one of the worst buys since the war.' Luckily the Lazio *tifosi* felt otherwise.

The tale of Gascoigne's time at Lazio is one of frustration and missed potential. There's no doubt that, when Lazio first decided to bring the Englishman to what was the leading league in the world, he was a fantastic player with huge potential. One can completely understand why, after seeing his performances at Italia '90, he was viewed as a significant coup for the Roman club. That excitement would only have been fuelled by that 1991 FA Cup run when Gascoigne scored six goals and almost single-handedly pulled Tottenham to the final. And then that crazy 'tackle' on Gary Charles changed everything. To be fair to Lazio, they could easily have walked away from the whole situation, but they stood by Gascoigne, waiting patiently for him to recover and then giving him chances in the first team. But whenever it seemed like things might be getting back on track, he suffered another setback. From the moment of the Gary Charles tackle, Gascoigne was never the same player again. But there will always be that equaliser against Roma – and that buys you a lot of love from the Lazio faithful!

Chapter 15

Golazo!

I remember thinking that James Richardson had just about the best job in the world. I'd be watching Gazzetta from some freezing cold flat in Edinburgh, surviving on kebabs and baked beans, and every week there he would be in some upmarket Roman coffee house sipping a Campari and soda and talking Signori, Baresi, Maldini, Baggio – players that seemed impossibly gifted and unattainably cool.

Charles Cumming, author

GAZZAMANIA HAD swept England. Following on from his peaks and tears during Italia '90, it seemed as if overnight he had become an English icon with his return to the First Division at Tottenham becoming the centre of media attention. Every neutral wanted to see highlights of his games, to see this maverick talent working his magic. And, after all, he was one of them – a genuine world superstar in the making right in their own backyard.

And how English football needed this injection of glamour. After all, it had been stuck in the dark ages following on from its ban from the European stage post-Heysel. Five seasons in the wilderness had caused it to fall behind its continental brethren. Sacchi had redefined football at Milan, bringing them back-to-back European Cup success. Sampdoria, Juventus and Fiorentina had all reached European finals. The world's greatest footballer, Maradona, had led Napoli to the holy land, while outside of Italy, Cruyff had built his Barcelona Dream Team, Ajax and Benfica continued to impress and Red Star Belgrade's young side were thrilling the continent. And during all this time, the only ray of light in England had been Manchester United's success in the 1991 Cup Winners' Cup. Dark days indeed.

But just as English fans finally had a spark, it was announced that Gascoigne would be joining Lazio in 1992. Once again, the Italian league was stealing away a superstar to join its ranks, meaning Gascoigne's skills would be lost to the English public. After all, they couldn't watch Italian football, which surprisingly hadn't been an issue up to this point, even though most of the world's top players plied their trade there. Most English football fans still had entrenched views on the Italian game, and it wasn't pretty. Italian football was viewed as defensive, boring, *catenaccio*, full of diving and complaining – unlike their own blood-and-thunder entertainment. Why watch teams stroke the ball around patiently when you could go to Vicarage Lane or Plough Lane and watch good, old-fashioned, route-one direct football. But losing Gascoigne? Now that was a concern. How could Gazzamania continue if he played in a league that wasn't covered in England?

* * *

Apparently, it was Gascoigne himself expressing his sadness that no one could watch him that set ideas in motion. According to an article in *FourFourTwo* written by James Horncastle, those concerns got staff at Chrysalis, an independent production company, thinking about whether Lazio games could be broadcast in the UK. Contacting Italian broadcaster Rai, they were told that the only way would be to buy the rights for a whole Serie A package, not just Lazio, and those UK rights currently sat with Sky.

But this was 1992 and Sky had other things on its plate, namely the launch of the Premier League. However, there was a fledgling channel in the UK that might be interested. Channel 4 showed product that was edgy and fresh and could potentially be the perfect place to show Italian football to its younger audience. They were interested and a deal was struck to purchase the rights for one year – for what now sounds like the ludicrous amount of just under £1 million. They had just six weeks to prepare before the 1992/93 Serie A season kicked off.

Sky had a young producer at the time who had a friend at Chrysalis. The friend thought the youngster should contact upper management about coming over and becoming involved on the show, mainly because he could speak some Italian. James Richardson took his friend's advice and suddenly found himself the face of a new programme, while colour was added by ex-Serie A players such as Ray Wilkins and Trevor Francis. *Gazzetta Football Italia* was born.

Unlike the traditional studio panels debating games, Channel 4 went for a more casual approach. *Gazzetta* was set up as a highlights show, to be shown on a Saturday morning, in which James Richardson would typically sit in an Italian café with a cappuccino and perhaps an ice cream, bringing the latest Serie A news from the Italian press and showing highlights from the previous weekend. There was the iconic theme music, punctuated by the words '*Campionato … Di Calcio … Italiano*' and finished with the extended cry of '*Goallllazzo!*', which, funnily enough, while meaning great goal, also hinted at 'Go Lazio' as well as 'Gazza'.

Like the Italian stadia, the show radiated just how cool Italy was compared to England – the piazzas, the coffee, the weather. As a viewer, you wanted to be part of it, to associate yourself with this lifestyle and *La Bella Figura*. Sitting in a pub, talking about your love of Milan, and maybe wearing the shirt, made you stand out as a hipster. Or a pretentious snob, depending upon your viewpoint. It would be the style of the show that helped to cement its cult status.

James Richardson would offer viewers interviews with such Italian greats as Roberto Baggio or Marcello Lippi. Often, players would enter the laid-back spirit. Attilio Lombardo was persuaded to do the lambada, while David Platt agreed to dress up as the Terminator. Gascoigne was up for absolutely anything, sinking his face into a chocolate egg in one episode, waking up surrounded by fake sex toys in another. It was all so refreshing for a generation brought up on *Football Focus* and *Saint and Greavsie*.

Following on from *Gazzetta* on a Saturday morning, Sunday afternoon saw the screening of a live match to the Channel 4 audience, titled *Football Italia*, again introduced by James Richardson, with Peter Brackley and Gary Bloom on board as match commentators. The opening match would, of course, involve Lazio, who were scheduled to play away at Sampdoria on the first day of the season. Unfortunately for the show, Gascoigne wouldn't be playing because of injury, creating angst about how many would tune in. A dull opening match without Gazza could spell death for the show before it had even really started. Fingernails were being chewed.

Happily for the Channel 4 brass, 3.4 million tuned in and were treated to a thrilling 3-3 draw – a great response to all those fearing *catenaccio* stereotypes. And lots more goals were to come in quick succession. Steve Gowans, a *Football Italia* producer, later recalled in a *Guardian* interview: 'People thought Italian football was boring, that it was *catenaccio*. That there was no way it could compare with the cut and thrust of English football. And then we got a 3-3 in week one, a 4-5 in week two. Milan later won 7-3 at Fiorentina. It had everybody hooked.'

There was a clear sexiness to the product that attracted a loyal audience. This was not football played in the wind and rain on a Tuesday night in Stoke. This was football played in the sun, in modern stadia filled with ultras and their incredible banners and pyrotechnics. And it was only two years after Italia '90, the tournament that made the English fall in love with football again after the dark days of the 1980s, helped by England's run to the semi-finals against a backdrop of New Order's 'World in Motion'. Italian football was cool.

If that start hadn't been good enough, the moment all Gascoigne fans had been hoping for arrived on 29 November 1992 – the *Derby della Capitale*, Lazio at home against fierce city rivals Roma, a match filled with colour and spectacle. English viewers watched transfixed as Roma appeared on course for a win, until Gascoigne scored his header, before rushing off to receive the worship of the Lazio Curva. It was *Boys' Own* stuff.

As the show grew in popularity, it was helped by the fact that Sky had also launched its own Premier League coverage. Available through their satellite network, it meant subscribing to their service, as terrestrial networks no longer had access to the games. In these early days, subscription levels were low as the public became familiar with the concept, leaving many football fans deprived of their weekly fix of English football. But they could tune to Channel 4 and satisfy that urge by watching the best players in the world playing in Serie A. And they did. Let's remember, the 1992/93 season was one when Milan played in the European Cup Final, Juventus won the UEFA Cup and Parma won the Cup Winners' Cup. English clubs hardly made an impression on the European stage. While Sky was advertising 'Watch the Premier League live and exclusive on Sky Sports', Channel 4 was able to counter with 'Watch the World's Premier League live and exclusive on Channel 4'.

It was through *Gazzetta* that a slice of English football aficionados fell in love with the Italian game. And who could blame them when Serie A teams were at the peak of their powers and all the best players plied their trade there, including some top English talent, such as Des Walker, David Platt and Paul Ince. There was nothing better than settling on your couch on a rainy Sunday afternoon and leaving the gloom of England behind for *la dolce vita*.

Sadly, those halcyon days weren't to last. With the emergence of satellite TV in the UK, it was only a matter of time before countries such as Italy followed suit. Games began to be staggered, so while Channel 4 could in the past show a marquee game on a Sunday afternoon, these top match-ups now often moved to Sunday evening or even Saturday, when Channel 4 already had scheduled programming. Also, the Premier League started to take off as most football fans gave in and bought subscriptions to Sky, meaning they could once again watch the English game, now packaged in a slicker, modern way.

It transpired that the 2000/01 Serie A season was the last broadcast, a season that saw Roma pip Juventus to the title, driven by the goals of Gabriel Batistuta following his move from Fiorentina. Needing to win their last match against Parma to be assured of the championship, *Gazzetta*'s final airing came from the Stadio Olimpico. Viewers were enthralled as Roma took a 3-0 lead after 78 minutes and prepared to watch the *Romanista* celebrate their first Serie A title for 18 years. However, the match was running behind schedule due to an earlier Roma pitch invasion, so it was at that moment that the Channel 4 transmission suddenly ended – to allow the screening of a black-and-white movie pencilled to commence at that time, a sad end to a fabulous show. But it had been fun while it lasted, producing a generation of fans for whom James Richardson's voice still produces misty eyes.

'Campionato ... Di Calcio ... Italiano.'

The Greatest Job in the World– *James Richardson chills with a brick phone and a gelato*

Gli Invincibili Overawe the Dream Team – *Milan make a statement*

Head and Shoulders Above the Rest – *Baggio and Juve celebrate winning the 1993 UEFA Cup*

Can You Feel the Heat – *Sacchi feels the pressure as Baggio looks on*

What a kit, what a player – *Asprilla brings joy to the Parma faithful*

Worth the Wait – *Juve players finally return to the summit in 1996*

La Dolce Vita – *Platt and Gascoigne enjoy life in the sunshine*

O Fenomeno – Ronaldo caps a brilliant night against Lazio in the 1998 UEFA Cup Final

Buon Viaggio – Lazio fans pay tribute to the late, great Sven-Göran Eriksson

BUON V

MISTER

An Italian World –
Marco van Basten with one of his three Ballons d'Or won with Milan

Before the Crash *– Calisto Tanzi in Parmalat's prime*

Chapter 16
Gli Invincibili

Perfection in football does not exist but this season
we came pretty close.

Marco van Basten

WHEN WE were last within the boardrooms of Milan, it was the summer of 1991 and Berlusconi had decided to part ways with Sacchi, despite all the success that he had brought to the *Rossoneri*. Sacchi would move on to manage the national team, leading them to USA '94 (more about that later), while Milan would move into a new era under a different manager.

The person selected to take over from Sacchi was Fabio Capello. As a player, he had played for Milan at the end of his career, having made his name with Juventus, before moving into management with the Milan youth teams in the early 1980s. Those teams enjoyed success under his leadership, developing a few players such as Alessandro Costacurta and Paolo Maldini into the first team. In 1987, Capello moved up to become assistant coach to Nils Liedholm and then managed the first team for six matches as interim coach between the dismissal of Liedholm and the employment of Sacchi.

For your first high-profile management job to be coaching the top team in Europe would have been a daunting task to most. Like the appointment of Sacchi, Berlusconi was gambling on a manager with little experience, but, unlike Sacchi, Capello had enjoyed an illustrious playing career. While Capello was used to the Milan way and knew the players well, he was unused to the public and press glare that he would now face and would have to combat a perception that he was a Berlusconi 'yes man' appointment. But he was lucky enough to be blessed with a highly talented team and he was smart enough to know not to overly mess with that initially. He promoted youth by bringing in 20-year-old Demetrio Albertini to replace Carlo Ancelotti and moving Daniele Massaro from midfield to attack, but otherwise tinkered little. He also had the advantage of no European football, following on from Milan's histrionics against Marseille, which meant he could fully focus on trying to win Serie A once again, something which, after all, Sacchi had only achieved once in his four seasons. Sticking with his predecessor's 4-4-2 system, his training regime was slightly more relaxed than Sacchi's but Capello did have the reputation of being a tough character. The question was whether he could hold his own in such a high-profile role under such a demanding boss.

* * *

With all eyes on Capello, Milan kicked off 1991/92, and their first five games were not overly impressive. After winning their first two by a single goal, they then drew the next three 1-1, thanks to late goals. While extremely fortunate to remain unbeaten, they had successfully ridden their luck, with the team now beginning to settle under Capello. After game seven, they moved to the top of Serie A.

With no European fixtures, Capello could field his best team most weeks, while also rotating his squad to avoid burnout. Most encouragingly of all for him, Marco van Basten was fully fit and back to his goalscoring ways, while the famous defence of Tassotti, Costacurta, Baresi and Maldini were available starters nearly every game. As the season progressed, Milan appeared to be getting stronger and stronger, winning most games comfortably without any major scares.

With three games remaining, Milan effectively clinched the title, beating Lazio 2-0 to open up a six-point gap over Juventus and a plus-20 better goal difference. Milan were still undefeated, having won 20 and drawn 11. If they could avoid losing in their last three matches, they would complete an unbeaten season, a feat that had only ever been achieved by Perugia in 1978/79, although they didn't actually win the league title that year. It meant that, even as already crowned champions, Milan couldn't let up over the final run-in.

The toughest of these last three games was the first, away at Napoli. Milan travelled to the San Paolo and came away with a 1-1 draw, having taken the lead through Rijkaard. That would represent the last hurdle as Milan then finished the season in style, hammering Verona 4-0 at home before thrashing Foggia 8-2 away, despite being 2-1 down at half-time. It was an incredible achievement for Capello – his first year of Serie A management and he had led Milan to an unbeaten season and a Scudetto. Come the summer, the only game that Milan would lose during those nine months was a Coppa Italia semi-final to Juventus by a single goal scored by Salvatore Schillaci.

Marco van Basten ended the season with 29 Serie A goals, playing in 31 of the 34 games. Several other key players also played over 30 times, including goalkeeper Rossi, defenders Tassotti, Baresi and Maldini and midfielder Rijkaard. Capello had benefitted from an extremely settled first XI, possibly aided by a less demanding training regime than under Sacchi. The press soon gave this Milan side an appropriate nickname – *Gli invincibili* (The Invincibles).

There was no doubt that Capello was the man to continue the Milan dynasty. Having proved himself during his first season, the main question now was whether he could continue that while also leading Milan in Europe's top competition. With four foreign players now allowed within an Italian club squad, Berlusconi wasn't shy in his financial support, breaking the world record transfer fee twice that summer in bringing in Jean-Pierre Papin from Marseille for £10m, followed shortly after by Gianluigi Lentini from Torino for £13m. Dejan Savićević was also brought in from Red Star Belgrade to boost the midfield, along with Fernando De Napoli from Napoli.

The 1992/93 season started with some furious attacking displays from Milan over the opening two months. In Serie A, they won eight of their first nine games, drawing the other. Their first away game was at Pescara, where Milan found themselves 4-2 behind after just 23 minutes, before a Van Basten hat-trick secured a 5-4 win. Their next away game was in Florence, where another goal fest ensued, Milan running out 7-3 winners, with two goals each for Gullit and Van Basten. Returning to the San Siro, they beat Lazio 5-3, including two Van Basten penalties. The ninth game saw Milan travel to Napoli and thrash them 5-1 in their own stadium – Van Basten this time netting four times.

In their opening nine Serie A games, Milan won eight, by an aggregate score of 27-11 – a fantastic spectacle for those who love goals but a heart-attack-inducing spectacle for fans of *catenaccio*. Marco van Basten had scored 12 of those 27 goals, proving himself to still be one of the deadliest strikers in world football. And just to add to that furious start, Milan returned to European action in the newly branded Champions League, eliminating Olimpija Ljubljana 7-0 on aggregate, followed by Slovan Bratislava 5-0 on aggregate, to reach the group stage.

Everything was going swimmingly for Milan as the season moved into December. They were top of Serie A, still unbeaten, and into the group stage of the Champions League. And then they faced Ancona in a home fixture on 13 December.

Marco van Basten's strong 1991/92 season and red-hot form in the first months of the new season resulted in him winning the European Player of the Year for 1992, his third such award, as well as FIFA World Player of the Year, a new award that had just been introduced the year before. Everything seemed to be going perfectly until he went down in the Ancona game. His recurring ankle problem had resurfaced, and he now faced another frustrating period of several surgeries, meaning he would sit out most of the season, eventually returning for the final run-in. It was another devastating blow for the player and meant that Jean-Pierre Papin would have to lead goalscoring responsibilities.

With Van Basten injured, Milan's goalscoring calmed down over the next few months, but still they continued to rampage through their Serie A fixtures, winning most of them. Following a 2-2 away draw at Lazio on 14 March 1993, Milan stood top of Serie A, ahead of Inter, with a huge 11-point advantage, having won 17 games, drawn six and lost none. That meant that their last Serie A defeat was way back on 19 May 1991, almost two years and 58 games ago, an unbeaten league run record that still stands in Italian football today. Capello had still to lose a Serie A game when in charge.

All great things must end eventually, and so it was on matchday 24, which saw Milan play a resurgent Parma at the San Siro and fall behind in the second half to a Faustino Asprilla free kick. Try as they might, Milan couldn't find an equaliser, so Capello experienced his first defeat. Milan then went into a mini-slump, winning only one of their last ten games, although drawing eight, but they had already opened up such a lead that they still ended as Serie A champions, ahead of Inter by four points. They had led the Serie A standings virtually from start to finish, with both Marco van Basten and Jean-Pierre Papin scoring 13 league goals apiece. Capello's first two seasons in charge had yielded back-to-back Serie A titles.

* * *

In Europe, meanwhile, Milan were part of the newly branded Champions League in which the final eight teams now played within two groups, with the two group winners facing each other in the final – a format that was in its second season of implementation. Milan were placed into a group alongside Swedish champions IFK Göteborg, Dutch champions PSV Eindhoven and Portuguese champions Porto, with the games commencing 25 November. That meant that Van Basten was available for Milan's opening match at home against IFK Göteborg. By the end of the evening, the Swedes would be sick of the sight of the Dutchman.

After half an hour, Van Basten gave Milan the lead, which they took into the half-time break. Seven minutes into the second half, they were awarded a penalty, which Van Basten struck home. But those two goals were just a teaser for what was to come eight minutes later, when Stefano Eranio crossed from the right. As the ball came across the area, Van Basten lurked close to the edge of the box, the ball slightly behind him. Without hesitating, his back to goal, the Dutchman launched into a bicycle kick, sending the ball into the bottom corner to complete his hat-trick. It was audacious, it was spectacular, it was Van Basten at his finest.

Unfortunately for the Swedes, he wasn't finished yet. Just one minute after this spectacular third, Van Basten calmly rounded the keeper and side-footed the ball into the vacant net. He became the first player to score four goals in a Champions League game. 'I never give a player 10 out of 10,' Capello said after, 'but Van Basten can have 9½.' A tough boss to impress!

Despite then losing Van Basten for four of the next five Champions League matches, Milan made easy work of the group, ending with a 100 per cent record over the six games, scoring 11 goals and conceding only once. Three years after their back-to-back European Cup successes under Sacchi, Capello had now taken Milan back to the promised land. Their opponents would be their nemesis from 1991 – the team that had defeated them in that quarter-final, Marseille. Berlusconi and Tapie, those two competitive businessmen, would be facing each other once again.

On 26 May 1993, Milan stepped out into the Olympiastadion in Munich to face Tapie's Marseille. Van Basten was back in the starting line-up after recovering from his ankle injury, while Papin started on the bench against his old team. The first half was uneventful and appeared to be heading for a goalless stalemate when Marseille won a corner. As the ball was swung in, Marseille defender Basile Boli rose highest to nod them ahead just before the break. First blood to the French as the stadium became awash with blue and white.

While Milan were the more aggressive after the break, they failed to make any clear-cut chances. Papin came into the game after 58 minutes to partner Van Basten but still they could find no way through the organised Marseille defence. With four minutes remaining, Van Basten limped off after a tackle involving Boli, and with that went Milan's last hope. The final whistle blew, signalling Marseille as champions of Europe. Capello and Milan had come so close to an almost perfect season, only to fall at the last hurdle.

But if everyone thought that was the last we would hear of the 1993 Champions League Final, they were sadly mistaken. After the match, a scandal started to unravel in France concerning Marseille's pre-final league game against Valenciennes. It transpired that Tapie had asked one of his squad to contact players at Valenciennes with whom he had played at Nantes and pay them to go easy on Marseille to avoid any injuries ahead of the Champions League Final. Two of the three players contacted agreed to do so, with Christophe Robert as club captain giving the message to the team ahead of the Marseille match.

At half-time, Jacques Glassmann, the player who had refused to cooperate, told manager Boro Primorac about the bribe, and by the end of the match the police had entered the Marseille changing room with questions. Soon after, Robert admitted his part in the scheme. As the full extent of the scandal unravelled, Marseille's 1993 league title was taken away, while UEFA banned them from the 1994 Champions League, although they didn't remove their

1993 title as the bribery had occurred in a French league game and not the Champions League. There was also a later allegation from within the team that most Marseille players had taken performance-enhancing drugs ahead of the 1993 final.

* * *

Capello could now move into the 1993/94 season feeling more comfortable in his role, having won back-to-back Serie A titles in considerable style, while finishing runners-up in his first season managing in the Champions League. As Paolo Maldini summarised, 'Capello was very strict and rigid, but he perfected the mechanisms of Sacchi and he prompted the leap in quality.' The summer would be a big test, though, as the end of an era arose. Sacchi's Milan had been powered by the famous signings of the *Tre Tulipani* – Ruud Gullit, Marco van Basten and Frank Rijkaard. While they hadn't always been constant starters every season, mainly due to injury issues, they did represent the glamorous overseas element to Milan. But now was the time to overhaul the squad, and that would see the end of the trio, the end of an era.

Gullit had become somewhat sidelined under Capello's first two years, not even part of the matchday squad for the Champions League Final. There were rumours of interest from Torino and Bayern Munich, but eventually he moved on loan to Sampdoria. Frank Rijkaard, meanwhile, returned home, going back to Amsterdam and his beloved Ajax. That left Marco van Basten as the last 'tulip' standing, but he was on the sidelines following the recurrence of his ankle injury in the Champions League Final. Sadly, for both the *Rossoneri* and him, he would play no part in Milan's 1993/94 season.

On the plus side, Capello still had the heart of his famous defence to call on. His new-look team would see this defence combined with a midfield of Roberto Donadoni, Demetrio Albertini, Croat Zvonimir Boban, Frenchman Marcel Desailly and Stefano Eranio, with Brian Laudrup also making some appearances. For goals, Capello would need to look to Daniele Massaro, Marco Simone, Jean-Pierre Papin and Yugoslav Dejan Savićević. It was a Milan squad that was evolving under Capello's leadership, but one that the rest of football could only stand and admire. Even Capello admitted: 'It's very difficult for all these great players. At most clubs, there's a squad of 15 or 16. Here we have 24.'

The season started well enough, with Milan unbeaten during their first nine Serie A games, but there was a notable change in style. While goals weren't as forthcoming without Van Basten in the line-up, the defence was becoming impenetrable. Their wins were all either 1-0 or 2-0, while their draws were all either 0-0 or 1-1 – after the first nine games they had scored ten goals but only conceded two – a remarkable defensive record. Sampdoria then inflicted Milan's first defeat of the season, beating them 3-2 in Genoa, with the winner coming ironically from on-loan Gullit, before Milan then went on an 18-game Serie A streak in which they won 14 and drew four, opening up a huge nine-point lead over both Juventus and Sampdoria. They then coasted through the last six league games, drawing four and losing two, but with such an advantage that they still ended up winning Serie A for the third consecutive season, three points ahead of Juventus.

What was remarkable about the season was Milan's defensive record. They conceded just 15 goals in 34 games, ten fewer than Juventus in second place. On the other side of the ledger, they scored just 36 goals, the fewest of all the top six teams and only one more than two of the relegated teams that season. They didn't score more than two goals in any Serie A game and only conceded more than two in that defeat to Sampdoria. They were ruthlessly efficient but perhaps the San Siro wasn't the place to be that season for a fan of attacking football. As Jean-Pierre Papin put it, 'If Capello's system looks boring from the stands, it's even worse to play in.'

* * *

Milan's Champions League campaign began in Zürich with what should have been a run-of-the-mill tie against FC Aarau, who had narrowly overcome Cypriot minnows Omonia in the preliminary round just to get this far. The tie proved trickier than expected as Milan squeaked a 1-0 win in Switzerland, courtesy of Papin, before a goalless game back in the San Siro saw them narrowly advance. However, normal service was resumed in the second round as Milan spanked Copenhagen 7-0 on aggregate, the damage being done in the first leg in Denmark, where Milan ran out 6-0 winners thanks to Papin and Simone doubles, to secure a place in the Champions League group stage. Under a slightly new structure, there would be two groups as before, but instead of the top teams from each group meeting in the final, this time the two top teams from each group would advance to semi-finals. Milan were placed into Group B to face Porto, Werder Bremen and Anderlecht.

Milan set the early pace in the group, following up a goalless draw at Anderlecht with home defeats of both Porto and Werder Bremen. However, they then drew their next two games, meaning that in their final group match away at Porto, they needed to avoid defeat or Porto would top the group, placing Milan second. Milan's defence mimicked its league form, securing a goalless draw to ensure they capped the group, their third goalless draw in the six group games. As in Serie A, they were ruthlessly efficient, if not mesmerising, finishing with six goals scored but only two conceded, earning them home advantage in a one-off semi-final match against Monaco.

Milan went into the semi-final with the Serie A title already wrapped up, allowing them to focus on European success. Over 78,000 fans packed the San Siro for this one-off tie and were rewarded with another ruthless Milan performance. After 14 minutes, Desailly rose highest to head Milan into the lead from a corner, setting off a Mexican wave of celebration around the stands. Then disaster struck when, firstly, Franco Baresi received a yellow card, meaning he would be suspended for the final, before two minutes later Alessandro Costacurta received a red card for a studs-up challenge. If Milan were to reach the final, they would be missing two of their famous back four that had shut down so many opponents.

Milan booked their place in that final, doubling their lead early in the second half when Albertini rifled home a free kick, before Massaro finished Monaco off with a bullet into the top corner. It meant Milan would play in their fourth European Cup/Champions League Final in the space of six seasons – an incredible record. But on paper this would be their toughest yet, given the quality of opponent they would be facing in Athens.

If any team could claim to be Milan's equal within Europe at this time, it was Barcelona. Legendary ex-player Johan Cruyff had been brought in as manager ahead of the 1988/89 season to try to inject some success back into the Catalan club. He did so immediately, guiding them to victory in the Cup Winners' Cup, where they defeated Sampdoria 2-0. From that initial triumph, Cruyff's side evolved into a powerhouse, the 'Dream Team'. Cruyff led them to four successive La Liga titles as well as lifting the European Cup for the first time – Sampdoria again their victims. They had sensational players, such as Michael Laudrup, Ronald Koeman, Hristo Stoichkov and the Brazilian sensation Romário.

The two strongest teams in Europe faced each other on 18 May 1994 in Athens, a mouthwatering prospect. Both had just clinched their domestic titles, so could fully focus on becoming champions of Europe. Capello's biggest headache was having to rejig his defence in the absence of Baresi and Costacurta, bringing in Christian Panucci and Filippo Galli, while handing the captain's armband to Tassotti. But in Capello's mind there was one piece of good news – the non-inclusion by Cruyff of Michael Laudrup – a move that he would later claim made the difference.

Cruyff was confident ahead of the final. As later recalled by Sid Lowe for *The Guardian*, Cruyff said, 'Barcelona are favourites. We're more complete, competitive and experienced than [in the 1992 final] at Wembley. Milan are nothing out of this world. They base their game on defence, we base ours on attack.' Comments that would surely have been pinned to the Milan changing-room walls for motivation. He then doubled down with a team talk that consisted of: 'You're better than them. You're going to win.' Capello on the other hand urged Milan to command the match: 'We must show our claws.'

Milan settled into the game quicker, looking the more attacking early on, while keeping Stoichkov and Romário quiet. Desailly in particular was everywhere, one minute snuffing out an attack before the next heading narrowly wide. The breakthrough came after just 22 minutes when Savićević broke into the area, before chipping across the face of the goal, where Massaro was lurking to slide home at the far post.

Barcelona started to control the game more, but still created few chances of note, while Milan looked dangerous on the break. It looked like Milan would take their narrow lead into half-time until the end of a 13-pass move that began with the keeper and saw every Milan player involved except for Desailly. It ended with Donadoni hitting the byline before pulling the ball back for Massaro to slam home his second. 'That has to go down as one of the best European Cup goals ever,' said Liam Brady for the BBC. A stunned Barcelona headed for the changing rooms, accompanied by a backdrop of red flares around the stadium. Capello appeared the only calm Italian in the stadium.

Barcelona needed to get back into the game swiftly, but whatever changes had been discussed at half-time were almost immediately destroyed by a piece of magic from Savićević. A key member of the exciting young Red Star Belgrade team that had conquered Europe in 1991, the midfielder had made the high-profile move to Milan in the summer of 1992 for around £9.4m. But his time under Capello had been frustrating, unable to secure a regular place in the midfield, while being hamstrung by the three-foreigner rule. Now he had already impressed in the first half but his moment to show Capello what he had been missing came.

On the ball out wide, just outside the Barcelona penalty area, Savićević hardly glanced up before sending an inch-perfect lob over Zubizarreta, the ball dropping into about the only spot that would result in a goal. It was magical – in one fleeting moment, Savićević had shown all his Italian critics his true talent. As the Italian commentators put it, 'Un gol incredibile,' the moment that saw the Catalan dream die. As the Milan faithful bounced in the stands, Miguel Nadal took the opportunity to exact some revenge on the Montenegrin genius, flying right through him to leave him prostrate. But Savićević was having the game of his life, going straight up the other end and hitting the post, before Desailly got in on the party, breaking through from midfield to slot home Milan's fourth, ensuring he would become the first player to win back-to-back Champions Leagues with different clubs. Cruyff could only watch on in shock as Capello's side handed him a footballing lesson.

As the final whistle sounded, European press marvelled at the Milan performance. A team that had largely relied on a rock-solid defence and narrow victories had humiliated Cruyff's Dream Team. Even with Baresi and Costacurta missing, they had been impenetrable, while scoring four times against the Spaniards.

Milan had their third European Cup/Champions League title in six seasons, Capello had cemented a growing reputation and Berlusconi could admire the fruits of his investment. For Cruyff, the dream ended – his Barcelona side would not win any further trophies under his stewardship.

* * *

The 1994/95 season saw Milan strive for a fourth successive Serie A title as well as playing another season in the Champions League, as defending holders. The start of the campaign saw the return of Ruud Gullit from his one-year loan at Sampdoria, as well as the purchase of a young striker from Napoli who had moved there after 'an animated exchange' with the Juventus manager Giovanni Trapattoni. Such exchanges would become a common thread in the career of Paolo Di Canio. But for once Milan resisted the urge to make a big signing, placing faith in the squad that had, after all, just won the Serie A and Champions League double. Instead, they focused on moving on some players, especially overseas ones, which resulted in the sales of Jean-Pierre Papin to Bayern Munich, Brian Laudrup to Rangers and Florin Răducioiu to Espanyol.

The Serie A campaign didn't start as hoped at the San Siro. Like the previous season, Milan still found problems scoring, but this time their defensive record wasn't as strong. By the end of 1994, they had played 13 matches and only scored ten goals, only twice scoring more than one. That left them stranded in ninth place, with the realisation that any retention of their title for a fourth consecutive season was now extremely unlikely. Fans' focus, therefore, turned swiftly to the Champions League.

Milan were in a group alongside an exciting young Ajax team under the leadership of Louis van Gaal, as well as Austrian side Casino Salzburg and Greece's AEK Athens. With the top two qualifying for the knockout stages, Milan and Ajax were favourites to progress. But if Milan fans were hoping for a stress-free set of matches, they were to be disappointed. Just like Serie A, this would be a struggle.

It all started with a trip to Amsterdam to face Van Gaal's young team. Rijkaard appeared happy to see his old team-mates, while Gullit greeted his Dutch international colleagues, before the teams emerged into a sea of red flares, smoke and chanting. Rain fell, making the pitch slower than usual, and the Ajax fans greeted Gullit's first touch with a cacophony of whistles to commemorate his past PSV and Feyenoord days. Even with the wet conditions, Ajax's passing was slick, the team appearing to always be one step ahead of Milan in every challenge. Marc Overmars tortured Milan on the wing, while Edgar Davids bossed the midfield, Milan having difficulty getting hold of the ball. It was mesmerising and finally paid off six minutes into the second half when another patient move saw Patrick Kluivert play in Ronald de Boer, who finished with the outside of his foot. Ajax kept applying pressure and 14 minutes later doubled their lead as Overmars burst to the byline before pulling back a cross that Finnish striker Jari Litmanen fired home.

With the score remaining 2-0, Milan had received an early warning of what was to come. The European champions had been thoroughly outplayed, unable to compete with Ajax's speed of passing. *Rossoneri* fans could only hope that it was a conservative away performance and normal service would resume at home to Salzburg. Instead, things got even worse.

A resilient Salzburg held Milan at bay until five minutes before half-time, when Giovanni Stroppa broke the deadlock, heading the *Rossoneri* in front. But as he wheeled away to celebrate, the cameras showed the Salzburg keeper, Otto Konrad, furiously rubbing the back of his head. As he applied a sponge, the referee ran over and picked up a plastic bottle lying in the penalty area, handing it to an official. The game restarted among furious protests from the Salzburg players.

Marco Simone added a second after 59 minutes and immediately Salzburg substituted Konrad, bringing on their reserve keeper. Simone struck again just five minutes later, and Milan seemed to have recovered from that initial shock in Amsterdam, registering a 3-0 home win. But the celebrations were premature. UEFA took a dim view of the bottle-throwing incident and inflicted a two-point penalty on Milan, resetting them back to zero points after two games, as well as mandating that their next two home games must be played away from the San Siro. Milan's European dream was in serious trouble.

Their cause wasn't helped by a goalless draw in Athens, who they then faced again in a must-win back in Italy – the game being played at the Stadio Nereo Rocco in Trieste before a crowd of just over 17,000. To the horror of Milan fans, AEK Athens took a 15-minute lead, and with 22 minutes remaining they remained ahead. It was then that an unlikely hero stepped forward, Christian Panucci grabbing two headed goals in the space of six minutes to register Milan's first official win in the group, providing a lifeline before the dreaded visit of Ajax.

If Milan were hopeful of revenge against the Dutch champions, it took just two minutes to remind them of Ajax's ability, Litmanen breaking through the middle of the Milan defence before lashing them into the lead. Once again, it was an easy night's work for the Dutch, running out 2-0 winners for a second time, helped by a Baresi own goal. It was clear that Milan couldn't match their Dutch rivals, who secured their place atop the standings and a knockout-round berth. Milan now only had one way to join them – they had to go to Salzburg and secure a win, to finish in second spot.

A cold December night saw Milan travel to Vienna with their season on the line. Nerves were jangling when Salzburg almost scored within the first minute before Milan then had a goal ruled out for offside. And then Milan finally got a stroke of luck. Savićević saw his shot smothered by Konrad but, unable to hold it, the ball squirmed loose, and it looked like Simone must score. However, his close-range shot hit the post before ricocheting across the goal straight to Massaro to head home. It was messy but it was the vital goal Milan needed, and they managed to see out the game to scrape through into the knockout rounds ahead of Salzburg on goal difference. But it was an unconvincing defence of their title thus far – a marked improvement would be needed if they were to go any further.

Finishing second in their group meant that Milan would face one of the other group winners. However, in an ironic twist, the runners-up pot was probably more formidable than the group winners. Barcelona, Bayern Munich and Hajduk Split had all also come second, meaning that Milan could at least avoid the Spanish and German champions. Instead, they would face a quarter-final against one of IFK Göteborg, Paris Saint-Germain

(PSG) or Benfica. Fate threw Milan a clash against the Portuguese champions.

With home games now allowed at the San Siro, Milan hosted Benfica on 1 March 1995. Marco Simone was at his predatorial finest, snatching two second-half goals to give Milan a strong advantage to take over to Lisbon. There, Milan's defence did what it did best, carving out a goalless draw to take them into the semi-finals with little fuss. The final four had now boiled down to a strong quartet – Ajax, PSG, Bayern Munich and Milan – and Milan were rewarded with a trip to the City of Light.

The name PSG will be associated by younger readers with a European superpower, funded by the considerable financial resources of the Qatar Sports Investment group – a club that has been able to buy the likes of Neymar, Lionel Messi and Kylian Mbappé. But back in the 1990s, this wasn't the case. Following a takeover by television group Canal+ in 1991, PSG became one of the richest clubs in France overnight. Then, in 1993/94, PSG won only their second Ligue 1 title, as well as achieving a Cup Winners' Cup semi-final finish. A change in management would see legendary player Luis Fernández lead PSG to their semi-final clash with Milan with a team boasting talent such as Bernard Lama, Alain Roche, Paul Le Guen and an especially fearsome attack of Liberian George Weah, Brazilian Raí (younger brother of Brazilian legend Sócrates) and David Ginola.

However, Milan suffocated PSG's trio of attackers, similar to how they had dealt with Benfica, Ginola coming closest with a late curler that rebounded back off the crossbar. As the game entered the final minute, it appeared that Milan were going to take a valuable goalless draw back to Italy, until Savićević slipped a clever ball through to Boban, who took one touch before firing home. It was a classic smash-and-grab by Milan.

The second leg took place two weeks later and, following on from his superb performance in the 1994 Champions League Final and setting up Boban two weeks prior, it would be another great night for the mercurial Savićević. Firstly, after 21 minutes, he received the ball near the right wing at speed, before cutting outside of PSG defender Ricardo and slipping it past Lama. Then, with 22 minutes remaining, Savićević sealed the tie, calmly slotting the ball past Lama after some great set-up play from Desailly. It was a reminder of just what he was capable of when in the mood.

Despite their Serie A malaise, Milan were once again heading to a Champions League Final. Ominously for the Italians, the other semi-final had seen their group foes, Ajax, travel to Germany and secure a goalless draw with Bayern Munich before then hammering them 5-2 back in Amsterdam. Given that performance and their two victories over Milan during the group stage, the Dutch should have been clear favourites. But it also had to be borne in mind that theirs was a young team, while Milan were playing in their third consecutive Champions League Final. Milan had been there and done it – would the inexperienced Dutch be overwhelmed?

While Milan had been struggling in Serie A, Ajax had been enjoying an incredible season as Van Gaal's young bucks swatted aside all before them. In the Eredivisie, they would go unbeaten throughout the season, winning 27 of their 34 games and scoring 106 goals. That form continued into the Champions League, where they were also unbeaten. In fact, their only defeat of the season before the final had been in the Dutch KNVB Cup quarter-finals, when rivals Feyenoord had managed to beat them 2-1 after extra time. This was an amazing Ajax side who were eyeing a league and Champions League unbeaten double – a formidable opponent for the Italians.

Given his performances in the semi-finals, Savićević could rightly feel frustrated when he was excluded from Capello's line-up for the final. According to Capello, the Montenegrin was injured, but according to Savićević he was fit to play – another incident to add to the catalogue of their worsening relationship. Instead, Roberto Donadoni was recalled into midfield, behind the attacking duo of Massaro and Simone.

The final wasn't a classic. While both sides probed, neither made any real goalscoring chances, with the keepers unduly troubled throughout. As the game entered the final 20 minutes something needed to change, so Van Gaal decided to bring off Litmanen and throw in an 18-year-old kid by the name of Patrick Kluivert.

This season had been Kluivert's first within the senior squad and he had got off to a terrific start, scoring 19 goals over 34 appearances. Nick Ames for *The Guardian* wrote that ahead of the final, Kluivert's mother, Lidwina, had told Van Gaal, 'You know my son will score the winning goal.' But Van Gaal had decided to start Kluivert on the bench, instead going for experience. However, now was the time for fresh young legs and Kluivert recalls that Van Gaal's instructions were: 'Be there as a target man, make sure you're available but don't come too much to the ball, try and get into the spaces behind.'

With just five minutes remaining, Overmars picked up the ball on the left wing. Cutting the ball back to Davids on the edge of the penalty area, he faced a line of six Milan defenders in a well-rehearsed structure. As the Milan defenders started to move out, Davids fed Rijkaard, who spotted Kluivert in a pocket of space. Playing it to his feet, Rijkaard accelerated into the area, expecting a return pass, but instead Kluivert turned and headed towards goal. A tackle from Boban seemed to throw him off balance but he still managed to poke a toe at the ball and prod it past a despairing Rossi. And with that toe poke, Ajax sealed a phenomenal season.

* * *

For Milan, it was the end of a European dynasty. Following on from the defeat, they wouldn't reach another Champions League Final until 2003. Under Sacchi and Capello, they had played in five finals over the past seven seasons, despite being banned for one of those. Three times they had lifted Europe's premier prize. But Capello would remain in charge for just one more season, securing a fourth Serie A title under his watch before moving on to manage Real Madrid.

The Champions League Final would be the final appearance of Massaro in a Milan shirt. He later looked back on the match, commenting that 'after that final, ten great years ended where we won everything and wrote pages of history in world football'. He was devastated by the defeat, after needing two painkilling injections to play. Massaro's exodus from Milan wouldn't be the saddest story, however.

Marco van Basten had missed the whole of 1994/95 with his recurring ankle injury. In an interview with Donald McRae of *The Observer*, he recalled those dark times in harrowing detail. He described how it would take him over two minutes just to crawl from his bed to the bathroom, his ankle in agony: 'The door sills are the most challenging part because my ankle has to go over them without touching them. Even the slightest touch makes me bite my lip to prevent a scream.' In his mind, the problems all stemmed from the ankle surgery he decided to have at the end of the 1991/92 season, just after receiving his third Ballon d'Or. He had chosen to go to a Swiss doctor who had worked on his ankle years before. The suggested procedure would be to clean the ankle and heal the cartilages but, following the operation, Van Basten began to experience a sharp pain in his ankles. Although he had managed to play towards the end of the 1992/93 season, the discomfort still bothered him, so he went to another surgeon, this time a Belgian, who recommended further surgery after the Champions League Final. For that reason, Van Basten played in the final with pain-killing injections in one ankle, before limping off after the Desailly challenge.

The Belgian doctor performed the surgery on Van Basten after the final, but the Dutchman had been unable to recuperate during the 1993/94 season. He tried everything in desperation, including Eastern herbs, faith healing and acupuncture, but with no success. It was therefore decided to try fitting a brace with pins, pulling bones apart for connective tissue to develop. In all, 22 pins were placed into Van Basten's foot and shin, causing him agony for the next three months. When the tortuous device was finally removed, the ankle was still unable to bear weight. He, and all around him, finally came to the realisation that his career was over.

And so it was that, on 17 August 1995, a press conference was called ahead of a Milan friendly and Van Basten uttered the fateful words: 'The news is short. I simply decided to stop being a footballer.' Then one of the greatest strikers to ever grace the game walked out into the San Siro for one last time. Dressed in a pink shirt, brown jacket and jeans, the legendary Dutchman followed the teams out onto the pitch, waving to the *Rossoneri* faithful before a lovely handshake with famous Italian referee Pierluigi Collina. As he ran to the centre circle, applauding the fans, the stadium erupted into song, flares burning – hardly a dry eye in the house. Even Capello, known for his stoic demeanour, couldn't control his emotions, shedding a tear in the Milan dugout. And then, just like that, the Swan of Utrecht disappeared back down the tunnel and into the bowels of the San Siro. He was just 30 years old.

MILAN (1991–96)

European Cup winners – 1993/94
European Cup runners-up – 1992/93, 1994/95
Intercontinental Cup runners-up – 1993, 1994
Serie A champions – 1991/92, 1992/93, 1993/94, 1995/96

Chapter 17

The Old Lady Awakens

One game stands out in particular, one against Udinese which we won 5–1. Baggio scored four goals. I don't think I've seen a better performance from any player in any game I've ever played in. As footballers go, he's a genius.

Former Juventus team-mate David Platt

SINCE THE tragic events of Heysel, the story of Italian dominance has excluded that most famous of Italian teams, Juventus – the reason being that following on from their European Cup win over Liverpool, the Old Lady went into something of a slump by her usual high standards. The season after Heysel saw Juventus once again crowned Serie A champions, for the fourth time in six years, but after that, manager Giovanni Trapattoni departed to work his magic over at Inter. It was the end of ten seasons in which Trapattoni had delivered six Serie A titles and each of the three European trophies – christened the 'Golden Decade'.

In his place came Rino Marchesi, who had managed both Napoli and Inter in the early 1980s before overseeing an outstanding 1985/86 season at Como, where he impressed in achieving a mid-table finish for the Serie A minnows with an attractive brand of football. But Trapattoni would prove to be a hard act to follow, given his success, and so it proved. Marchesi's first season saw Juve finish second behind the Maradona-powered Napoli, ending just three points behind them as Napoli defeated the *Bianconeri* both home and away. In Europe, meanwhile, a tough second-round draw in the European Cup saw them eliminated on penalties by Real Madrid.

For the first time in seven years, no trophies were making their way to the Stadio delle Alpi.

Marchesi's second season in charge saw the retirement of talisman Michel Platini, at only 32 years of age, meaning an end to the days of the Platini and Boniek partnership that had proved so successful. Platini's replacement as the foreign superstar was Liverpool's Ian Rush, scorer of 211 goals for the Reds over the previous six seasons, signed for a British record transfer fee of £3.2m. Sadly for the Welshman, he failed to make any significant impact in Italy, lasting just one season, during which he scored just seven Serie A goals before returning to another prolific period back with Liverpool. That one season saw him partner with Michael Laudrup up front.

Marchesi's second season proved even more frustrating as Juventus slipped to sixth place in Serie A, their worst showing since 1962, and again fell in European competition in the second-round stage – this time to Panathinaikos in the UEFA Cup. They also suffered elimination in the semi-final of the Coppa Italia to hated rivals Torino. Rush's disappointing season was seen as a symbol of Marchesi's struggles. The Agnelli family had seen enough – Marchesi was relieved of his duties.

In a somewhat surprising move, Juventus turned to a former club legend who had little coaching experience – ex-goalkeeper Dino Zoff. A stalwart over 11 seasons in Turin, Zoff had only retired from playing professional football five years before, during which time he became goalkeeping coach with Juve before managing the Italian Olympic team. Coming in to head up the *Bianconeri* would be his first senior club role – quite the debut job.

With Rush returning to Merseyside, Alessandro Altobelli was brought in from Inter, where he had been a proven goalscorer for 11 seasons. Also added were two new overseas players. Midfielder Oleksandr Zavarov who had played for the Soviet Union during the 1988 European Championship Final against the Netherlands was signed from Dynamo Kyiv, while midfielder Rui Barros joined from Porto.

Barros enjoyed a strong debut season, representing a bright spot along with Michael Laudrup's renaissance, as a fourth-place finish and UEFA Cup elimination at the hands of Napoli represented a disappointing 1988/89, although Zoff was given a second season at the helm to try to prove himself. Juve's league campaign had ended with just 51 goals from 34 games, showing the continued need for a proficient striker. Their attention turned to Sicily, where Serie B's top scorer for the prior season was plying his trade at Messina. Deciding to see whether that form could be translated into goals at a higher level, Juve signed Salvatore Schillaci, while another striker who had impressed at Serie B level, Pierluigi Casiraghi at Monza, also made the move up. To make room, Altobelli was moved on to Brescia, while Michael Laudrup left for Barcelona. Finally, another of the USSR's 1998 European Championship Final team also came aboard, as this time Juve plundered Dinamo Minsk to bring midfielder Sergei Aleinikov to join up with fellow countryman Zavarov. Given his mediocre first season, the pressure would be on Zoff to deliver silverware.

* * *

Ahead of the 1989/90 season, Juventus were rocked by tragic news. Zoff had appointed as his assistant coach club legend Gaetano Scirea as his assistant coach, who had gone on a scouting mission to watch Poland's Górnik Zabrze ahead of their September meeting in the UEFA Cup. On 3 September 1989, a car in which he was a passenger collided head on with a gasoline truck, exploding on impact and killing Scirea and two other passengers. Scirea was just 36 years old.

The Serie A season started well, with three wins and a draw, before Juventus settled into a third-place to seventh-place range from that point onwards, eventually finishing fourth as Napoli sealed their second Scudetto. But Zoff's team proved much more effective in the cup competitions. Entering the 1989/90 UEFA Cup, Juventus negotiated the first three rounds in relative comfort, eliminating Górnik Zabrze, PSG and East Germany's Karl-Marx-Stadt to set up a quarter-final tie against Hamburg in March. At the same time, Juventus reached the Coppa Italia Final, overcoming Roma in the semi-finals, with Casiraghi making a name for himself, scoring both goals in the home win. The first leg of the final, at home against Milan, took place in February, ending in a goalless draw. The return leg would be a whole two months later.

April saw Juventus host Köln in their UEFA Cup semi-final and everything appeared to be going smoothly for the Italians. A

Barros opener and an own goal put Juve two goals up at half-time, and when Giancarlo Marocchi scored a third early in the second half, it seemed all over. But German teams are famous for never giving up and Köln were no exception, scoring twice in the last ten minutes to grab two away goals and make the return leg back in Germany a much more tense affair. Juventus reverted to a solid Italian defensive performance and came away with a goalless draw, meaning Zoff's side now had the possibility of a cup double.

First came the Coppa Italia Final return leg away at the San Siro. With the odds against them, Juve lined up against Sacchi's powerhouse and snatched an unlikely early lead when midfielder Roberto Galia broke Milan's offside trap after just 16 minutes. They then managed to hold off the likes of Van Basten and Massaro to earn Zoff his first silverware, as keeper and captain Stefano Tacconi lifted the trophy in front of a sizeable travelling support. One cup in the cabinet, next up the UEFA Cup Final.

The final was against Roberto Baggio's Fiorentina and, as discussed in a previous chapter, Juventus prevailed courtesy of a controversial 3-1 first-leg victory in Turin, with Fiorentina fans then further inflamed by the signing of Baggio by Juventus. Despite being only the fourth-best Italian team in Serie A, Juventus had demonstrated the strength of the league by winning the UEFA Cup in an all-Italian final, in a season where Italian teams swept all three European competitions. Zoff had delivered two trophies to the Agnelli family in just his second season in charge. There wouldn't be a third, though, as he accepted an offer to join Lazio, announcing the move just ahead of the UEFA Cup Final.

Schillaci, however, could look proudly back on a season in which he netted 21 goals across all competitions for the Old Lady. The gamble in bringing him up from Serie B had paid off, earning him a place in Italy's World Cup 1990 squad, where, as we saw earlier, he took his chance with aplomb.

Elsewhere in Serie A, while Juventus were finishing fourth, recently promoted Bologna continued to impress, qualifying for the UEFA Cup with an eighth-place finish. Managed by Luigi Manfredi, they played an attractive brand of attacking football, so it was to him that Juventus turned, hoping to discover the next Arrigo Sacchi. As well as a new manager, the squad also underwent a significant overhaul. Out went the Russian pair, along with Barros, and in came Roberto Baggio for a world record fee, along with German midfield star Thomas Hässler from Köln, Brazilian defender Júlio César from Montpellier and a young Paolo Di Canio from Lazio. Juventus could approach 1990/91 with an impressive attacking trio – Baggio, Schillaci and Casiraghi.

Commencing the new campaign with a Supercoppa tie against Napoli, Juventus were thoroughly humiliated 5-1, Baggio getting their only goal. Nevertheless, Juventus then found their groove for the remainder of 1990. By the end of the year, they had lost just two of 14 Serie A games, placing them third in the standings, as well as reaching the Cup Winners' Cup quarter-finals after eliminating Bulgarian side Sliven and Austria Wien, with a combined aggregate scoreline of 16-1.

But then their season swiftly fell away. After topping the table in January, Juventus slumped to a seventh-place finish, below neighbours Torino and insufficient to earn a European place for next season. The Cup Winners' Cup quarter-final did, though, see the *Bianconeri* again inflict a thrashing, this time against Liège of Belgium, 6-1 on aggregate, meaning Juve had now scored 22 goals in the six games to date – an average of almost four goals per game as Baggio led the way with eight. He would add one more in the semi-final, making him the tournament's top scorer, but it wasn't enough, as Juventus exited to Cruyff's Barcelona. With no silverware and no upcoming European football for the first time since 1971, Manfredi's brief sojourn was over – the only bright spots of the season being Baggio's 27 goals across all competitions and the continued development of Casiraghi, as Schillaci disappointed following his stellar World Cup. It was time to bring back a legend.

* * *

As mentioned earlier, ten seasons under the management of Giovanni Trapattoni had seen Juventus claim six Serie A titles (along with three second-place finishes), as well as winning each of the three European competitions. It had been an unforgettable period, after which he had departed to Inter and helped them secure their first Scudetto for nine years as well as the UEFA Cup with the three Germans – Brehme, Matthäus and Klinsmann. Maybe he could bring the good times back to Stadio delle Alpi – it was worth a gamble.

Perhaps in order to mirror Inter's success, Juventus boosted the German influence within their squad from one to two. While Hässler departed to Roma, Jürgen Kohler and Stefan Reuter arrived from Bayern Munich, both of whom had been members of West Germany's 1990 World Cup-winning squad. With no European football to distract them, Juventus could concentrate fully on their domestic campaign, where the season turned into a two-horse race for the title between themselves and Milan. Sadly for Juventus, while they did top the table early in the season, they were up against Capello's Invincibles, who went the whole season unbeaten to finish eight points ahead of second-placed Juve. Trapattoni had improved their performances markedly, Baggio especially impressive with 22 goals across all competitions to finish second in Serie A behind Marco van Basten, also leading Juventus to the Coppa Italia Final, where they fell to Parma. There was growing optimism within the club, as all realised that there was no shame in being unable to overhaul an imperious Milan that year.

The potential shown meant the Agnelli family were ready to invest heavily to challenge Milan. While Reuter headed back to Germany and Schillaci moved on to Inter, three big summer signings were made. A new world record fee of £12.5m was splashed out on prizing Gianluca Vialli from Sampdoria (the second time Juventus had broken the record in two years, although shortly thereafter superseded by Milan's purchase of Lentini) while another German, midfielder Andreas Möller, was brought over from Eintracht Frankfurt. Further boosting the midfield was the acquisition of David Platt from Bari for £6.5m. Less heralded at the time, but just as importantly, Fabrizio Ravanelli and Antonio Conte joined from Reggiana and Lecce, respectively. Juventus now had a manager and a squad strong enough to seriously challenge anyone in Europe. And it would be in Europe that they would make their mark.

Playing in the UEFA Cup, the first three rounds at the back end of 1992 saw Juventus eliminate Cypriot side Anorthosis Famagusta, Greek side Panathinaikos and Czech side Sigma Olomouc with relative ease, only Panathinaikos causing minor problems. The quarter-final in March, though, would provide stiffer opposition as Juve were drawn against Benfica. The first leg in Lisbon saw Juventus suffer their first UEFA Cup defeat of the campaign, beaten 2-1, meaning a tense night back in Turin. With the smoke from pre-match flares still swirling, Juventus got off to the perfect start when a defensive mix-up from a corner provided Kohler with an easy finish after just two minutes. Later, another corner found its way to an unmarked Dino Baggio, who gratefully doubled their lead, before Ravanelli wrapped things up. European glory was beckoning in the distance.

The semi-finals pitched Juventus up against a PSG side that contained a precocious young talent. Liberian striker George Weah had been recommended to Monaco manager Arsène Wenger by Cameroonian manager Claude Le Roy, and signed for just £12,000. His four seasons in the south of France saw him net 66 goals, help Monaco reach a Cup Winners' Cup Final and win African Footballer of the Year in 1989. That earned him a move to PSG in the summer of 1992 and he had made his mark on the UEFA Cup to date, scoring six goals in their run to the semi-finals. While PSG boasted a team including other talented players such as David Ginola, Weah gave Juventus most food for thought.

Over 40,000 packed the Stadio delle Alpi, and while Juventus were aware of the threat from Weah, they were powerless to stop him when played through by Ginola, slotting the ball past Juve keeper Michelangelo Rampulla. The goal spurred Juve into life, with Dino Baggio hitting the post shortly after from an audacious lob; however, Ginola and Weah continued to create problems as they guided PSG into the break still one goal ahead. But ten minutes into the second half, Juventus found their equaliser. A ball into the box saw Ravanelli set the ball up perfectly for Roberto Baggio to strike into the bottom corner. Both sides then continued to create chances, but with the game drifting towards a first-leg draw, Juventus earned a late free kick just outside the penalty area. Roberto Baggio sized up the situation before hitting a perfect strike into the top corner to earn Juventus a precious home victory. With just one goal in it, and a PSG away strike, the second leg was beautifully poised.

Two weeks later, PSG came flying out of the traps back at the Parc des Princes. Playing at a furious pace, they bombarded the Juventus goal in the first half, unlucky not to score. The second half followed the same pattern, PSG swarming all over a deep Juve defence, until finally Weah broke through, only to seemingly be fouled in the area as he set to shoot. To the shock of the PSG players, the referee waved away their vehement protests, but it looked like just a matter of time before PSG would score, Ginola's wing play and Weah's strength in the air causing all manner of problems. But then a rare excursion into the PSG half saw Juve earn a free kick. With the PSG wall lined up, Giancarlo Marocchi surprised the PSG defence by chipping the ball to the left of the area, where the ball was headed by Platt to Vialli. Spinning, his shot was deflected by Roberto Baggio past PSG keeper Bernard Lama to secure Juventus's passage to the final. It had been a classic Italian smash-and-grab – backs to the wall for 77 minutes before snatching a winner against the run of play. Awaiting them in the final would be Borussia Dortmund.

Borussia Dortmund had already overcome Italian opposition on the way to the final, defeating Roma 2-1 on aggregate in the quarter-finals, before scraping through the semi-final on penalties against Auxerre. Their line-up for the final was almost 100 per cent German, the only overseas player being Swiss striker Stéphane Chapuisat, and included Stefan Reuter after his return from Juventus. Managed by Ottmar Hitzfeld, Dortmund had narrowly missed out on winning the Bundesliga the season before on a dramatic last day where any one of three teams could have lifted the trophy, Stuttgart eventually prevailing over Dortmund on goal difference.

The first leg took Juventus to the intimidating Westfalenstadion where Dortmund's passionate support held court. And if the atmosphere was terrifying to start with, it ramped up even more when Michael Rummenigge, brother of Karl-Heinz of Inter fame, scored after just two minutes. But Juventus kept their cool, Möller almost scoring against his former club with an audacious chip that clipped the bar before a well-worked free-kick routine saw Dino Baggio strike low and hard into the corner for the equaliser. Having weathered the early storm, it only took three minutes more for Juventus to go in front, Marocchi setting off on a lightning-fast break from his own penalty area before slipping the ball to Vialli, whose cross fell to an unmarked Roberto Baggio on the penalty spot. *Il Divin Codino* gratefully tucked the ball away to give Juventus the lead after 30 minutes.

Roberto Baggio was now in the mood, having an effort cleared off the line early in the second half, and with 16 minutes remaining he sealed a great away performance with another goal. Juventus had gone to Dortmund and come away with a comfortable victory, including three away goals, effectively placing one hand on the trophy.

If expectations were that Juventus would take their foot off the gas for the return leg in Italy, it wasn't to be. This time it was their turn to strike early, Dino Baggio slamming the ball into the roof of the net after just five minutes, after which Juve continued to dominate before Dino Baggio doubled his tally with a header shortly before half-time. At this point, Dortmund just wanted to get out of there.

Möller had been outstanding over both legs and finally got his reward, scoring midway through the second half, albeit via a lucky deflection. Dortmund were finally put out of their misery by the referee's whistle, leading to wild celebrations with the Stadio delle Alpi, Roberto Baggio carried around the field on his team-mates' shoulders before lifting the UEFA Cup high into the Turin night. Just three seasons after becoming UEFA Cup champions under Zoff, Juventus were again flying the flag for Italy, this time with Trapattoni back at the helm.

* * *

Trapattoni and Juventus's upper management had constructed a fantastic side, albeit assisted by two record-setting transfers. Angelo Peruzzi was establishing himself as a top keeper behind a defence including César and Kohler. Dino Baggio was the rising midfield star, while ahead of him, playing just behind the front two, Möller was in imperious form. But it was in attack that Juventus were especially impressive. Vialli and Roberto Baggio, the two record signings, were the usual pairing, but Juve also had options in Ravanelli and Di Canio. Roberto Baggio in particular was in a fine vein of form. Having scored 22 goals in all competitions the previous season, 1992/93 saw him add another 30, six of which were in the UEFA Cup. In recognition of this, Baggio received the Ballon d'Or, FIFA World Player of the Year and World Soccer Player of the Year award – an extraordinary haul.

While not as successful as his first decade at the club, a gifted Trapattoni-led team had now won the UEFA Cup, although it was seven years since they had been able to secure a Scudetto. The 1993/94 season saw another valiant effort but again Juve fell just short, losing only four Serie A games all season, of which one was a vital home loss to Milan, who eventually pipped them to the title by three points. Perhaps more surprisingly, Juve's defence of their UEFA Cup title ended in the quarter-finals, at the hands of fellow countryman Cagliari, who secured a shock 2-1 victory in Turin after Kohler was red-carded in the first half, before going on to lose to eventual champions Inter in the semi-final.

A lack of silverware saw Trapattoni unable to agree a new contract with Juve management, resulting in his second departure from the club, heading off to Germany and Bayern Munich, but he had put into place the pieces for a successful future. It just needed the right man now to come along and develop those pieces further. His replacement would be Marcello Lippi, and Juventus fans were about to enter a stupendous period.

JUVENTUS (1986–1994)
UEFA Cup winners – 1989/90, 1992/93
Coppa Italia winners – 1989/90

Chapter 18

Prosciutto, Parmigiano and Parmalat

We neither had the mental stamina nor resilience to win the Scudetto, but in a one-off game, I can honestly say we were as good as anyone.

Nevio Scala, Parma manager

WHEN YOU think of the Italian lifestyle, what images come to mind? Sipping espressos in a streetside café. An evening *passeggiato* and *aperitivo* as the sun sets. And food, great food. Italy has a deserved reputation for its cuisine, rivalled perhaps only by its neighbour France, with each region having its own specialties and wines. One of the foremost of those regions is the northern Italian region of Emilia-Romagna, home to two great culinary cities: Bologna and Parma.

Parma is best known for two famous specialties, prosciutto di Parma, and Parmigiano-Reggiano cheese, known to those outside of Italy as Parma ham and Parmesan cheese, respectively. For its residents, it was a great place to enjoy a family meal, eating impressive local produce washed down by a glass of red wine. What it was not, though, up to the 1980s, was a great place to watch football.

Parma had a team, Parma FC, which had been formed in 1913 as the wonderfully named Verdi Foot Ball Club after one of Parma's most famous sons, the opera composer Giuseppe Verdi (at times Parma used to come out onto the pitch accompanied by Verdi's 'Marcia Trionfale'). Following the conclusion of the Second World War, they were permanent residents of the lower divisions, bouncing between Serie B and Serie C, even dropping into Serie D for four seasons in the late 1960s. And that wasn't really a surprise, given that Parma is the 18th-largest city in Italy, overshadowed by nearby Bologna. The fans were used to their lot – they enjoyed meeting at the stadium, their rivalry against Reggiana and some fine local cuisine after. And then along came Parmalat.

* * *

In 1961, a young college dropout named Calisto Tanzi inherited the family-run ham retail company after his father passed away and he decided to expand by opening a small pasteurisation plant just outside of Parma. By the 1980s, the small plant had grown into a multinational company, dealing in dairy, bakeries and milk, which led to a public listing on the Milan Stock Exchange in 1990. It had become one of Parma's biggest employers and Tanzi was heralded as an example of aggressive business growth typical of many companies during that era. His company was pulling in money and looking for suitable places in which to invest. And like many Italian businessmen at the time, he turned to football and his local team, Parma.

In 1986, Parma made one of their periodic promotions from Serie C back to Serie B under the guidance of their new coach Arrigo Sacchi. As mentioned earlier, his Parma side made quite the impression on Milan's new owner, Silvio Berlusconi, when beating them twice in the Coppa Italia. That led in 1987 for a move for Sacchi over to Milan but he left a team in much better shape than before, attracting Parmalat to become their sponsor. It was the beginning of a connection between the two parties. Following on from Sacchi's success, Parma stabilised within Serie B over the next two seasons under the guidance of Giampiero Vitali, finishing 11th and ninth, respectively, but the decision was made to try to push on by appointing a new manager. For that they went to a former midfielder who had played for several Italian clubs during his career before a season of management with Reggina, who he led to promotion to Serie B. His name was Nevio Scala.

Scala would later recall his remit under club president Ernesto Ceresini: 'The first thing he said to me was that he had a dream. He wanted to see Parma in Serie A.'

Scala's first key change at the club was to move away from Sacchi's beloved 4-4-2 formation and implement a 5-3-2. To the joy of Parma fans, the change led to greater success on the pitch. Parma found themselves battling for promotion to Serie A during 1989/90 and it all came down to the final weekend when they played their local rivals Reggiana. There could be no sweeter way to win their first-ever promotion to the promised land than by beating their rivals, which they duly did 2-0. Long-time Parma fans could hardly believe it – after 77 years of existence, they were finally going to see their side compete in the top flight.

Sadly for Parma, club president Ernesto Ceresini wouldn't witness this historic moment, having passed away just months earlier. He had become club president back in 1976, making his money in construction before the death of his wife led him to consider a new passion.

It was under his leadership that Arrigo Sacchi had been appointed and it was tragic that he never got to enjoy Parma's promotion. But his death would result in Parmalat, who had until then been just sponsors, deciding to take control of the club. Buying the Ceresini family's ownership stake, Calisto Tanzi became the new owner, placing the day-to-day presidency under Giorgio Pedraneschi, just as Parma were about to embark on their Serie A adventure. It would prove perfect timing for the business magnate – a chance to invest Parmalat's wealth into a Serie A club and see whether he could not only help them to survive but to prosper within their new environment.

The summer of 1990 therefore saw major changes on the pitch as well as in the boardroom. With funds available, Parma went into the transfer market, and among their initial signings were two internationals, Belgian defender Georges Grün and Brazilian goalkeeper Cláudio Taffarel, who had both been to the 1990 World Cup over the summer. But the most interesting signing was a young 20-year-old Swedish midfielder by the name of Tomas Brolin, who they bought from IFK Norrköping. In one summer, Parma had picked up three foreign players to boost their otherwise all-Italian squad. They would also be sporting white shirts with a new logo, Parmalat, proudly displayed across the front. However, the newness of the whole situation was encompassed by the fact that Parma still didn't even have a fixed training location – they still borrowed grounds from other clubs or even used parkland.

Their season kicked off with a mouthwatering opener, the visit of Juventus to Parma's compact Stadio Ennio Tardini. Parma didn't embarrass themselves, narrowly losing 2-1, before then going on a six-match unbeaten run, including defeating Napoli, taking them to the giddy heights of fourth as Brolin demonstrated his potential with three goals over the period. They continued the season in the same vein, holding their own, until a late burst saw them secure sixth spot, one point ahead of both Juventus and Napoli, and qualification for the UEFA Cup. As far as debut seasons in a top division go, it was quite the achievement, powered by 13 goals from Italian striker Alessandro Melli, while young star Brolin contributed seven from midfield.

As Scala developed his team, he favoured his 5-3-2 formation being able to quickly morph into a 3-5-2 formation when attacking, by pushing up the full-backs. To help cement that, the summer of 1991 saw Parma purchase two fine Italian full-backs in the shape of Antonio Benarrivo from Padova and Alberto Di Chiara from Fiorentina. Benarrivo would go on to play for Parma for over a decade, becoming one of their key players across that era and earning him international caps. And once again, Parma enjoyed a strong start to the season, losing only one of their first 12 matches, away to the mighty Milan, placing them sixth in the table. Unfortunately, their European adventure wouldn't be as successful. Drawn in the first round against CSKA Sofia, Parma were one minute from progressing when an equaliser put Sofia through on away goals.

Like the previous season, Parma sat on the edge of European qualification for most of the campaign, eventually finishing in seventh, just one place lower than before. That league placing wouldn't earn them a repeat visit into Europe – but they would get there through another route.

The Coppa Italia had seen Parma progress smoothly through to the semi-finals, eliminating Palermo, Fiorentina and Genoa en route. But that then threw up a tough semi-final against defending Serie A champions Sampdoria. With 25,000 fans squeezed into the Stadio Ennio Tardini, Brolin grabbed a second-half goal to give Parma victory ahead of travelling back to Genoa. There, with just 13 minutes remaining, Sampdoria cracked Parma's defence, sending the game into extra time in front of a pulsating crowd. The odds were in favour of a Sampdoria victory.

But then, in the space of six extra-time minutes, a raking pass from Brolin put Melli through to equalise before Melli again scored, through a cheeky Panenka penalty. Suddenly Sampdoria needed two goals to progress. They got one through Pietro Vierchowod but it was almost the last kick of the game and therefore not enough. Parma found themselves in the Coppa Italia Final, where their opponents would be Juventus, who had eliminated Milan in their semi-final. Only a Roberto Baggio penalty would separate the two teams in Turin in the first leg, so all eyes turned to the second leg and the possibility of Parma winning their first-ever silverware.

On the stroke of half-time it was ace striker Melli who headed Parma into the lead from a corner. And then, with half an hour remaining, a beautiful Parma move saw Marco Osio double their advantage. Juventus pushed forward, off-the-line clearances and the woodwork saving Parma, but to no avail. Parma held on and wild celebrations broke out in their small stadium as they celebrated a first trophy, and entry into the 1992/93 Cup Winners' Cup.

Scala described it to *Corriere della Sera* as a key moment:

> We didn't just win the Coppa Italia. We pulled off our greatest coup. Our players have understood that you can win here, and other players saw it too. In future, they will not view us as a provincial club with an uncertain future.

The small team from Emilia-Romagna had made their mark on Italian football – would they now be able to do the same on the European stage?

* * *

One of the issues that had hampered Parma in 1991/92 was their lack of goals – 32 goals across 34 games in Serie A was low even by Italian standards, and when your leading goalscorer, Melli, is sitting on just six goals, there's an obvious problem. If Parma were to push on in addition to having a greater impact in Europe than their previous campaign, they needed more firepower. But where to get it from? The answer would be an intriguing one.

There are certain characters in football who just bring a smile to everyone – those players who perform with *joie de vivre* and happiness across their face. Those players who defy convention, where you never quite know what they will do from one minute to the next, but you can't wait to see. And often they have a madcap side to their personality that makes them even more fun. Think Paul Gascoigne, George Best, Rodney Marsh.

There was a young striker in Colombia who was beginning to garner attention from European clubs. He was only 22 years old but had been playing for Colombian team Atlético Nacional for three seasons, over which time he had scored an impressive 32 goals in 75 appearances. He had great pace as well as a dangerous free kick, with his goals already celebrated by a trademark somersault. But going from the Colombian league to Serie A would represent a huge step up for anyone, especially someone so young – still Parma beat off others to secure his signature for just under $11m, meaning Faustino Asprilla joined to boost their attack in the summer of 1992. It would prove to be an influential signing and one that would certainly liven up the Parma nightclubs.

The league campaign saw a slow start by the *Gialloblu* as six defeats in their first 12 games left them in ninth place, but at least this time they successfully navigated the first round of the Cup Winners' Cup, eliminating Hungarian side Újpest 2-1 on aggregate, with a goal scored by new boy Asprilla, before then also eliminating Portuguese side Boavista 2-0 on aggregate. They also reached the quarter-finals of the Coppa Italia as they attempted to retain that trophy. If they were going to win anything this season, a cup was looking the most likely.

The period up to mid-February continued to be a frustrating one for the Parma faithful. Their sluggish form in Serie A continued, leaving them still ninth after matchday 20, and their Coppa Italia run ended in the quarter-finals at the hands of Juventus. Fans' hopes therefore turned to Europe, with their Cup Winners' Cup quarter-final scheduled for March, where they would face Sparta Prague, needing to progress to keep their season alive. And as luck would have it, as March started, Parma suddenly clicked into gear, firing both in Europe and domestically.

A goalless draw away in Prague put Parma in a strong position for the second leg, and it would prove to be a night when Asprilla justified the belief Parma had placed in him. After just ten minutes, the Colombian was played in by Brolin and saw his shot parried by the Sparta keeper. It looked as if the ball might still creep inside the far post, but Melli slid in just to make sure and claim the strike. Then, 23 minutes later, Asprilla received the ball in the area before lashing a first-time unstoppable shot into the top corner, leading to his usual somersault and a hug for the corner flag. It would be enough to send Parma into the semi-finals and a date with Spanish giants Atlético Madrid.

Ahead of that clash, Parma also went on a streak of five wins and one draw in Serie A, lifting them to third in the table. Most famously, the streak saw them defeat Milan by a single Asprilla free kick in the San Siro – the defeat that ended Milan's record 58-game unbeaten run. It meant that Parma went into the Atlético game full of confidence.

The first leg was in Spain and a prickly first half saw English referee Philip Don brandish four yellow cards. As the half-time interval approached, disaster struck for Parma when Mexican striker Luis García shot Atlético into the lead. The first five minutes of the second half saw another two yellow cards flourished as Parma tried to fight back into the tie. Then, on 57 minutes, it was Asprilla time again, as he hit a low shot into the bottom corner before the obligatory somersault and celebration with the bench. Five minutes later, the Colombian was at it again, this time heading Parma in front. It would be enough to secure a valuable away win, along with two away goals.

If Parma fans were hoping for a calm return leg, they wouldn't get their wish. Marco Osio had a great chance to put the tie to bed early but saw his attempt cleared off the line when it really should have been settling in the back of the net. Parma continued to pressurise the Atlético goal, both Brolin and Melli coming close. But as the game moved into the second half, Atlético started to come back into it, creating chances as they sought the two goals they needed. Finally, the breakthrough came in the 77th minute when a high cross into the area saw Parma keeper Marco Ballotta unable to catch under pressure, the ball dropping to Juan Sabas to hook into an empty net. Atlético still had 13 minutes to find a winner.

Then came the defining moment of the game. Atlético defender Solozabal Villanueva broke into the Parma area, only to go down under the challenge of defender Lorenzo Minotti. It looked a possible penalty but was waved away by the referee, despite strong Atlético protests. As their frustration escalated, the game entered the final minute, when they had another penalty claim ignored. As the referee blew for a free kick to Parma instead, Atlético's defender Juanito lost the plot, kicking the nearest Parma player right in front of the official, who had no choice but to brandish a straight red. Finally, his whistle ended the madness, Parma fans celebrating wildly as Atlético players continued to harass the referee. The team that had been in Serie B just three seasons ago were now in a European final.

Their opponents would be Belgium's Royal Antwerp in what would be the last European tournament final to ever be played at the old Wembley Stadium in London. Only 37,000 fans would make the trek to the ground, which could hold 82,000, but the majority were from Parma as they enjoyed their big day in only their second-ever European competition. The bad news for Parma fans was that Asprilla would be unable to start, sitting on the bench as a substitute due to a minor injury. Incredibly, Parma's starting XI contained five players who had been with them when still in Serie B. As fans settled in for the big night, the game got off to a furious start.

Right away Parma threatened, a header from Melli being saved at the near post. The resulting corner could only be parried by the Serbian keeper Stevan Stojanović, falling at the feet of Parma captain Minotti, who hooked it home beautifully before celebrating in front of the yellow hordes, it having taken just nine minutes for Parma to unlock the Belgian defence. But then, just two minutes later, Antwerp equalised, adding to the breathless start.

Twenty minutes later and Parma were back in front. What looked a harmless floated ball into the area by Osio saw Melli outjump both a Belgian defender and the keeper to head Parma into the lead. Melli looked to have added another just before half-time, only for Antwerp to be saved by the linesman's flag, despite the replay showing that Melli was in fact onside.

Parma went into the break 2-1 up and enjoying the majority of chances. The second half saw them continue to dominate, Melli spurning a couple of clear opportunities. Then, with just four minutes remaining, Stefano Cuoghi broke Antwerp's offside trap and coolly sent the keeper the wrong way to secure victory. The Parma fans could finally relax and enjoy the final few minutes within a sea of yellow scarves.

As the final whistle blew, manager Scala celebrated with his staff. Once again, an Italian club had emerged to lift a major European trophy, testament to the strength of Serie A at the time. Financial backing had helped but it was still a fact that a previously lower league team had gone from Serie B to a European trophy in just three years. Yet more silverware was travelling to Italy.

* * *

While conquering Europe, Parma also ended the Serie A season strongly. Following on from ending Milan's record unbeaten run, they lost only once in their last ten games, propelling them up to an unprecedented third place, behind only the two Milanese heavyweights. Parma fans must have been rubbing their eyes in disbelief – suddenly they were a major power within Italy and therefore Europe. The question now was whether they could continue to develop this squad. Once again goalscoring had been their Achilles heel, although the ever-reliable Melli notched up another 15 across all competitions, while new boy Asprilla weighed in with 11. But another talented striker wouldn't hurt.

When Maradona departed Napoli, he left a huge hole to fill. It would take a big player to inherit both his position and, even more, his vaunted No.10 jersey. But the challenge was accepted by a young 5ft 6in Sardinian who would serve Napoli well – Gianfranco Zola. Under new manager Claudio Ranieri, Zola played in every Serie A game in 1991/92, finishing with 12 Serie A goals and helping Napoli to finish fourth. The next season saw the return of Ottavio Bianchi as manager and Zola again hitting double figures. But it was a disappointing season for Napoli and, with Zola looking for a new challenge and Parma requiring another proven striker, a transfer made sense. By now Napoli were suffering financial problems, so an offer of £13m was enough to clinch the deal. Maradona's replacement was heading north.

So, Parma went into 1993/94 with an attack of Melli, Asprilla and Zola. Carrying on from the previous season, Parma continued their strong league form, losing only two games out of their first 13, placing them equal top with Sampdoria and Milan. In Europe, meanwhile, the first two rounds of their defence of the Cup Winners' Cup saw them first looking in some trouble against Swedish side Degerfors before two goals from Asprilla in the last three minutes of the first leg calmed nerves. They then needed penalties to overcome Israeli side Maccabi Haifa to reach the quarter-finals. A date with Dutch giants Ajax would await them in March.

Before then Parma faced Milan to contest the European Super Cup, played between the previous season's Champions League and Cup Winners' Cup champions, and not surprisingly for the era an all-Italian affair. With both fielding full-strength sides, it looked like Milan would continue their usual winning ways when they travelled to Parma and came away with a single-goal victory, thanks to Papin. But Parma then enjoyed a famous night at the San Siro as Argentine Roberto Sensini scored to take the contest to extra time. Five minutes in and Massimo Crippa ensured that Parma had another European trophy to place in their new cabinet.

Parma's league form stuttered during December and early January, dropping them to fourth, but thankfully, with the Ajax tie looming, they got back into the groove with four successive victories. They then travelled to Amsterdam to face Van Gaal's emerging young Ajax team on 3 March 1994. Parma left well pleased with a goalless draw ahead of the return leg two weeks later.

Back at home, Parma got off to the perfect start when, after just 16 minutes, Ajax keeper Edwin van der Sar completely misjudged a Minotti free kick, the captain coming up with another important goal for the Italians. Four minutes into the second period, Parma wrapped up the tie with a beautiful second. Picking up the ball deep in his own half, Brolin powered forward, crossing the halfway line before playing the ball out wide to Zola. Cutting across the area, Zola took out three Dutch defenders before seeing his shot saved. But Brolin had continued his run and was on hand to slot into an empty net. Once again, Parma were heading to a European semi-final.

The final four were all fearsome – Arsenal, Benfica, PSG and Parma. The draw pitted the Italians against Benfica, facing a first-leg trip to Lisbon. Benfica's side included the skilful Rui Costa, and after just 11 minutes, a great run and pass from the Portuguese wizard put Brazilian Isaías through to score. But if Parma were shocked by the early goal, it didn't show as they immediately equalised when Asprilla battled for a ball in the area before it was worked out to Zola to strike home. The last laugh fell to Rui Costa, though, who scored the winner in the second half. It left the tie deliciously balanced – Benfica one goal ahead but Parma with an away goal.

Two weeks later, the teams re-emerged in Parma's small but packed stadium to see whether the Italians could continue the defence of their trophy. It was a tense affair, with Benfica reduced to ten men in the first half following a red card, and with 16 minutes to go it was still goalless. But it was then that Parma won a corner, which was swung in for Argentine defender Roberto Sensini to sneak in at the back post, stooping to head the ball home and send the Parma crowd into ecstasy. Parma would be returning to a second successive Cup Winners' Cup Final – this time facing Arsenal in Copenhagen. Before that, Parma finished the season in fifth spot, enough to earn them a place in the following season's UEFA Cup, should they fail to retain the Cup Winners' Cup.

Just over 33,000 Parma and Arsenal fans made their way into the Parken Stadium in Copenhagen for the showdown on 4 May 1994. George Graham's Arsenal had already beaten Italian opposition on their route to the final, defeating Torino 1-0 on aggregate in the quarter-finals, before then eliminating PSG in the semis. It was the Arsenal side of the legendary back four – Dixon, Adams, Bould and Winterburn – backed up by David Seaman in goal that had only conceded three goals in the competition to date. But they would be missing Ian Wright up front, who was suspended after receiving a red card in the semi-final second leg.

Scala went with Zola and Asprilla up front, with Melli available from the bench, supported by a midfield including Brolin and Crippa. After just 20 seconds, Parma almost took the lead, a fantastic tackle by Bould denying Asprilla after he was played through by Brolin. Parma kept on the front foot, Brolin next coming close with a header before then hitting the post following a lightning-fast breakaway. But then, against the run of play, Dixon hit a hopeful ball forward, which Lorenzo Minotti tried to clear with an overhead kick, only to see the ball fall nicely for Alan Smith, who chested it down before firing into the top corner to give Arsenal the lead after 20 minutes.

Parma went back on the attack, this time Zola coming close on a couple of occasions before the half-time whistle blew. This pattern of play continued through the second half – Parma pressurising Arsenal, but the Gunners' defence as resolute as ever. It appeared that Parma had grabbed a late equaliser, only to be denied by the linesman's flag. Eventually the referee blew, allowing Arsenal to celebrate a famous night for them, serenaded by their anthem 'one-nil to the Arsenal'. Parma had done brilliantly to reach a second successive Cup Winners' Cup Final and had dominated the play, but in the end couldn't penetrate that legendary Arsenal defence. But they had done Italian football proud and could look forward to more European nights in the following season, this time in the UEFA Cup.

The addition of Zola to the Parma side had been an outstanding success. His initial season in yellow saw him score 22 goals across all competitions, the second-highest scorer in Serie A; and owners Parmalat were ready to invest still more over the summer to improve the squad even further.

Alessandro Melli moved on, heading to Sampdoria, to be replaced up front by a new signing, Marco Branca, who was in his third spell at Udinese. But the most significant signings of the summer were in defence and midfield. Fernando Couto was a Portuguese international defender, playing at Porto, before Parma lured him over to Italy, while Dino Baggio had been part of Juventus's 1993 UEFA Cup-winning side, scoring three goals across the two legs of the final. In one of those 'what might have been' moments, Juventus didn't want to sell Dino Baggio to Parma, so they offered them a young striker on their books instead. Parma agreed to that arrangement but then Dino Baggio decided to accept a move away, leaving the young striker to remain with Juve. That young striker was Alessandro Del Piero, the future Juventus club legend. With a strengthened squad in place, Parma went into 1994/95 full of confidence. It would prove to be a season that saw them, and Juventus, locked in competition in every field.

* * *

The opening four months of 1994/95 saw Parma firing on all fronts. Their 14 Serie A games at the back end of 1994 saw them suffer just one loss, away at Sampdoria, placing them top of the table at the start of the new year, one point ahead of Juventus. Their home form was especially strong, with all seven games at the Stadio Ennio Tardini resulting in victory for the *Gialloblu*. Zola again led the way with seven goals but new boys Branca, Couto and Baggio also found the net. They had also overcome Perugia, Cagliari and a strong Fiorentina to earn a place in the last four of the Coppa Italia, alongside Lazio, Foggia and, again, Juventus. And then there was their latest assault on Europe in the UEFA Cup.

The opening round had proved a little nervier than Parma fans would have liked. Travelling away to Vitesse in the Netherlands, Parma went down to a second-half goal, while also losing Couto to a red card. Thankfully, a Zola double back in Italy saw Parma move on to the next round and a tie against AIK of Sweden, which proved less stressful due to a 3-0 aggregate win. The third round, however, supplied stiffer competition. For the third consecutive time, Parma went on the road for the opening leg, this time travelling to the famous San Mamés stadium, home of Athletic Bilbao. The 45,000 packed into the intimate arena cheered on a 1-0 victory for the Basques, setting up a tense second leg.

Any crowd nerves were settled by two first-half goals for the home team from Zola and Baggio, and when Baggio scored a third early in the second half, it looked like the game was done and dusted. But then momentum shifted back and forth, as first Bilbao pulled one back, then Couto restored Parma's three-goal lead, and then Bilbao scored again with 14 minutes remaining. It meant one more goal for the Spaniards and they would be through. The Parma defence proved stout, however, booking the Italians a place in the quarter-finals, one of three Italian teams to reach that stage, alongside Lazio and, yes, Juventus again.

Parma's first league game of 1995 saw them face a top-of-the-table clash against Juve. Defending their 100 per cent home record, Parma took the lead 12 minutes into the second half through Baggio. But then, in the space of just 13 minutes, Juventus fired in three goals, including two from Fabrizio Ravanelli, to inflict Parma's first home loss, worsened by the loss of Couto to a second yellow card late on. It meant that Juve leapfrogged Parma to the top of the standings – a position that they would retain for the rest of the season, also beating Parma again, 4-0, late on in the season, powered by another Ravanelli double. Parma would eventually finish their season in third place, behind Lazio on goal difference, equalling their best finish of just two years earlier and proving that they were now a consistent top-five team within the Italian league.

On the cup front, Parma defeated Foggia in the Coppa Italia semi-final to set up an end-of-season final against, well, obviously, Juventus – a repeat of the final of 1992 that had seen Parma win their first-ever silverware. But before that could be played, there was Parma's annual assault on Europe to be continued.

The last eight of the UEFA Cup was dominated by German and Italian teams – six of the eight from those two countries. However, any all-Italian or all-German ties were avoided by a draw that saw Parma paired against Danish side Odense BK, while Juventus faced Eintracht Frankfurt, and Lazio faced Borussia Dortmund. The first leg saw Parma narrowly win through a second-half Zola penalty, despite dominating the game, meaning a tense trip to Odense to follow. On a cold, Scandinavian evening, chances were few and far between, and anything that did get close to the Parma goal was well dealt with by keeper Luca Bucci. A goalless draw meant that Parma were through to the semi-finals, along with Juventus, Bayer Leverkusen and Borussia Dortmund. Once again, the nationalities avoided each other as Parma were drawn against Bayer Leverkusen, who had just thrashed Nantes 5-1 on aggregate in their quarter-final. On paper, it appeared to be a tough tie. But football isn't played on paper.

Leverkusen had only once before reached the semi-final stage of a European competition, back in 1988 when they won the UEFA Cup following a penalty shoot-out against Espanyol. Their record in the 1995 UEFA Cup had been impressive to date, scoring an incredible 25 goals over the eight matches to reach the semi-final – an average of over three a game. Striker Ulf Kirsten was responsible for ten of those, one of the first East German players to move to a Western club after reunification, moving over from Dynamo Dresden. He had a prolific scoring record and, along with Brazilian partner Paulo Sérgio, represented a huge threat to the Italians. If they wanted to overcome Leverkusen, Parma would have to quieten the pair of them.

Things started badly for the Italians in the first leg in Germany when Sérgio pounced on a loose ball from a corner to fire Leverkusen ahead after just 20 minutes. Parma were able to reach half-time without conceding any further goals, allowing them to regroup, and whatever instructions Scala gave to them produced a new team in the second half. Right from the kick-off Parma attacked, and after just three minutes they grabbed an equaliser, albeit somewhat luckily as a loose ball fell nicely to Baggio. The keeper parried his shot but the ball still looped into the net. Spurred on, Parma continued to push and three minutes later took the lead when Benarrivo arrived into the Leverkusen area. Beating a defender, he managed to head the bouncing ball away from Leverkusen's keeper before stepping aside to let Asprilla hit the bottom corner, followed by the traditional somersault celebration. Leverkusen responded shortly thereafter by bringing on veteran striker Rudi Völler, but to no avail – Parma were able to hold out and take a valuable away win back to Italy.

Any second-leg nerves were quickly calmed when, after just four minutes, Leverkusen's keeper couldn't hold a stinging shot from Crippa, and Asprilla was on hand to tap the loose ball home. The Germans then self-destructed in the second half when a slack pass allowed Zola to run through, before passing across the area for Asprilla to again tap into an open goal. Finally, Asprilla returned the favour, playing Zola clean through to slot in Parma's third. It capped an impressive 5-1 aggregate win that had seen Leverkusen's deadly attack shackled and meant a third successive European final for Scala's Parma.

Therefore, Parma would finish their season playing two cup finals – and both against the team who had just pipped them to the league title, Juventus, while also doing the double on Parma during the Serie A campaign. The UEFA Cup Final would come first, scheduled over two legs in May, the first of which would be at the Stadio Ennio Tardini. This was a Juventus side that had plenty of attacking talent, including Didier Deschamps, Paulo Sousa, Roberto Baggio, Fabrizio Ravanelli, Gianluca Vialli, and a young Alessandro Del Piero on the bench. Over 22,000 fans packed the small stadium to see whether Parma could finally overcome their league nemesis.

They couldn't have asked for a better start. After just five minutes, Zola's wand of a foot played through Dino Baggio, who calmly slotted the ball past the onrushing Michelangelo Rampulla to send the Parma faithful into raptures. Juventus couldn't find a response, so the final was beautifully balanced as the return leg came around two weeks later.

Instead of Turin, Juventus chose to play the second match at the San Siro due to an ongoing dispute with their landlords. The change of location didn't prevent the Juve hordes from travelling the 88 miles to fill Milan's stadium with over 80,000, of which only a small minority were Parma fans. Juventus made all the early running, Ravanelli again causing problems for the Parma defence that he had ravaged so successfully during the league meetings. With 35 minutes on the clock, Juve right-back Moreno Torricelli received the ball deep in his own half. With a quick look up, he launched a long ball forward that Vialli raced after. Without breaking stride, Vialli blasted the ball first time into the top corner to level the tie on aggregate. It was a breathtaking finish that caused the stadium to erupt in a cauldron of noise.

Early in the second half, Torricelli missed a golden opportunity to put Juve further ahead as the *Bianconeri* continued to dominate. With Juve coach Marcello Lippi watching pensively, smoking furiously on the sideline, Parma started a flowing move, patiently playing the ball around until able to release full-back Mussi down the right. Reaching the byline, Mussi chipped the ball into the area where first-leg hero Dino Baggio was arriving for an easy header into an open net. Suddenly Juve needed two goals to win, given Parma's vital away goal, with just 37 minutes to find them.

Tensions began to flare as Vialli and Massimo Susic tussled on the ground, players rushing in to confront one another. The controversy continued as Torricelli appeared to pull a goal back, only for the linesman's flag to deny him. But Parma held strong, celebrating with the pocket of Parma fans at the end before captain

Lorenzo Minotti lifted the UEFA Cup high into the Turin night sky. The team that had won nothing before 1992 had now played in three successive European finals, winning two. It was infuriating for the rest of Europe – here was yet another club from the Italian peninsula dominating European competition.

The season ended with a last Parma vs Juventus confrontation as the two met across two legs in the Coppa Italia Final, which saw Juve prevail 3-0 on aggregate. So, as the season closed out, Juve had pipped Parma to both the Serie A title and the Coppa Italia. But on the European stage, Parma had won out over their Turin rivals – a compromise that I'm sure Parma fans could live with.

In the space of just five seasons, Parma had gone from being a Serie B team that had never experienced top-flight football to winning four major trophies. It seemed as if Italy could produce European champions from any corner of the country.

PARMA (1991–1995)
Cup Winners' Cup winners – 1992/93
UEFA Cup winners – 1994/95
Cup Winners' Cup runners-up – 1993/94
European Super Cup winners – 1993
Coppa Italia winners – 1991/92

Chapter 19

USA '94

*As for taking the penalty in the first place, I was
knackered, but I was the team's penalty taker.
I've never run away from my responsibilities.
Only those who have the courage to take a penalty
miss them. I failed that time. Period. And it
affected me for years. It is the worst moment of
my career. I still dream about it. If I could erase a
moment from my career, it would be that one.*

Roberto Baggio in a 2002 interview with *The Observer*

WHEN WE last met Arrigo Sacchi, he had just left Milan to
take the job as coach of the national side, having enjoyed great
success with the *Rossoneri*. Italy had high hopes of winning the
1990 World Cup, being played at home, but had come unstuck at
the semi-final stage – and worst of all had fallen to a poor Argentina
side led by Napoli's Maradona, beaten at the Stadio San Paolo.
Coach Azeglio Vicini had struggled to hit upon a successful attack,
changing between Roberto Baggio, Andrea Carnevale and Gianluca
Vialli, while lucking out on finding a surprise talent in Salvatore
Schillaci. Following on from that disappointment, Vicini was tasked
with ensuring Italy qualified for the 1992 European Championship
finals, to be held in Sweden.

Placed into a qualification group alongside the Soviet Union,
Norway, Hungary and Cyprus, it was expected to be a race between
Italy and the Soviet Union for the single qualification spot. And
so it was, although Norway would cause problems for the *Azzurri*,
beating them at home before then earning a draw in Genoa. Those

dropped three points would be enough to ensure Italy finished second in the group, behind the Soviet Union, missing out on a trip to Sweden for Euro 1992. It was a huge embarrassment at a time when Italian clubs were dominating Europe and signalled the end for Vicini and the start of Sacchi's reign. The mission: to ensure Italy qualified for the 1994 World Cup, being held in the USA as FIFA moved away from their traditional Europe/Latin America cycle.

Sacchi wasted no time in implementing his preferred regime upon the players. Famed for his detailed preparation, he drilled the players at training camps, going over moves and tactics repeatedly. A 4-4-2 formation was employed, similar to his Milan side, and a high press encouraged. Italy at the time had incredible talent at its disposal – the problem for Sacchi was how to distil all that talent to a manageable squad that would complement each other.

Unlike the 1990 World Cup, this time Italy would have to earn their place at the big dance. They were in a six-team group, from which two would earn a ticket to the USA, with their main competition being Switzerland, Portugal and Scotland, while Malta and Estonia would make up the numbers. Italy's start to the campaign was faltering – kicking off with a 2-2 home draw against the Swiss, having been 2-0 down with seven minutes remaining, before Roberto Baggio and, in stoppage time, Stefano Eranio saved their blushes. This was followed by a dull goalless draw in Glasgow. Their third match produced a win, but again less than convincing as they narrowly beat underdogs Malta 2-1 away.

It was in early 1993 that the *Azzurri* finally hit their stride. A 3-1 win in Portugal, including goals from both Roberto and Dino Baggio, was swiftly followed by a 6-1 thrashing of Malta in Palermo and a 2-0 home win over Estonia. All was looking rosy until Italy travelled to Bern in May and lost 1-0 to Switzerland. As the campaign went into the final set of matches, played simultaneously on 17 November 1993, Switzerland looked favourites for qualification as they faced Estonia at home, while Italy met Portugal in Sacchi's old stomping ground of the San Siro. Switzerland would ultimately end the night with a 4-0 victory, earning them qualification, meaning the Italy vs Portugal game would decide the second qualification spot, with Portugal needing to beat Italy to steal it. It was a Portuguese side that was more than capable of doing so, containing such stars as Fernando Couto, Paulo Sousa, Rui Barros, Joao Pinto, Paolo Futre and Rui Costa.

The first half saw Italy do the bulk of the attacking, but with no success, meaning the game went into the break goalless. The second 45 minutes saw Italy come closer and closer to scoring, but they couldn't quite get the breakthrough and were aware that one slip at the back could cost them a place in the finals. And then, with just seven minutes remaining, the decisive moment occurred. A ball out wide to Dino Baggio saw him pass inside to Roberto Baggio, whose shot was deflected by the covering defender and just happened to fall right back at the feet of Dino to slot past a scrambling keeper. It was a moment of luck but also probably deserved given their second-half pressure. The last five minutes saw the game degenerate as the frustrated Portuguese took their pain out on the Italians. A flare-up in the Italy penalty area was followed by a straight red for Couto as he appeared to lash out at Casiraghi. When the final whistle sounded, the San Siro burst into celebrations, heavy with relief – it had been tight, but Italy would be joining Switzerland on a trip out west the following summer.

* * *

The lead-up to USA '94 was full of drama for Italy as Sacchi's performance to date underwent intense scrutiny from the Italian media. There were even calls for him to resign as accusations flew that he didn't know his squad. He had indeed called up 73 different players to the first team over the prior two and a half years, leading an Italian soccer magazine to show all of them, along with a picture of the pope, with the headline: 'Arrigo, have you forgotten anyone?' Performances in friendlies ahead of the tournament had been poor, including losses to both France and Germany. Worst of all, the Italy team had played a friendly against a Serie C team, Pontedera, in April 1994, and incredibly lost 2-1 – leading to *La Gazzetta dello Sport*'s headline: 'Let's send Pontedera to the World Cup'. The knives were out.

As well as the renowned Milan defence, Sacchi was blessed with a wealth of attacking talent to choose from. There were Lazio's Pierluigi Casiraghi and Giuseppe Signori, Parma's Gianfranco Zola, Milan's Daniele Massaro and Juventus's enigmatic and gifted

Roberto Baggio. In paring down his squad, two talented individuals were taken out of the equation by bust-ups with Sacchi – Vialli and Mancini. Vialli's crime was apparently a prank involving Parmesan cheese that wasn't appreciated by his manager, while Mancini had reacted badly to being substituted in the pre-tournament friendly against Germany, leading him to shout at Sacchi at the airport on the way home and then announce that it would be his last appearance for the *Azzurri*. And so it proved.

Sacchi left it late to name his 22-man squad, waiting until 12 May, just a month before the tournament, leading to more accusations that he didn't know his best team. When he finally did announce the 22 men for the tournament, it was perhaps no surprise that Sacchi relied heavily on Milan – a team he knew so well and where he felt the players would know his system. Seven of the 22 were Milan players, the most from any single Italian club, with Parma second best, represented with five. Among the Milan seven were five who had a material number of international caps already – defenders Alessandro Costacurta, Paolo Maldini and Franco Baresi, along with midfielders Demetrio Albertini and Roberto Donadoni.

* * *

The draw had placed Italy into Group E, playing in New York, Washington and Orlando, alongside Mexico, Norway and the Republic of Ireland. Italy's campaign would begin by facing Ireland at Giants Stadium in East Rutherford, a suburb of New York. The big question ahead of the game was the fitness of both Franco Baresi and talisman Roberto Baggio. Baresi had undergone knee surgery pre-tournament so his mere presence was somewhat of a miracle. In the end, both were declared fit to start, so Sacchi went with the attacking partnership of Baggio and Signori – the same pairing that had been involved in the Pontedera fiasco. The back four would be the classic Milan line-up of Tassotti, Costacurta, Baresi and Maldini.

The teams lined up on a hot and humid afternoon – weather conditions that the Irish would be unfamiliar with. So hot that, in fact, Irish defender Steve Staunton even took the precaution of wearing a baseball cap during the national anthems, determined to delay exposure to the searing sun as long as possible. If the hope was that Italy would receive sizeable support from the New Jersey location, it was Irish green and orange that dominated the stadium as over 75,000 packed it to the rafters. The two teams had met in the last World Cup, when Schillaci's goal separated them in the quarter-finals, and Jack Charlton was still in charge of the Irish, continuing to get impressive performances out of his squad. After all, England and Scotland hadn't even qualified for USA '94.

It took just 11 minutes for Sacchi's nightmare to continue. The ball fell to Ray Houghton outside the penalty area and his shot sailed over the head of Gianluca Pagliuca to give the Irish a shock lead. From then on, it was up to Italy to take the game to the Irish, who were quite happy to defend deep. And the Irish gave a sterling performance. They were well organised and resilient despite the searing heat. Italy tried boosting the attack, bringing on Daniele Massaro in the second half, while Dino Baggio had a penalty decision waved away. But despite that, it was Ireland who came closest to scoring near the end of the game as John Sheridan hit the bar. When the whistle sounded, Italy had suffered a humiliating defeat – their first ever in an opening game of the World Cup.

The Italian press was merciless. Expressions of disgust included 'legendary fiasco', 'betrayal' and 'Sacchi disaster'. They even ran a story that this was the worst Italian team of all time. Sacchi was on thin ice and desperately needed a result in their next game against Norway.

This came five days later, again at Giants Stadium, where this time the Italian *tifosi* were in the majority. Sacchi decided to stick with the Roberto Baggio and Signori partnership, although also starting Pierluigi Casiraghi. This time Italy started much brighter, creating early chances, and things seemed to be looking up – until the 29th minute. At that moment, Norway sprang the offside trap, only for Pagliuca to rush out and handle the ball outside the penalty area. The German referee had no hesitation in showing a straight red, meaning Italy were now looking at 60 minutes of play one man short – and Sacchi needed to decide who he would take off to bring on the substitute keeper Luca Marchegiani.

To the shock of many, he chose to take off Italy's most skilful player, Roberto Baggio. After the match, Sacchi claimed that he had taken him off because he was nursing an Achilles injury, so may not be able to help defensively, which Italy would now need with just ten men. But he was also the player who could turn a game suddenly with a piece of magic. To say Baggio wasn't amused is an understatement – furious, he trudged to the dugout, mouthing the words, 'This guy is crazy.' Sacchi had made a huge roll of the dice – one man down, if Italy now failed to win this game, he had just given the Italian press the ammunition with which to hang him. As Liam Brady said on the BBC commentary, 'Well, it's the most incredible decision, he's taken Roberto Baggio off. I think Sacchi with this decision is gambling his whole career.'

Norway had little intention of attacking Italy, having won their first group match, and Italy failed to find any path through during the first 45 minutes. Right at the start of the second half, Italian luck worsened further as captain Baresi pulled up and had to be substituted, unable to carry on, limping to the bench clutching his knee. Then, with 20 remaining, the other Baggio struck, as Dino headed home a free kick to give Italy a vital lead. It was enough for them to hold on for an essential victory.

The following day, Baresi couldn't straighten his leg, so was taken to a Manhattan hospital to have the knee scanned. While there was no ligament damage, his meniscus was fractured, meaning arthroscopic surgery would be required, a procedure that normally involved a six-to-eight-week healing process. The Milan doctor was flown out to perform the surgery, which, given Baresi's age, meant any further participation in the tournament was extremely unlikely, even if Italy were to get to the final. But the *Azzurri* captain decided to stay on with the squad and see whether he could regain fitness in time for a future game.

Going into the final group match, all four teams were tied on three points apiece, with Mexico having the best goal difference, while Ireland sat second above Italy due to the head-to-head result. Moving to Washington, Sacchi's team faced Mexico with Roberto Baggio once again starting. The highlights of a goalless first half were a dramatic overhead attempt from Signori, which unfortunately was fired straight at Mexican keeper Jorge Campos, clad in his usual colourful kit, followed by an outstanding save from Marchegiani from a vicious shot by Alberto García Aspe. Italian hearts were also in mouths when, right before the whistle, Costacurta headed into his own net, only for his blushes to be spared by the linesman's flag. It had been an entertaining half, but both final matches sat goalless after 45 minutes.

The second half couldn't have started better for the *Azzurri* as Massaro, who had been brought on during the break for Casiraghi, scored after just two minutes. Unfortunately, Italy could hold that lead for only nine minutes before Mexico equalised through a screamer from Marcelino Bernal. With the Norway vs Ireland game still goalless, the whole group still lay in the balance.

Italy pushed forward, willed on by a frustrated Sacchi on the sidelines, resplendent in green shirt and trademark shades. But the game ended one apiece and all awaited news from Giants Stadium. They soon learned that Ireland and Norway had also drawn, 0-0, to leave all four teams on equal points in the table: four apiece. Looking at goal difference and head-to-heads, the top two were Mexico and Ireland, who would therefore automatically move on to the round of 16. Italy were third and would have to wait to learn whether they would be one of the four best-ranked third-place sides – they narrowly made it, being the fourth-ranked.

Italy had limped into the last 16 as the worst side to make it that far. It was an incredibly disappointing showing from a team that contained players from Milan, Parma, Juventus and Inter, serial winners of European competitions. They had scored just two goals in their three games. Star player Roberto Baggio, who was the current holder of the Ballon d'Or, and coach Sacchi appeared to be at loggerheads. Juventus's owner Agnelli said that Baggio's performance against Mexico was that of a wet rabbit, even though he was a Juventus player! A round of 16 game against an exciting Nigeria, who had topped the group containing both Argentina and Bulgaria, awaited in Foxborough on 5 July. The predictions were not bullish.

Kicking off just after midday, Italy's woes continued when Nigeria opened the scoring after 25 minutes. A corner swung into the area bobbled off Paolo Maldini, who was captain for the game in Baresi's absence, allowing Emmanuel Amunike to hook it home. Thereafter, Italy had a couple of close penalty shouts for fouls on Roberto Baggio and Signori, but the Mexican referee was in no mood to award them, in fact giving Signori a yellow card for his dramatics. With 25 minutes remaining, Sacchi pulled Signori off, bringing on Parma's Gianfranco Zola, who at that time was still a fringe player nationally, having earned just six caps. Ten minutes later it was Dino Baggio's turn to have a penalty claim waved off. Immediately after, as Italian frustration built, Zola felt he was obstructed in the area. Losing the ball, he seemed to win it back well, but was inexplicably shown a straight red, causing him to drop to his knees and hold his head in disbelief. Italy were now a goal down and a man down with just 15 minutes remaining.

As the clock moved into the 88th minute, a move down the right released Mussi into the area. Pulling the ball back, he set up Roberto Baggio, who stroked the ball into the corner. The Divine Ponytail's moment had finally come just as Italy were staring defeat in the face, with his moment of magic taking the game into extra time. Roberto Baggio was now playing with an extra swagger in his step and, ten minutes in, he received the ball on the edge of the area, where he played a cute scoop into the penalty box for Benarrivo to chase, before being bundled to the ground. Finally, the Mexican referee awarded Italy a penalty, and who else but Roberto Baggio took responsibility, tucking it into the corner. Their most gifted player had finally delivered.

Still Italy lived dangerously, especially when Michael Emenalo lost his marker in the area and crossed into the six-yard box, where it seemed Nigeria must score, only for Rashidi Yekini to fluff his lines and allow Dino Baggio to clear. But eventually the final whistle sounded, and Italy could celebrate a famous victory, in which they had shown resolve and character to again win with ten men. They continued to look unconvincing, but they had scraped their way into the quarter-finals. And, most encouragingly of all, Roberto Baggio had awoken.

Sacchi wasn't excused from criticism, though, the Italian media still aware of how lucky the Italians were to still be in the competition. There was also worry that Roberto Baggio may be unavailable for the quarter-final due to cramping, but in the end he was in the starting XI as Italy faced Spain, again at Foxborough, on 9 July.

It was Roberto Baggio who almost opened the scoring after just 13 minutes, before his namesake obliged after 25 minutes, Dino hitting a rocket into the corner to give the *Azzurri* the lead. But if we were learning anything in this World Cup, it was that Italy would make life hard for themselves, as it proved when José Luis Caminero equalised after 58 minutes. Then, with just eight minutes remaining, Spain had a golden opportunity when Julio Salinas found himself clean through and the flag stayed down, only for Pagliuca to make himself big and save with his leg, keeping Italy alive. Spain continued to press for a winner, Italy desperately hanging on, before suddenly, with two minutes left, Berti played a great through ball to Signori, who managed to poke the ball on to Roberto Baggio before being clattered to the ground. Baggio faced up to Andoni Zubizarreta before calmly rounding him and firing in from an acute angle. Once again, he was the saviour of Italy.

The game didn't peter out calmly, however. A cross from Andoni Goikoetxea saw Luis Enrique suddenly drop to the floor, clutching his face in the penalty area. He got up, looking dazed but gesticulating furiously at his marker, Mauro Tassotti, who was a picture of innocence. Blood was clearly visible on Enrique's face due to a broken nose inflicted by Tassotti's elbow. No penalty or card was awarded, but Tassotti would suffer retroactive punishment from FIFA in the form of an eight-match ban and $16,000 fine. As Spain's physio, Senen Cortegoso remembered it, 'Luis Enrique wanted to kill the referee and Tassotti.' It would be 17 years before the two players shook hands.

As the final whistle blew, Sacchi let out a huge puff of his cheeks, while Baggio fell to his knees in celebration. Once again, *Il Divin Codino* had guided Italy through, and now, improbably, they faced a semi-final against surprise package Bulgaria. Two of the best players of the World Cup would be facing one another: Roberto Baggio and Hristo Stoichkov. And both would deliver.

Bulgaria had impressed to date in the tournament, defeating Argentina 2-0 in the group stage before then eliminating Mexico and World Champions Germany in the knockout stages. While the whole team was strong, their undoubted star was Barcelona's Hristo Stoichkov, who had bagged five goals to date, including a beautiful free kick against Germany. Both he and Roberto Baggio were classic No.10s, pulling the strings while also leading the way in goalscoring. It was a mouthwatering match-up.

The two sides lined up on 13 July at Giants Stadium, with Maldini still standing in as captain in the absence of Baresi, as the thermometer registered 100°F/38°C. The first 20 minutes saw neither side threaten as they sparred, before Italy won a throw-in. Tossed to Roberto Baggio, he immediately spun his marker, cut across the area, beat another defender and then curled a shot into the bottom corner. Immediately Italy threatened again, Albertini seeing his long-range effort rebound off the post before then almost chipping the Bulgarian keeper. Undeterred, Albertini then flicked a lovely ball over the Bulgarian defence for Roberto Baggio to fire home first time. The game was just 25 minutes old and Italy's talisman had struck twice, taking his tally to five goals in the knockout stages. Italy were playing their best football to date at just the right time.

Italy continued to threaten but then, just before half-time, Costacurta was deemed to have fouled Nasko Sirakov in the area. Stoichkov had already converted two penalties in the tournament and confidently sent Pagliuca the wrong way to halve the deficit. The match was turning into a personal duel between the two greats.

The second half was less eventful as Italy managed the game towards its conclusion, the main concern being when Roberto Baggio was substituted after 71 minutes, clutching his hamstring, looking a picture of misery on the bench as the possibility of missing the World Cup Final entered his mind. When the final whistle sounded, that emotion spilled out as he sobbed, both with joy and frustration. The big question now was whether Baggio and/or Baresi would be available for Italy's first final since 1982.

* * *

The final saw Italy face Brazil at the Rose Bowl, Pasadena in the midday heat. It would be a meeting of two great footballing powers, both of whom had won three World Cup trophies. For Brazil, it had become the holy grail, not having reached a final since the golden side of 1970 defeated the *Azzurri* so comprehensively. They were desperate to win, which had led to a more pragmatic approach than in previous tournaments – a side that was built to win in modern football but that lacked the flair that Brazilian fans usually demanded. Their attack was spearheaded by Romário and

Bebeto, an unlikely pairing with completely different personalities off the pitch but that gelled during USA '94. The game would also represent a rematch of the famous 1982 clash when Paolo Rossi broke hipster hearts by beating Brazil's talented team of Zico, Sócrates, Falcão and Éder.

Italy's final training session included Baresi, who looked to have miraculously healed, but Roberto Baggio sat it out. According to Sacchi, the final decision was made on the morning of the final, when doctors put both through final tests – both players passed. Sacchi would, however, be without two players due to suspension: Costacurta and Tassotti. With those suspensions, Sacchi went to a back four of Mussi, Baresi, Maldini and Benarrivo, while Roberto Baggio and Massaro were partnered up front. Italy had ridden their luck in getting to the final – could they now finish the job and bring the trophy home?

The Rose Bowl was the largest venue used during USA '94 and was packed with over 94,000 fans at kick-off, which was just after noon. Unsurprisingly, given the southern California summer, the stadium was roasting – 97°F/36°C – which was as brutal for the fans as it was for the players, given that the stadium is uncovered. The combination of the heat and the magnitude of the occasion meant that the game was largely a disappointment. Italy's woes in defence continued when Mussi had to be substituted after 35 minutes, replaced by Luigi Apolloni, but on the plus side Baresi seemed to be moving well, always following Romário to snuff out the dangerman.

Both sides appeared exhausted, this game coming at the end of a long tournament involving much travel, heat and not enough rest between matches. The key chance came with just 15 minutes remaining when Mauro Silva hit a speculative shot from distance, which Pagliuca fumbled. He could only watch as the ball spun out of his grasp, struck the post and rebounded back into his thankful arms. Pagliuca kissed his glove and touched the post in gratitude – it would have been a cruel way to lose a World Cup Final.

The game moved on into extra time, Roberto Baggio taking on strapping to his hamstring, which was still obviously causing him discomfort. Again, chances were few and far between as both sides suffered, cramp beginning to set in. Romário came close twice, while Roberto Baggio hit a shot from distance that Taffarel tipped over, but otherwise the game petered towards the inevitable penalty shoot-out. The players grabbed fluids while leg muscles were massaged as they prepared for a final duel under the sun, Baresi especially suffering from cramp, having somehow managed an imperious 120 minutes in the sweltering heat.

Baresi was chosen to be the first penalty taker. With socks rolled around his ankles, he looked spent and dropped to his knees as his attempt flew high over the bar. Given his injury issues and playing for two hours, no one could question his commitment on this day. If Italian heads dropped for a minute, the sight of Pagliuca saving Brazil's first penalty from Márcio Santos would have revived them. The next four penalties were all converted, keeping it all square with two apiece to go. Next up for Italy was Massaro. His low shot was saved by Taffarel and suddenly Italy were behind the eight-ball again. Brazil's captain, Dunga, fired home confidently, so Italy had to score their final penalty and hope Brazil missed to stay alive. All eyes turned to their next penalty taker.

Roberto Baggio placed the ball on the spot and strode back; Baggio, who had virtually single-handedly dragged Italy to this point; Baggio, who had played with a hamstring injury through 120 minutes under a blazing sun. Could he provide one more piece of skill for the *Azzurri* under enormous pressure? Feigning to shoot to his right, he sent Taffarel in that direction, while switching his shot to the left at the last second. Sadly, like Baresi, his effort flew over the bar, and he stood in disbelief, hands on hips. As he slowly turned his face downwards, that image became the defining shot of the tournament, Baggio's despair as the Brazilians celebrated. At that moment, that penalty area must have felt like the loneliest spot on the planet to Italy's talisman. Finally, he was accompanied off the pitch, a haunted look on his face.

Italy had come so close. And what a roller-coaster ride it had been. Looking back, it was astonishing that they had even reached the fifth penalty of a shoot-out in the World Cup Final. They had struggled to qualify for the tournament, resulting in a final tense game against Portugal. Sacchi's team selections had been questioned for months as the Italian press despaired. They had lost their opening game against the Republic of Ireland and then gone down to ten men against Norway, having to take off Roberto Baggio. But then they had rescued a win and done enough against Mexico to qualify for the knockout stages, albeit as the worst of the 16 teams. They were two minutes from being eliminated by Nigeria before Roberto Baggio suddenly awoke and took the competition by the horns, leading them to the Rose Bowl and Brazil. And all this despite having a squad boasting some of the world's best players, playing in the world's strongest league.

The 1994 World Cup had commenced with Diana Ross missing a penalty and ended with Roberto Baggio missing one. The conclusion was especially cruel on such a great player. The image of him after the penalty miss became iconic and many people still associate him with that moment, forgetting how his five goals in the knockout stages took Italy to the final. His was already a career that had seen him overcome many physical obstacles, before having the hopes of a nation placed upon his slim shoulders. Thankfully, the Italian press were understanding, appreciating his contribution and spirit in getting so far.

It may not have been convincing but once again Italian football had shown itself to be among the best in the world. While their clubs continued to dominate European football, the national team had come within a penalty shoot-out of becoming world champions. Italy was still the gold standard against which other footballing nations had to measure themselves.

ITALY (1994 WORLD CUP)
Losing finalists

Chapter 20

The Old Lady Soars

Marcello Lippi is one impressive man. Looking into his eyes is enough to tell you that you are dealing with somebody who is in command of himself and his professional domain. Those eyes are sometimes burning with seriousness, sometimes twinkling, sometimes warily assessing you – and always they are alive with intelligence. Nobody could make the mistake of taking Lippi lightly.

Sir Alex Ferguson's book, *Managing My Life*

AS TRAPATTONI'S plane departed for the short flight from Turin to Munich, the eyes of the Agnellis turned to his replacement and the season ahead. Changes were being made at the top of Juventus, with ex-player Roberto Bettega replacing Giampiero Boniperti as vice-president, which heralded the arrival of Luciano Moggi as general manager and Antonio Giraudo as CEO. The trio were tasked with finding a suitable managerial replacement. A defender at Sampdoria back in the 1970s, Marcello Lippi had managed eight Italian clubs over the past nine seasons, only staying more than a year at one: Cesena. Most had been lower-level sides but in 1992 he secured the Atalanta job, guiding them to an eighth-place Serie A finish, which earned him the Napoli job at a time when they were undergoing turmoil following the departure of Maradona, and financial meltdown, with players unpaid for six months. A respectable sixth-placed Serie A finish and UEFA Cup spot secured him the Juventus appointment, even though he was by no means an obvious choice, given his limited top-level experience to date. He would need to hit the floor running to make his mark.

Lippi cut a dashing figure on arrival. Usually dressed in a suit, he was often seen puffing away on a cigar, even during matches. He had a strong winning mentality despite his average playing career and could be utterly ruthless, both traits that would be invaluable at a club like Juve. Known for being a strict disciplinarian, he kept close relationships with his players, which some viewed as helpful, while others viewed as smothering.

The lead-up to the 1994/95 campaign saw heartbreak impact the Juventus squad. During the previous season, Andrea Fortunato had established himself as a key member of the Juventus defence, playing 35 games across the campaign. An extremely popular player with both team-mates and fans, Arrigo Sacchi described him as 'a revelation of Italian football', calling the defender up for a 1994 World Cup qualifier against Estonia. However, his form fell away over the second half of the season as he complained of fatigue, which, following tests, was diagnosed as a rare form of leukaemia. It was a sickening blow for the youngster, resulting in chemotherapy and two bone marrow transplants. He seemed to be making a recovery, so Lippi included him within the squad, although with no intention of playing him at this early stage.

Heading into his first season, Lippi's squad underwent considerable refreshment. As mentioned in the chapter on Parma, an initially reluctant Dino Baggio eventually made the move there, while Borussia Dortmund brought Möller back to their club once more, along with César. Coming into the squad were four significant additions – defender Ciro Ferrera, along with midfielders Paulo Sousa, Robert Jarni and, most significantly, Didier Deschamps from Marseille. There was also a young attacker moving up from the youth system who would become an important part of the team from this time onwards – Alessandro Del Piero. Now it was up to Lippi to get a tune from them all.

If there were any concerns about Lippi needing a bedding-in period, those were blown away by Juventus's start to the season. The 1994/95 Serie A season saw the introduction of three points for a win, resulting in more attacking football, and by the end of 1994, Juve had won nine of their 13 Serie A games, losing just once, away at Foggia. Ravanelli and Vialli terrorised Italian defences, while Del Piero became a first-team mainstay after Roberto Baggio was injured in a game away to Padova, scoring the winner the following week in an amazing 3-2 comeback against Fiorentina. Two goals down with 17 minutes remaining, Vialli netted a swift brace to level the scores before Del Piero scored one of his and Italian football's greatest goals with just three minutes remaining. Alessandro Orlando fired a long ball into the area where Del Piero was flanked by two defenders. As the ball dropped over his shoulder, he struck it on the volley with the outside of his right foot, chipping Fiorentina keeper Toldo, who later stated that it was the best goal he ever conceded. Del Piero had officially arrived.

Locked in a title race with Parma, the first game of 1995 saw Juventus travel there and inflict a 3-1 defeat, despite Dino Baggio opening the scoring for his new club. Juventus were back atop of the standings. They had also eliminated Roma in the Coppa Italia to reach the semi-final stage, as well as smoothly progressing to the quarter-finals of the UEFA Cup. It seemed as if Lippi had the golden touch.

Usually opting for a 4-3-3 formation, Lippi had the luxury of a front three of Ravanelli, Vialli and either Baggio or Del Piero. He stressed the need for these players to press when out of possession. Vialli would later recall in his book *The Italian Job* that 'we had to work harder, both mentally and physically. When you're one of three forwards, you have to run that much more to help out the midfield.'

While Juventus's league form slowed down over the remainder of the season, it was still enough for them to comfortably win their first Scudetto since 1986, ahead of Lazio by ten points. That huge lead had allowed Juventus to focus more on both the Coppa Italia and UEFA Cup, with Roberto Baggio returning to the side in March. But the title win was tainted by the tragic news that, on 25 April 1995, Andrea Fortunato passed away from pneumonia, which his weakened immune system couldn't fight. He was only 23 years old. In his memory, the team referred to the success as Fortunato's Scudetto.

Lazio were defeated in the Coppa Italia semi-finals to set up a final against early Serie A rivals Parma. That would be the finale of the season, as first Juventus had their UEFA Cup campaign to complete, starting with a quarter-final match-up against Eintracht Frankfurt. Returning from Germany with a 1-1 draw, Juventus struggled to break down a resilient side back in Turin. It took until the 77th minute for Antonio Conte to eventually break the deadlock, before late goals from Ravanelli and Del Piero put a gloss on the scoreline.

The semi-final saw Juventus once again matched up against Borussia Dortmund, two years after beating them so comprehensively in the 1993 UEFA Cup Final. This time it would be a much more competitive affair. Playing the first leg at the San Siro, former team-mate Stefan Reuter broke Juve's offside trap to fire the Germans ahead after just eight minutes, sending a considerable travelling army into flare-lit celebrations. A foul on Ravanelli 20 minutes later allowed Baggio to coolly level from the penalty spot, but this was a resilient Dortmund, for whom Möller repeated the infliction of pain from old team-mates by launching them back ahead with 19 minutes remaining. Staring defeat in the face, it would take another German, Jürgen Kohler, to grab Juve's equaliser with just two minutes left. It wasn't an ideal night for Juve – a home draw with two away goals conceded – made even worse by a last-minute red card for defender Moreno Torricelli. They would need to up their game considerably back in Germany.

The second leg couldn't have got off to a better start for the Old Lady. With just six minutes on the clock, Baggio swung in a corner that defender Sergio Porrini headed home. It was just the start Lippi had been hoping for, but the early optimism was swiftly dashed when César rifled an indirect free kick into the corner four minutes later. It seemed that ex-Juve players were determined to make a mark against their former club. But Juventus could always draw on the genius of Baggio, and once again he delivered. Half an hour into the game, Juventus won a free kick around 30 yards from goal. Facing a considerable Dortmund wall, Baggio struck the ball perfectly into the top corner, leaving the keeper rooted to the spot. It was a magnificent strike, worthy of winning any match, and so it proved. Baggio continued to dazzle, almost scoring a second from an impudent lob from distance, while Paulo Sousa struck the post, as Juventus sealed their third UEFA Cup Final place in six seasons. An all-Italian affair against Parma awaited them.

The final would be one of Parma's finest moments as Dino Baggio stuck the knife in, scoring in both legs to secure a 2-1 aggregate win as discussed earlier. The dream of a treble died but Juventus quickly gained some revenge, beating Parma 3-0 over two legs to lift the Coppa Italia. That capped a remarkable debut season for Lippi – a first Serie A title for nine years, the Coppa Italia and a UEFA Cup Final appearance. Juventus had returned to the top of their game and there would be no stopping them over the next few years.

* * *

The Serie A title allowed Juventus to compete with Europe's elite once again in the Champions League, so the management decided on a summer shopping spree, primarily focused on Genoa. Since their glory days at the start of the 1990s, Sampdoria had begun to tail off following the death of their beloved owner Paolo Mantovani in October 1993. An eighth-place finish for Sampdoria in 1995 allowed Juventus to sweep in, as they picked up three of their starters: midfielder Vladimir Jugović, defender Pietro Vierchowod and winger Attilio Lombardo. But the biggest headline would be the departure of Roberto Baggio to Milan.

Baggio wasn't a huge fan of Lippi's approach to man management, and Lippi wasn't a huge fan of over-reliance on an injury-prone star. During Lippi's first season, the midfield genius had suffered at times from injury, leading Lippi to rely more upon Del Piero, which gave him the ammunition to convince the Juve board that the youngster represented the future. The decision was made to focus upon youth potential, with Baggio told that he would no longer be a guaranteed starter and would need to accept a significant pay reduction. Given his talent and still being only 28 years old, Baggio was never going to accept such a proposal, resulting in Berlusconi swooping in to add *Il Divin Codino* to Capello's Milan squad for £6.8m. The Juve faithful weren't pleased but, given Del Piero's later longevity at the club, it turned out to be a smart move.

Kohler also exited, returning to Germany and Borussia Dortmund, as Juventus commenced their second season under Lippi. Their early league form was solid but not spectacular, sitting fifth at the end of 1995, having lost a vital away game at top team Milan. In the Champions League, meanwhile, fate intervened to again place Juventus and Borussia Dortmund in conflict, this time within the group stage, partnered with Steaua București and Glasgow Rangers.

Juventus romped through, winning all their first four games by an aggregate score of 14-2 as Del Piero repaid the management's faith in him, delivering four of those goals. The highlight was a 3-1 away victory in Dortmund, where Del Piero was in sensational form. As well as setting up goals for both Padovano and Conte, he scored an extraordinary goal of his own, cutting in from the left wing before hitting a long-range shot into the top corner – a move he would repeat so often during his career that it became known as the Zona Del Piero. The Germans did get some revenge in Turin, leaving with a 2-1 victory, albeit Juventus had already qualified for the knockout stages by that point. Dortmund eventually finished second in the group behind the Italians as both teams moved on to March's quarter-finals.

Heading into that quarter-final, Juve's league form had improved significantly. Losing just once in January and February, away at Vicenza, saw the *Bianconeri* climb to fourth as Milan ran away with the title. Juventus would need that improved confidence, as awaiting them in March were Real Madrid – a side that they had been drawn against twice previously in Europe, eliminated both times.

The first leg in the Bernabéu saw Raúl inflict a one-goal win for Real, setting up the return leg perfectly. A bank of red flares and smoke greeted the players into the Stadio delle Alpi as Lippi watched the early exchanges, cigar held in mouth. And it was Del Piero who levelled things on aggregate with a 17th-minute free kick into the bottom corner, after which Michele Padovano sealed the deal for Juve with a second-half strike. Dortmund, meanwhile, were eliminated by defending champions Ajax, who were again showing themselves to be the team to fear under Van Gaal. Juventus fans would be praying to avoid the Dutch in the semi-final, and their prayers were answered.

While Ajax drew Panathinaikos, Juventus found themselves pitted against French champions Nantes, who had won Ligue 1 by ten clear points the previous season, while also reaching the quarter-finals of the UEFA Cup. The first leg in Turin saw Juventus gain the advantage with a 2-0 win, making them favourites to progress, provided they avoided any unnecessary drama back in France. An early Vialli goal followed by another from Sousa meant Nantes would require five goals to move on – they managed three to finish winners on the night, but Juventus had done the job. In just his second season, Lippi was taking the Old Lady to a Champions League Final.

Juventus finished their league season strongly, ending second, albeit eight points behind champions Milan. But it was all about the Champions League now, the final being held down in Rome, inevitably against Van Gaal's young Ajax side, who had defeated Capello's Milan in Vienna the year before. With Edwin van der Sar in goal, Danny Blind in defence, the De Boer brothers alongside Edgar Davids in midfield and an attack boasting Finidi George, Nwankwo Kanu and Jari Litmanen, with Patrick Kluivert available from the bench, it would be a serious test for just how far Juventus had come under Lippi.

The Juventus side that lined up that night included Angelo Peruzzi in goal, Ciro Ferrera and Vierchowod in defence, Conte, Sousa and Deschamps across the midfield and the fearsome attack of Vialli, Del Piero and Ravanelli. Juve fans from around the country descended upon Rome, as 70,000 packed the Stadio Olimpico. It took just 13 minutes for Juventus to open the scoring when a mix-up between Van der Sar and Frank de Boer allowed Ravanelli to steal the ball, before scoring from an extremely tight angle. The 'white feather' had struck once again and it appeared that Juve would get into the break ahead, until a De Boer free kick fell to Litmanen, who made no mistake from close range, the deadly Finn grabbing his ninth goal of the tournament.

Both sides had chances during the second half but eventually the game moved through extra time and into a penalty shoot-out. 'After full time, I was calm,' Lippi would later remark. 'Everyone came towards me and told me they wanted to take a penalty.' Edgar Davids began the shoot-out and missed, handing the advantage to Juventus, which they then never relinquished. Ferrara, Gianluca Pessotto and Padovano all netted, meaning that as Jugović stepped forward to take the fourth, after Sonny Silooy's miss for Ajax, the title was in their grasp. He hit it to Van der Sar's right. The keeper guessed the correct way but the ball nestled into the corner. After years of enviously watching Milan play in five finals and even Sampdoria reach a final, Juventus were the champions of Europe for the first time since that horrific night in Heysel. The Old Lady was back at the top.

As players and staff celebrated, there began the first sprouts of accusations that would rumble on in the future. Ronald de Boer would subsequently say that Marc Overmars felt the Juve players looked like they 'were on something'. Finidi George would add years later that he was amazed by Juve's energy levels. But at the time nothing more came of it – maybe Juve were just fitter on the day. The blowback would really start when, in 2004, Juve were prosecuted for doping after club doctor Riccardo Agricola was given a suspended prison sentence for providing performance-enhancing drugs to players – although subsequently acquitted. A Dutch documentary, *Andere Tijden Sport*, broadcast in 2013, talked with the expert medical witness at that trial, haematologist Giuseppe d'Onofrio, who looked at Juve players' haemoglobin levels between February and June 1996, and concluded that they could only have registered as they did if explained by using blood transfusions or EPO (erythropoietin). In the eyes of Ajax, therefore, the final has always remained 'questionable'.

* * *

The key to success in football is to never rest on your laurels. Despite lifting Europe's ultimate trophy, senior club management and Lippi were ready to undertake another major rehaul of the squad during the summer of 1996. They were never shy to move players on as soon as it was felt expedient to do so. With the Premier League starting to strengthen following its formation in 1992, two of Juve's star strikers were prised away to England as Vialli headed to Stamford Bridge and Ruud Gullit's Chelsea revolution, and Ravanelli, in a much more surprising move, headed up to Middlesbrough in the North East. As part of the seeming relationship between Juve and Dortmund, Sousa exited for Borussia Dortmund, 'Because they didn't believe in my quality anymore. I picked up a knee problem and they believed that I could no longer achieve the same high levels.' With Vierchowod also off, to Perugia, Juventus was not a place of sentimentality.

With those high-profile exits, Juve fans would be looking for some serious talent to move back into the club. Probably the most celebrated new signing was Croatian striker Alen Bokšić, who had been part of an exciting Lazio side managed by Zdeněk Zeman. The attack was also bolstered by the acquisition of a young Christian Vieri from Atalanta as well as Nicola Amoruso from Padova. In defence, an exciting young talent named Mark Iuliano came in from Salernitana, along with Argentine Paolo Montero from Atalanta. And then there was a young French midfielder who had caught the eye of Kenny Dalglish at Blackburn, but he had been allegedly rebuffed by owner Jack Walker and his immortal line of 'Why do you want to sign Zidane when we have Tim Sherwood?' Zinedine Zidane had played four seasons with French club Bordeaux, helping them reach the 1995/96 UEFA Cup Final, where his fame rose considerably. Suddenly he was in demand at several top European clubs, but he decided on a move to Juventus. It would be the commencement of a beautiful relationship.

Juventus stood atop of Serie A at the end of 1996, having lost just once, away at Vicenza, although they hardly set the league alight, scoring more than two goals just twice in those first 14 games, with Zidane especially struggling to shine. That would all change when Conte suffered a serious injury, forcing Lippi to change his midfield structure, pulling back an attacker from his 4-3-3 and instead pushing Zidane forward to play just behind a front pairing in a 4-3-1-2, which suited his skills much better.

Again, the early part of the season was dominated by the Champions League group stage. Finally avoiding Borussia Dortmund, Juventus were placed into a group alongside Rapid Wien, Fenerbahçe and key rivals for the top spot, Manchester United, who Juventus entertained at home on the opening day. In a bitterly cold Stadio delle Alpi, Manchester United boss Sir Alex Ferguson recalled in an interview with *FourFourTwo* magazine how he held Juventus in esteem. 'I stood in the tunnel before kick-off and the Juventus players made ours look small,' he remembered, an impression seconded by Gary Neville in his autobiography: 'Big names, big players, in every respect.' 'Juventus were the model for my Manchester United,' Ferguson would also state. The start of a European rivalry would commence with a Bokšić goal sealing an opening group win for Juventus. It could have been a lot worse, Neville recalling that United didn't register a single shot on goal: 'It could have been 10-0. It was the biggest battering I've ever had on a football pitch.'

A Bokšić goal then also secured an away win in Turkey, after which a draw in Austria was followed by a 5-0 thrashing of Rapid Wien back in Turin, Bokšić grabbing another two goals, while Del Piero also scored a brace. That set up a trip to Old Trafford where, despite United putting in a much better performance, Juventus again emerged winners by a single goal, this time a Del Piero penalty. A home win against the Turks secured first place in the group via five wins and a draw, with United following in second. Unbeaten in their Champions League group and top of Serie A, Juventus were enjoying a strong end to 1996.

November of 1996 also saw Juventus lift their first silverware of the campaign when they travelled to Tokyo to take on Argentina's River Plate in the Intercontinental Cup. With just nine minutes of the game remaining, Del Piero slammed home from a corner to crown Juventus as world champions. The season just kept getting better and better.

The start of 1997, however, saw an irritating Serie A loss to Parma, but Juventus still retained top spot and continued to do so as they went through the rest of January and February unbeaten, before returning to Champions League action. The last eight of Europe saw some familiar recent Juventus rivals, with both Ajax and Borussia Dortmund present; however, Juventus lucked out in avoiding both, instead drawing surprise package Rosenborg of Norway. Falling behind in Trondheim, Vieri saved Juve's blushes to secure a draw before Zidane gave them a first-half lead back in Turin. But Juve struggled to add another, meaning that, as the game approached the end, one goal from Rosenborg would mean extra time. Finally, in the last minute, Juventus won a penalty that Amoruso gratefully converted, allowing Juve fans to breathe once more. They were into the last four, but what a last four it was. Borussia Dortmund, Ajax and Manchester United all joined the Italians – all of whom they had recently played. And it would be Ajax that Juventus would face in a repeat of the previous year's final – could Juve overcome the Dutch again?

Travelling to a passionate Amsterdam Arena, Juve took the lead after just 14 minutes when a magical spin from Jugović put Amoruso in to open the scoring. Zidane was denied a second as Van der Sar saved brilliantly before Vieri doubled Juve's lead with a low strike into the corner just before half-time. There was still time for Van der Sar to deny Amoruso at close range before the teams headed into the break. Litmanen broke the offside trap in the second period to halve the deficit, but Juve saw the game out, leaving with a valuable away win.

The return leg would be the Zidane show – his true rise to glory as a Juve star. For the opening half an hour, Ajax dominated, taking the game aggressively to the Italians. But then a Juve corner saw the balding pate of Lombardo rise to put Juve ahead, after which Vieri slid in a second just two minutes later, effectively ending the tie. Requiring four goals, Mario Melchiot did head one in, in the second half, before Juve again struck twice in two minutes, Amoruso tapping home from Zidane's cross, before Zidane closed out the night by rounding Van der Sar. It had been a ruthless performance from Juve, Zidane later telling Messi in an interview that it had been his best career performance for the Old Lady.

An outstanding Ajax team had been crushed 6-2 on aggregate as Juventus lay claim to being the hottest team in Europe by vanquishing the Dutch masters for two successive seasons. The other semi-final saw Dortmund defeat Manchester United 1-0 both home and away, so, once again, Juventus would face the Germans in European competition, their seventh meeting in the last five seasons, in which, to date, Juve had won four, drawn one and lost one. And for the second consecutive year, Juventus would be playing in the biggest European match of them all.

The final was played at the Olympiastadion in Munich, situated roughly halfway between Dortmund and Turin. Dortmund's starting XI contained four players who had all worn the black and white of Juve in the past: Jürgen Kohler, Stefan Reuter, Paulo Sousa and Andreas Möller, heightening the familiarity between the two sides. Lippi decided to start with the attacking duo of Vieri and Bokšić, with Del Piero on the bench, while Ottmar Hitzfeld had a host of injury issues to deal with. But strangest of all was the situation with midfielder Lars Ricken.

At this time, Ricken was combining playing with serving time in the German Bundeswehr (Federal Defence) twice a week. In fact, he needed to get permission to leave for both the Champions League quarter-finals and semi-finals. Two weeks before the final, he suffered a motorcycle accident and then, compounding that, he forgot to lock his army locker, which contained his firearms card, the weekend before the final.. The penalty for such an offence was three days in military prison, but Ricken managed to get away with doing night shifts instead, allowing him to be on the subs' bench for the final.

In the end, Hitzfeld was able to field a side containing Sammer (as captain), Kohler, Reuter, Sousa and Möller, with an attack comprising Karl-Heinz Riedle and Stéphane Chapuisat. There was also a Scotsman in midfield. Paul Lambert had played for St Mirren and Motherwell before a trial in the summer of 1996 landed him a place in the Dortmund squad, where he had shone as a defensive midfielder. The Scot would play an integral part in the upcoming 90 minutes.

Juventus were clearly the favourites as the game commenced and made the better start to the final, with Zidane controlling the tempo and flow of the match. For 20 minutes they dominated, until Dortmund realised they needed to make a tactical change. Sousa recalled in a later interview with Sky Sports: 'I took one decision on the pitch with Paul Lambert. We decided that he would take care of Zidane and I would take care of the rest of the midfield.' Lambert added: 'We spoke during the game to change it. The two of us looked at it. Zidane was playing on the other side to where I was. Paulo and I switched it because that allowed Paulo the freedom to do what he wanted to do. It gave me the role that I was used to doing.' It would be an influential call.

Zidane's authority began to wane as Lambert shackled him, allowing Dortmund back into the match. With almost half an hour played, Dortmund won a corner. As the ball swung in, Peruzzi's punch fell to Lambert, who crossed to the far post, where Riedle was lurking. In one movement, Riedle chested the ball down before blasting under Peruzzi to give Dortmund the lead against the run of play.

If that wasn't shocking enough for Juventus, Riedle then doubled Dortmund's lead just five minutes later with a header from another Möller corner, sending the black-and-yellow end into delirium. Even the German commentator sounded shocked, expressing the feelings of many: 'Riedle! 2-0. What is going on here?' Zidane did manage to free himself to hit a shot against the post, before Vieri had a goal disallowed for handball, but as the half-time whistle blew, Juventus were staring at a surprise two-goal deficit. Change was needed.

Juventus's second-half intention was clearly signalled as Lippi withdrew right-back Sergio Porrini, to be replaced by Del Piero, and 20 minutes later the change resulted in a lifeline as Bokšić broke down the right before pulling the ball across the area, where Del Piero converted with a cute backheel. Suddenly it was game on once more.

Riedle had to be substituted as a previously broken toe was causing him discomfort; then five minutes after Del Piero's goal, Hitzfeld made another change, throwing in Ricken to replace Chapuisat up front. Rarely has a substitution had such a swift effect. Ricken takes up the story: 'I noticed that Peruzzi was often standing too far from his goal, and I came on with that in mind.' Just 16 seconds after the substitution, Möller put Ricken through and he immediately chipped the ball first time over Peruzzi from distance. As Dortmund's players celebrated, Juve's looked stunned and they couldn't lift themselves from the canvas as the game petered out into a 3-1 victory for the Germans. Juventus had been denied a second successive Champions League success.

While their European campaign had ended in despair, more silverware did flow to the Old Lady. At the start of 1997, Juventus contested the UEFA Super Cup over two legs against Cup Winners' Cup holders PSG. It would turn out to be no contest, as Juve thrashed PSG 6-1 in Paris before finishing the job with a 3-1 home win. Meanwhile, in the league, Juventus held off Parma to clinch their second Scudetto in three years, losing just three times all season. Especially impressive during the run-in was a trip to the San Siro in April to face the mighty Milan. With Del Piero and Bokšić both unavailable through injury, Lippi went with an attack comprising Vieri and Amoruso, and a famous night in Juve history saw them humiliate Milan 6-1, with Vieri scoring a brace and Amoruso also on the scoresheet.

The gamble on Del Piero over Baggio had paid dividends as the young striker ended the campaign with 15 goals across all competitions, making him Juve's top scorer, one ahead of Vieri. In total Juve scored just 51 goals in 34 Serie A games, fewer than Lazio and Udinese in fourth and fifth, but it was their defence that was the key, conceding just 24 goals.

In the awards for 1997, Zidane placed third in the Ballon d'Or, reflecting his strong performances over the season. Interestingly, narrowly beating him for second place was Real Madrid's Predrag Mijatović – a name we will soon encounter again.

* * *

Another summer, another transfer merry-go-round at the Stadio delle Alpi. The seasonal clear-out included strikers Bokšić and Vieri to Lazio and Atlético Madrid, respectively, while midfielders Lombardo and Jugović departed for Crystal Palace and Lazio. The departing forwards were replaced by the Serie A Young Footballer of the Year Filippo Inzaghi, bought from Atalanta, along with Daniel Fonseca from Roma. Continually evolving, Lippi again changed Juve's formation, moving this season to a 3-4-1-2 structure rather than a back four based on how strong his defence had been across the previous campaign. It would allow the team to be more attacking as he trusted three defenders to cover the back.

The new boys settled quickly into the Juventus set-up as they purred along once more, ending 1997 unbeaten in their 13 Serie A games, placing them second, just behind Inter as Serie A looked to already be a two-horse race. Meanwhile, the Champions League group stage would see Juventus again pitted against Manchester United, along with Feyenoord and whipping boys Košice from Slovakia. Kicking off with a 5-1 thrashing of Feyenoord in Turin, fuelled by a Del Piero brace, Juventus then travelled to Old Trafford for the first of their two games against the English champions. For the 53,000 fans that witnessed the game that night, it would be an unforgettable encounter.

The game exploded into life right from the start when Portuguese midfielder Dimas played Del Piero through, although it looked suspiciously offside. He slotted Juventus into a lead after just 24 seconds. Deschamps then picked up a yellow card for a foul on Denis Irwin, which would become meaningful later. Manchester United settled down and had the ball in the back of the net when Teddy Sheringham headed home, only to be denied by the linesman's flag, which ironically looked closer to onside than Del Piero's opener. United continued to press, with the breakthrough finally coming just eight minutes before half-time through Sheringham.

Twenty minutes into the second half, United's Ronny Johnsen turned Deschamps, who inexplicably grabbed his shirt, leading to a second yellow, leaving Juve one man down. To make matters worse, United immediately took the lead as substitute Paul Scholes rounded Peruzzi and stroked home. Old Trafford exploded. United were now playing like men possessed, attacking Juve in waves. And with a minute remaining, Giggs picked up the ball in midfield, accelerated at a retreating Juve defence before rifling it into the roof of the net. As the United faithful serenaded their heroes, Zidane immediately grabbed back a consolation goal from a free kick but it was too little, too late as United registered a famous night under the lights.

Following that setback, Juventus beat Košice home and away, although each time by only one goal. There then followed a humbling night in Rotterdam as Feyenoord defeated the Old Lady 2-0, meaning Juve needed at least a point from their final game at home to United to progress. With six minutes to go, it remained goalless, until Zidane chipped in a cross for Inzaghi to head home, ruining United's 100 per cent record and sending Juve through to the knockout stages behind them in the group standings. It hadn't been a convincing group-stage performance from the *Bianconeri* but at least they were through.

The winter transfer window saw the addition of some steel into the Juventus midfield. While Zidane was providing silky performances, what better enforcer to have beside him than Edgar Davids, the 'Pitbull', so he was signed from Milan. The first week of 1998 saw Juve lose their unbeaten Serie A record when Youri Djorkaeff gave rivals Inter a valuable 1-0 home win. But that spurred Juve into a strong remainder of January and February, winning seven of their next nine to top the Serie A standings as the Champions League quarter-finals rolled around. A double header against Dynamo Kyiv was their reward for coming second in the group.

Dynamo Kyiv were a useful side, managed by their legendary coach Valeriy Lobanovskyi. It was a youthful team where all the players were younger than 30, but two were making a name for themselves – the attacking partnership of Serhiy Rebrov and Andriy Shevchenko. Ukrainian champions, they had topped a tough group containing PSV Eindhoven, Newcastle United and Barcelona, which included a famous 4-0 win at the Camp Nou in which Shevchenko fired a first-half hat-trick. They were a team not to be taken lightly.

With the first leg in Turin, Juventus dominated the first half but without really threatening against a well-organised Kyiv. Early in the second half, Del Piero hit the woodwork before Kyiv silenced the stadium, Andriy Husin volleying them ahead from a corner. Kyiv almost doubled their lead when Rebrov went down under a challenge in the area that looked like a penalty, although waved away by the referee, after which Inzaghi saw his close-range header saved, before tapping home the rebound to level the match. A draw meant a tough trip to the snowy wastelands of Ukraine lay ahead for the Italians.

A stellar performance from Juve saw Inzaghi bag a hat-trick and Del Piero add a fourth as they cruised past Kyiv, despite the cold, 4-1. It was Inzaghi at his best – goal poacher extraordinaire – securing them a semi-final against Monaco. Again, the first leg would be in Turin, but this time Juve would be much more ruthless than against Kyiv. Del Piero opened the scoring with his trademark free kick into the top corner, before Costinha levelled close to half-time. But just before the referee could blow for the break, Zidane broke into the area, only for keeper Fabien Barthez to bring him down. Del Piero stepped up to dispatch his second of the night.

The second half saw Del Piero grab his hat-trick with a second penalty and then Zidane added the gloss, scoring just before the end. It had been a thoroughly professional performance from the *Bianconeri*, overcoming a Monaco that included future Juve star David Trezeguet and a young Thierry Henry on the bench. Henry scored in the second leg as Monaco salvaged some pride with a 3-2 win, but Juve were never at risk of elimination. They had made it to a third successive Champions League Final, a remarkable achievement. All eyes now turned to the other semi-final, which involved Juve's nemesis from the previous year – Borussia Dortmund.

Dortmund were drawn against Real Madrid, who took a 2-0 win back to Germany, where they held out for a goalless draw and a place in the final, to be played at the Amsterdam Arena. Surprisingly, this was Real's first Champions League Final appearance. Their last European Cup Final had been back in 1981 when they lost to Liverpool, and they hadn't lifted the trophy since overcoming Partizan back in 1966. A 32-year drought for the *Madridistas* had become a monkey on their back that they were determined to end.

This was a Madrid side that included Italian Christian Panucci and Brazilian Roberto Carlos in defence, while Frenchman Christian Karembeu, Dutchman Clarence Seedorf and Argentine Fernando Redondo marshalled the midfield. The strike force consisted of club legend Raúl, Fernando Morientes and Serbian Predrag Mijatović, all overseen by German manager Jupp Heynckes. Still, going into the final, they were clear underdogs given Juve's record over the past four seasons under Lippi. Real had finished a distant fourth in La Liga and been eliminated by second division Alavés in the Copa del Rey, so all was not well within the club with the relationship between Heynckes and key players described as strained.

Unsurprisingly, the Italians started the stronger, Zidane especially dominating the midfield while coming close to scoring. But although controlling possession, it was Real who almost opened the scoring when Raúl missed from just six yards out, sinking to his knees at the realisation of what an opportunity it had been. The second half continued in the same vein, Juventus coming close, but slowly Real's midfield began to smother Zidane. And then came the 66th minute.

A Madrid corner was cleared only as far as Roberto Carlos on the edge of the area. The Brazilian fired hard and low, only to see his shot deflected into the path of Mijatović. Calm as you like, the Serb immediately took the ball around a diving Peruzzi before striking the ball past last-ditch defender Paulo Montero. 'Those few seconds after scoring were sheer happiness. I have never felt such a feeling in my life,' Mijatović would recall.

It would be enough to end the 32-year drought. Juventus were unable to find a way through the tight Madrid defence and faced the fact that they had lost a second successive Champions League Final. For Madrid, the win was huge. According to club captain on the night Manolo Sanchís, 'The 1998 Champions League Final was possibly the most important game in Real Madrid's history. That's not to say the others weren't, but the club had been waiting for 32 years. In all that time the hunger had been growing among the fans, the players and the club.' Ironically, Heynckes was sacked just eight days later. Managing Real Madrid is not for the faint-hearted.

While Juve's Champions League campaign had ended in another heartache, they had been unstoppable in Serie A. Following the January defeat to rivals Inter, they only lost one more game all season, away at Fiorentina, winning Lippi his third Serie A title in four years. But the championship wouldn't be without controversy. With just four games left, Juventus hosted Inter, with just one point separating first-placed Juve from the Milan side. It was the key game of the run-in and would take a place in infamy.

Del Piero put Juve ahead after 21 minutes and it stayed that way into the half-time break. But then, on 71 minutes, Ronaldo challenged for a ball on the wing. With lightning speed, Iván Zamorano picked up the loose ball and sped into the Juve area before a tackle pushed the ball invitingly back to Ronaldo. Poking the ball to the right, he was felled by the onrushing Iuliano, whose clumsy challenge looked an obvious penalty. To the astonishment of the Inter players and management, referee Piero Ceccarini waved play on and, to make matters worse, Juve immediately broke up the pitch and were awarded a penalty themselves after Del Piero went down under a challenge. Pandemonium broke out, Inter players surrounding and shoving the referee, but he was adamant, booking an incensed Inter manager Luigi Simoni for apparently calling him 'shameful'.

Some justice prevailed as Gianluca Pagliuca saved Del Piero's penalty but, shortly after, Inter's Zé Elias received a red card for elbowing Deschamps and Inter also had a goal disallowed for a foul on the keeper. It ended 1-0 to Juventus, effectively sealing the championship race, but Inter were in an uproar. *Gazzetta dello Sport* ran with 'L'Inter urla vergogna' (Inter cry disgrace), while two politicians almost came to blows in parliament over the affair. To this day, the game is known to Inter fans as 'la partita madre di Calciopoli' (the mother game of Calciopoli), while the season is dubbed 'la grande ruberia' (the great robbery). But to Juve, it was just another Scudetto.

The partnership of Del Piero and Inzaghi had netted 59 goals between them across all competitions as Lippi's new formation increased Juve's attacking effectiveness, Del Piero also ending as the leading goalscorer in the 1998 Champions League with ten.

* * *

The 1998 World Cup would see Zidane rise to global stardom as he led France to victory at home, his two goals in the final helping him win the 1998 Ballon d'Or. Didier Deschamps would have the honour of lifting the trophy as France captain. For once, Juve's summer transfer activities were muted, leaving Lippi to start the 1998/99 campaign with primarily the same squad. There were rumours that Lippi was unhappy, having seen his request for five new players over the summer rebuffed by Moggi, and that he had discussed leaving, only for Moggi to insist he honour his contract, which had one more season to run.

Juventus's season started with a 2-1 loss to Lazio in the Supercoppa before they seemed to get back into their usual groove, winning five of their first seven Serie A games to top the standings, until a trip to Udinese derailed them. At 2-1 ahead going into the final minute, all looked good until Del Piero stretched for a ball, after which he immediately signalled for medical assistance. Stretchered off in obvious pain, his season was over due to rupturing the anterior and posterior ligaments in his left knee, leaving Juve deprived of a key player.

If that wasn't bad enough, Zidane hit a spell of poor form. Also suffering from knee issues and a general malaise after such a historic summer, he drifted in and out of games, which, combined with the loss of Del Piero, sent Juve into a tailspin. Losing four of their next five Serie A games and failing to score in any of them, Juventus dropped to ninth, before also suffering Coppa Italia elimination to Bologna. Their Champions League form was also dire. In a relatively easy group alongside Galatasaray, Rosenborg and Athletic Bilbao, Juve drew all their first five matches, only qualifying for the knockout stages on goal difference by beating Rosenborg at home 2-0 in the final fixture. And then came the worst news of all.

In December 1998, Lippi announced that he would be leaving Juventus at the end of the season to take the managerial position at Inter. This was followed by the revelation from Deschamps that he had been involved in a violent fight with Lippi in the changing room. A stung board, watching Juventus's struggles, decided to terminate Lippi's position early, relieving him of his duties on 7 February after a 4-2 home loss to Parma and replacing him with Parma's Carlo Ancelotti.

It was a sad end to an incredible four-and-a-half-year spell at the helm for Lippi. He had taken over a club that hadn't won the Serie A title for eight seasons and delivered them three championships. He had taken over a club that hadn't reached a Champions League/ European Cup Final since the tragic 1985 night in Heysel, and taken them to three successive finals, winning one, plus a UEFA Cup Final appearance. He had built a team that constantly evolved but included Roberto Baggio, Zinedine Zidane, Alessandro Del Piero, Didier Deschamps and Gianluca Vialli. For four seasons, Juventus had preserved and built upon Italy's record of producing the strongest teams in Europe.

Like Alex Ferguson later, Lippi had always looked to improve the club, even when winning almost every trophy available. An example of this is summed up by his recollection of winning the Intercontinental Cup in 1996. Rather than basking in glory, he remembered 'turning to the bench, to [assistant coach Narciso] Pezzotti and my other staff members and saying that a new cycle starts now. I'm not a big fan of celebrations anyway. I prefer the day before the game to the evening after.' He was unafraid to change formations to suit the players he had, ensuring that the system matched the available talent. The team was expected to play for each other, each area helping another. For Lippi, his job was all about coaching – he didn't get deeply involved with transfers, viewing his task simply to get the best out of what he was given, which were highly talented individuals thanks to Agnelli's ambitious purchases.

Happily, for Lippi and Juventus, this wouldn't be the end of their relationship, with a successful reunion in the early 2000s still to come.

JUVENTUS (1994–1998)
Champions League winners – 1995/96
Champions League runners-up – 1996/97, 1997/98
UEFA Super Cup winners – 1996
Intercontinental Cup winners – 1996
UEFA Cup runners-up – 1994/95
Serie A winners – 1994/95, 1996/97, 1997/98
Coppa Italia winners – 1994/95

Chapter 21
Moratti and O Fenômeno

Ronaldo? Simple ... for me he was the best ever.
He was without a doubt the best player I have
ever coached in my career. He was a crazy talent.
He had an extra gear compared to the rest and
he used to do incredible things on the pitch. In
training he was even stronger than what you
could see in games. Sometimes I was left stunned
by the things he did. For him this was normal ...
but only for him.

Luigi Simoni, former Inter manager

WHEN WE last visited Inter, they had secured their first silverware for a decade as Trapattoni delivered them both a Serie A title and UEFA Cup, with a team that comprised the *Tre Tedeschi* as well as Walter Zenga, Giuseppe Bergomi, Nicola Berti and Aldo Serena. Having captured their first European trophy for 26 years, Trapattoni rode off into the sunset (actually, back to his first love, Juventus), leaving Inter chairman Ernesto Pellegrini to find a suitable replacement. The choice was somewhat surprising.

Corrado Orrico began his managerial career in 1966 at a host of lower-level, mainly Tuscan clubs, including five spells overseeing Carrarese, based in Carrara, home of the famous marble used by Michelangelo among others. In 1988, Orrico moved from Carrarese to manage Serie B's Lucchese, almost winning them promotion to Serie A for the first time in 36 years, which attracted the attention of Pellegrini, who appointed him to his first high-profile post following Trapattoni's departure. It was a huge step up along with big shoes to fill.

The appointment didn't work out as hoped. While Serena moved to Milan and Dino Baggio came in on loan from Juventus, the squad remained relatively unchanged, including all three Germans, but Orrico couldn't get the same tune from them. Players such as Matthäus and Bergomi were getting older, the team in need of refresh. After matchday 16 on 12 January, Inter had won just five Serie A games, drawing eight and only scoring more than one goal three times, leaving them languishing in eighth position. To make things worse, they had only narrowly scraped past minnows Casertana and Como in the Coppa Italia, drawing two of the four games, and crashed out of defending their UEFA Cup title in the first round to Portuguese side Boavista. While the team remained strong defensively, Orrico's defensive attitude was blunting their attacking prowess. Defeat to Atalanta on 19 January was the final straw – Orrico was unsurprisingly out.

Pellegrini next turned to an Inter legend, Luis Suárez, to oversee the remainder of the campaign, but little improved. Squad disharmony was the backdrop to a final league position of eighth, meaning no European football for the first time since 1976. Their 34 league matches had yielded a miserly 28 goals, along with 17 draws. It was a significant drop-off in performance from the prior year that would see Suárez join Orrico in leaving the San Siro.

The 1992/93 season would see seismic change within both team and management. Firstly, all three Germans left the club – Matthäus to Bayern Munich, Klinsmann to Monaco and Brehme to Real Zaragoza – a definite end of an era, the three having accumulated over 300 appearances for the *Nerazzurri*. The forward line was completely rebuilt through three summer signings. Darko Pančev moved over from Red Star Belgrade, where he had been an integral part of the exciting young team that won the 1991 European Cup, scoring 84 goals in his 92 appearances, Inter securing his coveted services for £7m. Joining him was 1990 World Cup hero Salvatore Schillaci from Juventus as well as Uruguayan Rubén Sosa from Lazio. In midfield, Russian international Igor Shalimov arrived from Foggia, while Matthias Sammer returned from loan at VfB Stuttgart. Put in charge of this new-look squad was Osvaldo Bagnoli, the manager who had overseen the historic 1984/85 Hellas Verona Serie A championship win before a successful spell with Genoa.

It was a bold overhaul that paid dividends, Inter sitting second in Serie A for most of the season behind rivals Milan and therefore earning UEFA Cup qualification. Goalscoring markedly improved with 59 as compared to the previous 28, Sosa tearing the league up with 20 goals, while, sadly, Schillaci struggled, netting just seven times. Having an upcoming European campaign, Pellegrini invested heavily over the summer to push Inter on to a title challenge and possible European silverware. Big money was spent on five new players, bringing in Dennis Bergkamp and Wim Jonk from Ajax, Francesco Dell'Anno from Udinese, Gianluca Festa from Cagliari, and Massimo Paganin from Brescia. It represented serious investment, especially the capture of Bergkamp, who had been a prolific striker in the Netherlands over the past three seasons. Everything was in place to attack Serie A and Europe.

The first half of the season saw Inter treading water in the league, leaving them in fifth as 1993 ended but only four points behind Milan, accentuated by a 2-1 loss to their bitter rivals. While Sosa was again prolific, Bergkamp was struggling to adjust to Italian football, scoring just twice from open play across those first 16 matches. But when Inter played their UEFA Cup games, a wholly different Bergkamp appeared. A first-round 5-1 aggregate elimination of Rapid Bucharest saw Bergkamp net a first-leg hat-trick, before a tricky 4-3 aggregate elimination of Cypriot side Apollon Limassol saw another brace from the Dutchman. That set up a quarter-final against a surprise package who were enjoying a rare moment in the sun.

The 1992/93 season had been the debut Premier League season in England, which saw the news dominated by Manchester United securing their first league title for 26 years. But also notable was the third-place finish earned by Norwich City. Having almost been relegated the season before, another battle for survival was expected at Carrow Road, but instead they earned a UEFA Cup spot, having led the Premier League by eight points towards the end of 1992 before falling away. Their 1993/94 UEFA Cup campaign would live on in Norwich supporters' hearts for decades to come.

Having negotiated Dutch side Vitesse in the opening round, Norwich drew a nasty second-round tie against Bayern Munich, who had narrowly missed out on winning the Bundesliga the year before and were one of the favourites for the competition, with former Inter hero Lothar Matthäus in midfield. Even hardened Norwich fans felt this would likely be the end of their adventure, but against all odds the Canaries travelled to Bavaria and returned with a famous 2-1 victory, thanks to goals by Jeremy Goss and Mark Bowen – the first time a British side had ever come away from the Olympiastadion with a win. Jeremy Goss's stunning volley was particularly memorable. He then scored again as Norwich secured a 1-1 home draw and a shocking aggregate win. After eliminating the mighty Bayern, surely things would get easier. But Norwich were then drawn to play Inter – two European superpowers in succession.

To be fair to Norwich, they made it difficult for the Italian giants. The first leg in Norfolk was only decided by a late Bergkamp penalty, given for a clear foul on Sosa, before the underdogs travelled to the San Siro and stayed in with a chance until two minutes from the end, when Bergkamp struck yet again, his seventh goal of the campaign already.

With Norwich out of the way, Inter could turn their focus back to Serie A for a while. January and February saw them continue to struggle, winning just two games out of nine, dropping to seventh. The situation became untenable for Bagnoli, so, on 7 February, he and Inter parted ways, leaving him to move into retirement. To cover the remainder of the season, Inter asked former player Gianpiero Marini to take the short-term reins – his first managerial post. His three-month reign would be eventful.

In Serie A, Inter's form nosedived even further, as they lost six of their final eight matches, causing them to flirt with relegation. Just one season after coming second, they had now finished 13th, just one point above relegated Piacenza. But they became a totally different team on European nights. Their UEFA Cup quarter-final took them first to Borussia Dortmund, where they came away from the intimidating Westfalenstadion with an impressive 3-1 win, thanks to a brace from Jonk in the space of four minutes. But what should then have been a straightforward second leg proved anything but. Dortmund took a 2-0 lead at the San Siro, meaning they required just one more goal to progress. As they pushed forward in pursuit of a third, Inter hit them on the break with nine minutes to go, Antonio Manicone securing a semi-final spot.

Their opponents would be Italian but not who Inter probably expected. The quarter-finals had seen Juventus paired against Cagliari, who were also in Serie A relegation danger. But against the odds the Sardinians defeated Juve both home and away to set up another all-Italian clash. It would be an intimidating place for Inter to travel.

Cagliari's Stadio Sant'Elia was aflame with flares as Inter entered the vast bowl on a sunny evening. Inter got off to the perfect start, Davide Fontolan heading them in front after just six minutes, but Cagliari quickly equalised. Sosa put Inter back in front early in the second half and it seemed as if Inter would take a one-goal advantage back to Milan. But then, in the last nine minutes, Cagliari scored twice to notch up a famous victory. Once again Inter were making things hard for themselves.

Luckily for the *Nerazzurri*, everything clicked in the return leg. A first-half penalty settled nerves, dispatched by Bergkamp, before the Dutchman set up both Berti for a second early in the second half and a third for Jonk, taking them to the UEFA Cup Final. Their opponents would be Austria Salzburg, who had defeated German opposition in the previous two rounds: Eintracht Frankfurt and Karlsruhe.

The first leg took Inter to Vienna, where some quick thinking from Sosa saw his free kick converted by Berti after 35 minutes. Inter then had to negotiate most of the second half with ten men after Alessandro Bianchi received a second yellow, but they held firm. Two weeks later, a second-half strike from Jonk saw Inter once again lift the trophy that they had secured just three seasons before under Trapattoni.

And so ended a strange season for the *Nerazzurri*. Their league form had been awful, taking them from second place the season before to almost relegated. They had changed manager during the campaign, appointing a temporary stand-in to take them to the season end. And yet they had still been talented enough to win the UEFA Cup, another example of just how strong Italian sides were during this era. Sosa had provided their Serie A firepower with 16 goals, but just one in the UEFA Cup, while Bergkamp had been the opposite, scoring just eight Serie A goals but ending as the joint-leading goalscorer in the UEFA Cup with eight. You sensed that something needed to change at Inter to drive them upwards once again.

* * *

Ottavio Bianchi would be the next manager who Inter turned to for leadership. Having successfully brought the first-ever Serie A title to Napoli, including overseeing Maradona, he had taken Roma to a UEFA Cup Final before returning south again, to briefly manage and then act as technical director. But with Napoli falling apart financially, he was attracted back to a coaching role by Inter, whose summer saw just one major purchase, the signing of keeper Gianluca Pagliuca from Sampdoria. It would prove to be a stabilising first season under Bianchi, commencing with disappointment as Inter crashed out of the UEFA Cup in the first round to Aston Villa, before an improved Serie A campaign saw them finish a respectable sixth, including a 3-1 *Derby della Madonnina* victory over their city rivals. The major event of the season, however, did not occur on the pitch but in the boardroom.

Inter's golden age of the late 1950s and 1960s, the *Grande Inter*, was overseen by chairman Angelo Moratti, who made his fortune in oil and energy. After his death in 1981, ownership of his company, the Saras Group, passed to his fourth son, Massimo. And it was during this 1994/95 season that Massimo decided to follow in his father's footsteps. In February 1995, he took over as owner of Inter, also relieving Pellegrini from his position as president to oversee that role too. Finally, Inter had an owner with the financial muscle to match the Berlusconis and Agnellis of Italian football. He had money and wasn't afraid to use it.

As soon as the 1994/95 season was over, Massimo produced his chequebook to fund part one of the squad refresh. Out went the Dutch pairing of Bergkamp and Jonk, to Arsenal and PSV Eindhoven, respectively. Bergkamp had endured a frustrating two years in Milan, where the second season had seen him struggling with injuries, compounded by tiredness following the 1994 World Cup. A shy individual by nature, he preferred to shun the limelight, alienating himself from Italian press and fans who viewed the Dutchman as cold and aloof. In a particularly cruel twist, an Italian publication renamed its award to the weakest Serie A player of the week from *L'asino della settimana* (donkey of the week) to *Bergkamp della settimana* (Bergkamp of the week) in recognition of his poor performances.

Recalling his time there in a *FourFourTwo* interview, Bergkamp explained:

> They made a lot of promises – which I found out later was something they did a lot. They said: 'We're going to play more offensive.' They did, but only for the first month! It wasn't what I'd hoped for. But Italy was good for my development. I learned to be more professional, learned to play against two or three defenders, and to play with players who are there for themselves rather than for the team.

Arsenal and Bergkamp would have the final laugh as his career would be reinvigorated under Arsène Wenger, although many forget that he was actually signed by Bruce Rioch.

Also sold to German clubs were Rubén Sosa, who had been Inter's top Serie A scorer for the last three seasons, and Darko Pančev. He had suffered an even tougher time than Bergkamp during his spell at Inter, especially under Bagnoli, with whom he had never seen eye to eye. Accused of not being committed enough, the Italian press hounded him too, changing his Red Star Belgrade nickname of the *Il Cobra* to *Il Ramarro* (the green lizard). In would come three foreign stars – midfielder Paul Ince from Manchester United, Argentine midfielder Javier Zanetti and Brazilian defender Roberto Carlos. The key question was where the goals would come from. With their whole attack of Bergkamp, Sosa and Pančev gone, the forward line now comprised the Italian duo of Maurizio Ganz and Marco Branca, which seemed on paper a weaker strike force.

With Moratti looking for immediate results, 1995/96 couldn't have started worse. Drawn in the first round of the UEFA Cup against lowly Logano of Switzerland, Inter once again crashed out early, humiliatingly beaten 1-0 in the San Siro. That was enough to provoke change as Moratti had been talking to Roy Hodgson, who had taken Switzerland to the last 16 of the 1994 World Cup and qualification for Euro 1996, about coming back to club management. Replacing Bianchi, Hodgson initially struggled, Inter sitting in

12th at one stage, before markedly improving over the second half of the season, including a 1-0 win over Milan, to finish seventh and narrowly secure UEFA Cup football for the following season. Their reliance on Branca and Ganz for goals was clear to all, the pair scoring 30 of their 51 Serie A goals for the season, with the next-highest scorer being Carlos with five. Inter had not won any silverware again, but at least Hodgson could point to a strong finish to the campaign.

After part one of the squad refresh, Massimo moved on to part two with a vengeance. Looking to significantly boost Inter's strike force, he brought in Chilean Iván Zamorano from Real Madrid, Nigerian Nwankwo Kanu from Ajax and Frenchman Youri Djorkaeff from PSG. The midfield was also strengthened by the additions of Swiss Ciriaco Sforza from Bayern Munich and Dutchman Aron Winter from Lazio. Hodgson couldn't complain that Massimo wasn't backing him in the transfer market. The key departure, after just one season, was Roberto Carlos, heading off to Real Madrid.

In a 2005 interview with *FourFourTwo* magazine, Carlos was asked about his one season at Inter and his reason for leaving so soon:

> My problem at Inter was Hodgson, Roy Hodgson. He wanted me to play as a forward when I'm a defender – I prefer to have space ahead of me to run into rather than be a winger already up there; for me it's better to have 80 metres to play in than 20. I didn't like the system or where Hodgson wanted me to play in it. I spoke to Massimo Moratti to see if he could sort things out and it soon became clear that the only solution was to leave.

Kanu's first season at Inter would unfortunately be brief, complicated by the fact that after returning from captaining Nigeria to an Olympic title and being named African Player of the Year, an Inter medical revealed a serious heart defect. Forced to undergo surgery to replace an aortic valve, Kanu would thankfully rejoin the club in April but play little part in their campaign.

With a clearly improved squad, the priority for Hodgson was to avoid a third successive early elimination in the UEFA Cup. In this he was successful, Inter comfortably knocking out French side Guingamp, but then the wheels nearly came off again. What should have been a calm second-round tie against Austrian side Grazer AK saw it go all the way to penalties in the second leg away in Austria. Luckily, Inter's penalty takers were calm enough to score five from five and scrape through, before then eliminating Portuguese side Boavista easily to book a place in March's quarter-finals. But it had been a close shave.

As March approached, Inter's league form was much improved, placing them fourth with only three losses, but unfortunately a significant number of draws. Their UEFA Cup quarter-final saw them face Anderlecht and, despite the new attacking faces, it was Ganz who stepped up, scoring all three Inter goals in a 3-2 aggregate victory. That set up a semi-final meeting against Monaco and once again Ganz was on the scoresheet with a brace as Inter secured a first-leg 3-1 win to take back to France. It would be a tense affair.

With Monaco knowing they had to attack, they went at Inter from the off. Goalless at half-time, they brought on their young striker, Thierry Henry, from the bench with half an hour remaining and he made an instant impact, scoring almost immediately, only to see the goal disallowed for offside. The decision took a while to reach and sparked off protests from the Monaco players as they scuffled with both officials and Inter players, Ince especially being heavily involved in the fracas. Shortly after, Monaco did get a legitimate goal, then they threw everything at the Inter defence, even sending keeper Barthez up for a late corner and keeping him there for a free kick, from which he almost scored a last-gasp winner, before taking the resultant corner himself. Somehow, though, Inter held on, earning themselves a third UEFA Cup Final appearance in seven years. Awaiting them would be German side Schalke, with the first leg to be played at the intimidating Parkstadion.

Hodgson went with an attacking duo of Ganz and Zamorano for the opener, backed up by Zanetti, Sforza and Winter in midfield. Schalke dominated the first half but were restricted to mainly long-range shots that Pagliuca dealt with easily. Then, with 20 minutes remaining, Belgian striker Marc Wilmots struck another long-range effort that finally nestled in the corner, giving Schalke a one-goal advantage to take over to Milan. Six minutes from defeat in the second leg, Zamorano saved Inter with a typical poacher's goal, shortly after which Inter went down to ten men when a second yellow card was issued to defender Salvatore Fresi. Despite the one-man disadvantage, Inter negotiated extra time to take the UEFA Cup Final to a penalty shoot-out. Three years after lifting the trophy in the San Siro, they were on the edge of repeating the feat.

Unfortunately, the pressure got to a tired Inter side. Zamorano saw his penalty saved by Jens Lehmann, Djorkaeff held his nerve but then Winter watched his shot fly wide. Schalke, meanwhile, converted four from four with German efficiency and raised their only major European trophy in the club's history to date. It was a sad finish to the season for Inter, worsened by the sight of their fans pelting Hodgson with coins and lighters.

Inter's Serie A campaign saw them finish strongly, ending a credible third behind champions Juventus and Parma. Hodgson had guided them to their best finish for four seasons and only penalty kicks away from winning the UEFA Cup, but he was stung by the fans' reactions after the Schalke game, leading him to resign, taking the Blackburn Rovers job. Moratti tried to persuade the Englishman to stay but his mind was made up. However, Moratti always expressed his admiration of how Hodgson had helped kick-start the Inter revival:

> Roy Hodgson was an important person in the development of Inter Milan to the point we have reached today. He saved us at the right time. When he came we were in trouble and things appeared dark. He didn't panic, he was calm and made us calm. Disaster was averted at the most important time. Everyone at Inter will remember him for that and his contribution. He is considered by us all as an important person in our history. He left an endowment to this club that's important in our history.

* * *

The summer saw Luigi Simoni brought in as manager from Napoli, but the news of his appointment was overshadowed by a much bigger announcement. Moratti was about to make the statement purchase of all statement purchases. Brazilian Ronaldo had become the hottest player in world football after setting Barcelona alight with a season of unsurpassed attacking skill. Moving over from PSV Eindhoven at the age of just 19 for a world record fee of $13.2m, he terrified European defences, netting 47 goals over 49 matches in all competitions as Barcelona secured the Cup Winners' Cup and Copa del Rey but finished two points behind Real Madrid in La Liga. His goals were breathtaking, manager Sir Bobby Robson declaring, 'I don't think I've ever seen a player at 20 have so much.' Ronaldo's 47 goals included the famous run against SD Compostela from the halfway line that had Robson holding his head in disbelief. Barcelona had the most exciting world talent on their books. All they had to do now was to renegotiate his contract.

Barcelona president Josep Núñez emerged from initial negotiations with Ronaldo's agents announcing that a deal was in place, only for the draft agreement to collapse the next day, causing Núñez to admit, 'It's all over. Ronaldo is going.' The words were music to Moratti's ears. Having considered buying him from PSV the year before, he now swooped in with a world record payment of £19.5m to secure himself the Brazilian sensation on a five-year contract. Suddenly Inter were on everyone's radar.

That wasn't the only business Moratti did that summer. Diego Simeone came from Atlético Madrid along with striker Álvaro Recoba from Argentina, while Ince headed back to England with Liverpool and Sforza departed to Kaiserslautern. Simoni had the pieces to challenge on multiple fronts as all eyes focused on Ronaldo – could the youngster deliver?

The first half of the 1997/98 season, leading up to the end of the year, saw Inter in blistering form. While Ronaldo failed to score on his Serie A debut, he scored in eight of the next ten matches, with Inter's first loss coming in the last game of 1997, away at Udinese. They sat atop Serie A from matchday two all the way to the end of December, as it looked like a two-way tussle between them and Juventus for the title. In the Coppa Italia, the first two rounds were easily negotiated to set up a quarter-final against rivals Milan. The quarter-finals of the UEFA Cup were also reached by beating Neuchâtel Xamax, Lyon and Strasbourg.

No Inter fan could have asked for more as the new year came around – Inter were on fire and Ronaldo was justifying his fee, becoming a media sensation in Italy. Unsurprisingly, his second successive FIFA World Player of the Year award and the Ballon d'Or were bestowed upon him – and he was still only 21 years old. Ronaldo had everything a manager could want from a striker – electrifying pace, coolness in front of goal and strength. But then came the 'wobble'.

The first sign of trouble was Inter's Coppa Italia first leg against Milan on 8 January, with Milan nominally the home team. They crushed Inter, scoring five unanswered goals in the first hour to put the tie to bed, including one from ex-Inter hero Ganz. It was a humiliating defeat that Inter couldn't possibly come back from, winning the second leg by a single last-minute goal. In Serie A, while 1998 started off with a crucial 1-0 home win over Juventus, Inter then lost four of their next 11, pushing them down to third, behind leaders Juventus and Lazio. Heading into March and the continuation of their UEFA Cup campaign, things suddenly looked much less rosy than two months prior. It was vital that Inter get back on track with a quarter-final win.

The game would see a rematch of the previous year's final as Inter once again faced Schalke. Immediately from the kick-off in Milan, bad blood appeared as Ronaldo was badly fouled and flare-ups arose around the pitch. But Ronaldo had the last laugh, scoring a fantastic first-half goal by playing a one-two with Djorkaeff, before powering into the area and rifling his shot into the top corner. It was typical Ronaldo: power, pace and a clinical finish.

Requiring at least a goal in the second leg, Schalke pressed in front of their home fans but as stoppage time rolled around, the game remained scoreless. With 92 minutes on the clock, the ball was played out to Michaël Goossens on the left wing. Looking up, the Belgian striker fired a beauty into the top corner, creating pandemonium around the tight stadium. As fans prepared for extra time, a last-minute Inter free kick was headed home by Taribo West. One minute the stadium had been jumping, the next … silence. Inter had snatched victory from the jaws of defeat, gaining some revenge for the previous year.

The result seemed to reinstall confidence in them. As well as the quarter-final win, they won three successive Serie A games during March, including a 3-0 thrashing of Milan, to move them above Lazio and only one point behind Juventus. Facing a tricky semi-final against Spartak Moscow, it was the perfect tune-up, and their hot form continued as a late strike from Zé Elias gave Inter a 2-1 home win to take to an icy Russia.

It may have been April, but the Moscow pitch was surrounded by snow banks. Players emerged in long sleeves and gloves to play on a threadbare pitch, Moscow getting the perfect start when Andrey Tikhonov scored after just 12 minutes. Needing at least one goal, Ronaldo, clad in a warming headband, fired home from close range just before half-time to renew Inter's advantage. And then, with 15 minutes remaining, a piece of pure Ronaldo magic. Picking up the ball from a throw-in, the Brazilian spun his marker before playing a pass to Zamorano on the edge of the area. Continuing his run, Zamorano slipped it back to him, after which Ronaldo accelerated between two defenders, rounded the keeper and slotted home the match-winning goal. Icy conditions be damned.

So, with a UEFA Cup Final booked, Inter could turn back to challenging Juventus for the Scudetto. With four games remaining, Inter remained just one point behind the Old Lady. It would all come down to the next match, Juventus at home to Inter and, as discussed in the previous chapter, that game lives in infamy among the Inter faithful. Ronaldo's claim for a penalty was denied and 'la partita madre di Calciopoli' was born. Inter ended the season second, five points behind Juventus, turning their focus on to the UEFA Cup Final and their last chance for silverware.

The 1997/98 UEFA Cup Final would be the first to be contested in a one-off final setting, played at the Parc des Princes in Paris. Inter's opponents were a familiar foe, the Lazio side that had finished seventh in Serie A. They will be discussed more in the next chapter, but it was the team managed by Sven-Göran Eriksson, including the likes of Vladimir Jugović, Pavel Nedvěd, Pierluigi Casiraghi and Roberto Mancini. For the third time during the 1990s, it would be an all-Italian UEFA Cup Final.

Inter got off to the perfect start when, after just five minutes, a long ball from Simone fell perfectly for an onrushing Zamorano to fire past Lazio keeper Luca Marchegiani. Dominating the first half, Ronaldo hit the bar before Djorkaeff headed narrowly over. The second half continued in the same vein, Zamorano again breaking the offside trap only to see his shot rebound off the post. It was all Inter, and with half an hour remaining Zanetti wrapped up the game with a screamer into the top corner. There was only one thing missing that would make the night perfect, and with 15 minutes remaining it came. Ronaldo again broke Lazio's offside trap and ran through alone to face Marchegiani. Giving him the eyes and throwing a couple of sublime stepovers, he eased past the keeper and rolled the ball into the empty net to set the seal on a historic night. It capped a wonderful night for the Brazilian, who had impressed all match with his surging runs and fancy footwork.

As Lazio faced up to their defeat, tempers flared. Taribo West reacted to a perceived foul, kicking out and receiving a straight red, before Lazio's Matías Almeyda hacked down Ronaldo in the final minute, earning the substitute his second yellow. As the whistle sounded, Massimo Moratti could look proudly on at his first piece of silverware, lifted by Pagliuca into the cool Parisian night. Meanwhile, Ronaldo could reflect on an incredible first season in Milan, scoring a phenomenal 34 goals across all competitions, allowing him to head off to the 1998 World Cup as the star attraction.

The win represented Inter's third UEFA Cup during the decade, following 25 years of European competition failure. The capture of these trophies, as well as the world's best player, showed once again that Italy was a dominant force in European football. Moratti's wealth had pushed Inter back into the top tier, as Italian clubs continued to use their money to attract top players from everywhere. It was an Italian world, and the rest of Europe could only continue to look on in envy.

INTER (1991–1998)
UEFA Cup winners – 1993/94, 1997/98
UEFA Cup runners-up – 1996/97

Chapter 22

'It Was Like Living in a Foreign Country'

I want to be an Italian, speak Italian, live like an Italian, and eat like an Italian.

David Platt, former Bari, Juventus and Sampdoria midfielder

FOOTBALL CAN be cruel – you can achieve much in your career and still be remembered for one random event, which in no way represents the sum of your work. The chances are that the name Ronny Rosenthal immediately conjures up an image of his open-goal miss against Aston Villa, despite his 21 goals for Liverpool. And so it is for Ian Rush, the Liverpool legend. The scorer of 383 goals over an illustrious 20-year career, he's one of football's greatest strikers. But he's always associated with one quote from his time at Juventus that continually haunts him. Moving to the Italian giants in the summer of 1987 for a British record transfer fee, he spent just one season with the Old Lady before returning to his beloved Merseyside. His sojourn abroad hadn't been successful and seemed to be encapsulated in a quote attributed to him about his time in Turin: 'I couldn't settle in Italy. It was like living in a foreign country.'

Since then, Rush has been at pains to point out that he never actually said that. In a 2005 interview with *The Observer*, he discussed the quote:

I was set up. It was someone's idea of fun – probably one of my Liverpool team-mates joked that I'd said it and things went from there. I had just re-joined the club [in August 1988] and wanted to get back to playing football, not worry what was being written about me.

287

Part of the reason that the legend has stuck is because there was a reticence during those days for British players to move abroad, so many journalists and fans can imagine such a comment being said. British footballers were viewed as insular, afraid of new environments. To be fair, there was some precedent for such a view. The first British player to enjoy huge success in Italy was John Charles, who joined Juventus back in 1957 and gained legendary status through his 108 goals over 155 appearances, leading fans to vote him their best foreign player during the club's centenary in 1997. The next phase of the British invasion occurred in 1961 when three players made the move – Denis Law and Joe Baker to Torino and Jimmy Greaves to Milan. It's these transfers that started the rumour that British players couldn't settle in Italy.

Jimmy Greaves moved to Milan from Chelsea, where he had proved a proficient goalscorer. Despite being given a very attractive salary and signing-on bonus, he didn't want to leave London and tried to get out of the move. Once in Milan, he clashed with coach Nereo Rocco, a fierce disciplinarian who inflicted strict training regimes and rules on his squad. Greaves lasted just one season, appearing generally unmotivated to play, before returning to London for a great career with Tottenham Hotspur. Denis Law experienced similar woes at Torino, not enjoying the football and especially the defensive nature of Italian football. Like Greaves, he fell out with the coach and ended up forcing a move back to Manchester United, also after just one season. Joe Baker joined him on a plane home, heading to Arsenal after a year in Turin where he almost died after a serious car crash left him needing life-saving surgery, resulting from driving the wrong way around a roundabout. Law had been in the car too, but was less seriously injured.

Following on from the single-season exodus of that trio, one can't be too surprised that Italian clubs became wary of dipping into the British market. However, the option was removed in 1964 by the Italian Football Federation when they placed a ban on buying foreign players – a rule that stayed in place until 1980 when one foreigner was finally allowed. As discussed earlier, one of the first foreigners to arrive after the ban was lifted was Liam Brady, when he joined Juventus. But, given the one-player restriction, there was hardly a flood of British players travelling to Italy.

One early import was Joe Jordan, the Manchester United striker who moved to Milan in 1981, spending two seasons there, including a second in Serie B after their shock relegation. The sight of 'The Shark' or 'Jaws', depending which nickname you preferred, must have been quite a shock to the cool Italians as the 6ft 1in forward elbowed aside defenders, his front two teeth missing to reveal a menacing gap. After Jordan's move to Verona in 1983, Milan again went shopping in England for a striker, this time bringing in Luther Blissett from Watford. He lasted just one season and was another player to build the myth of non-compatibility when he said, 'No matter how much money you have here, you can't seem to get Rice Krispies,' which he claimed was a joke. After Blissett moved back to Watford, Milan next signed striker Mark Hateley for £1m, who at the time was playing in the English second division for Portsmouth. He lasted three seasons with the *Rossoneri*, scoring 19 goals in his first two – a decent return in the notoriously defensive Serie A. He carved himself a special place in the hearts of Milan fans by scoring a match-winning header against arch-rivals Inter in October 1984, the first time Milan had beaten Inter in the *Derby della Madonnina* for six years.

Hateley was joined by another countryman during his three-year stint at Milan. While he patrolled up front, one of his midfield suppliers was Ray Wilkins, who had enjoyed a successful career with Chelsea and Manchester United. By this time, he was an experienced England international, having played at the 1982 World Cup. On arriving in Milan, the first thing that struck Wilkins was the training intensity as, working with the coaching staff, he reduced his body fat to a level where he felt in the best shape of his career. His first two seasons were relatively successful but, with the arrival of Berlusconi and strengthening of the squad, he fell down the pecking order in his third, leading to a move at the season's end to PSG. *Corriere della Sera* praised him as a 'serious and meticulous professional who was immediately appreciated for his long and precise passes'.

Elsewhere during the 1980s, southern Italian club Bari also experimented with bringing in English talent in the shape of the double signing of Gordon Cowans and Paul Rideout in 1985, both from Aston Villa. Bari had just won promotion back to Serie

A and were looking to progress upwards. Cowans had enjoyed a stellar career with Aston Villa up to that point, playing for nine seasons in which he was an integral part of their First Division and European Cup-winning side as a midfielder. He had missed the 1983/84 season through injury, however, recuperating from a broken leg, and Bari bought him in the summer of 1985 for just £250,000. Cowans enjoyed three seasons with the *Biancorossi*, playing 94 times. Rideout, meanwhile, was a striker who had joined Aston Villa after their league and European success. Like Cowans, he played at Bari for three seasons, before moving back to Southampton, playing 99 times and netting 23 goals, a decent return. Sadly for Bari, the signings didn't prevent an immediate return to Serie B.

The other key English imports into Italy during the 1980s were Trevor Francis and Paul Elliott. We've already mentioned Francis at Sampdoria, where he played alongside Graeme Souness in their 1984/85 Coppa Italia-winning team. After four seasons with the *Blucerchiati,* he then spent one season at Atalanta, before heading to Glasgow Rangers to join Souness once again in the revolution he was building there. Paul Elliott was another who made the move from Aston Villa to Italy, joining Pisa in 1987 for two seasons in defence, and who also experienced relegation in his second season, as Pisa fell out of the top division.

As Serie A became the dominant European league in the late 1980s and early 1990s, there was less focus on British talent as Italian teams could attract stars from any country in the world, and British players weren't setting the world alight, either domestically or internationally. Of course, there was Gascoigne, as discussed earlier at Lazio, coming off his hugely successful Italia '90, but he didn't exactly help to strengthen the reputation of the British abroad. The only other two British players who earned moves had also attracted attention through strong Italia '90 performances – defender Des Walker and midfielder David Platt.

We talked earlier about the infamous tackle by Gascoigne on Nottingham Forest's Gary Charles in the 1991 FA Cup Final that so nearly scuppered his move to Lazio. Despite being stretchered off, Tottenham went on to win the final 2-1 after extra time. The winning goal didn't come from a Tottenham player but instead from a Forest defender – Des Walker. It was a rare error from a sublime defender.

Walker was in his eighth season at Forest when he stepped out for the FA Cup Final, having initially been part of the youth system at Tottenham. An outstanding player, blessed with great speed, he played one further season at Forest, at the end of which he was named in the PFA Team of the Year for a fourth successive season, having also won Forest's player of the season in three of his last six. His final season with Forest saw him score his only goal over 346 appearances, against Luton Town on New Year's Day 1992. Like Platt, he had enjoyed a successful Italia '90, starting in all seven games, his perfect timing of a tackle becoming his trademark. As the terrace chant went at the time: 'You'll never beat Des Walker!'

The summer of 1992 saw Sampdoria begin their slide from recent footballing heights. The legendary manager Vujadin Boškov, having failed to secure European football despite taking them to the European Cup Final, had been replaced with Sven-Göran Eriksson, and star striker Gianluca Vialli completed his world record transfer to Juventus. It was within this changing environment that Des Walker finally left Nottingham Forest, moving to Genoa for £1.5m. Like Sampdoria, he would struggle during that 1992/93 season as the club finished seventh, powered by the goals of Mancini. Walker started 27 times within the 34-game season but found himself often starting as a full-back, rather than his usual Forest and England position at the centre of defence. His Italian sojourn lasted just the one season, before he returned to Sheffield Wednesday for £2.7m, reviving his career across eight seasons in south Yorkshire.

After so many false starts and quick burns for British players in Italy, David Platt would become the poster boy for British success abroad. He had made a name for himself at Aston Villa (there seems to be a recurring theme of moving from Aston Villa to Italy, swapping the Brummie lifestyle for *la dolce vita*), joining them in February 1988 as a midfielder from Fourth Division Crewe to help the Villans win promotion back to the First Division. The 1989/90 season was an outstanding one for Platt as he powered Aston Villa into a battle for the First Division title, eventually coming second behind Liverpool. Platt scored 24 goals that season across all competitions, ending as the club's top scorer, despite being a midfielder, winning him the PFA Player of the Year award, along with a place in the England squad flying to Italy that summer.

A substitute during the first few games, he made a name for himself in the round of 16 match against Belgium when he replaced Steve McMahon in the 71st minute. With the game goalless and just one minute from a penalty shoot-out, Gascoigne floated a free kick into the Belgian area. As it came over Platt's shoulder, he swivelled before hitting a sumptuous volley to earn England victory, gaining him instant fame back home. In a 2010 interview, Platt recalled:

> If I hadn't scored that goal, I might still have ended up playing in Italy, but, realistically, I'm sure it was the catalyst. Italian clubs were looking for international names and, before that goal, I was only really known as a club player with Aston Villa.

That performance earned him starting berths in both the quarter-final against Cameroon, where he scored England's opener, and the semi-final against Germany, where he had a headed goal disallowed before converting his penalty in the shoot-out. He then scored his third of the tournament in the third-place play-off against Italy, ensuring many European eyes were now firmly focused on him.

The 1990/91 season saw him once more lead the Aston Villa goalscoring charts, again with 24 goals, but the Villans couldn't repeat their heroics of the previous year, only narrowly avoiding relegation. It was time for a change, and a move to Italy beckoned. As in the 1980s, southern club Bari would again bring over English talent.

Bari paid a not-inconsiderable £5.5m to sign Platt, making him captain. Once again, he showed his goalscoring ability, netting 11 times in his debut season within Serie A, but mirroring Cowans and Rideout's first seasons in Bari after Aston Villa, Bari were relegated. Unlike Cowans and Rideout, though, Platt wouldn't be sticking around to play in the lower division. Juventus were interested and waving around a £6.5m transfer fee. Platt was off to Turin.

It would prove to be a frustrating 12 months with the Old Lady. Injury issues, causing him to miss the period from November to February, along with a strong squad limited Platt to just 28 appearances across all competitions, scoring four goals. Signed at the same time as such talent as Gianluca Vialli, Andreas Möller, Dino Baggio and Fabrizio Ravanelli, he missed out on Juventus's UEFA Cup Final success against Borussia Dortmund, so it was no surprise when he moved on to his next adventure at the end of the season. He would remain in Italy, with Sampdoria picking him up next for £5.2m.

Platt's move to Sampdoria had been championed by their star player, Roberto Mancini, who sold the idea to owner Paolo Mantovani. The move meant that, in the space of just over two years, Italian clubs had spent a combined £17.2m on the England midfielder. His time at Sampdoria was once again enjoyable, playing under future England manager Sven-Göran Eriksson and scoring 21 goals in his two seasons, while helping Sampdoria lift the Coppa Italia in 1994 and reach the Cup Winners' Cup semi-final in 1995, before losing out to Arsenal on penalties.

It was at that point that Platt ended his four years in Italy, moving to Arsenal for £4.75m just ahead of the appointment of Arsène Wenger, taking his transfer tally up to almost £22m. He did return one more time in December 1998 when he took over the managerial reins at Sampdoria, but this time the affair ended quickly, with Platt sacked after just six matches in which he failed to register a win. He was probably England's most successful export into Italy since Liam Brady and Trevor Francis. Embracing the culture, he quickly became fluent in Italian and was greatly respected by fans at all three of his clubs. If Gascoigne was the embodiment of all the problems that could beset an Englishman in Italy, Platt was the opposite – a calm, enthusiastic presence who soaked in the local colour. A man who embraced *la dolce vita*.

Chapter 23

The Final Season

A 0-0 is boring. It's better to lose 5–4, at least it
gives you some excitement.

Zdeněk Zeman, former Roma and Lazio manager

AS THE end of the 1990s approached, Italian teams had dominated
European football, with success enjoyed by a range of clubs. There
were the obvious powerhouses of Milan, Inter and Juventus but
there were also traditionally less successful clubs such as Napoli,
Fiorentina, Sampdoria and Parma. But there was an obvious
omission – Italy's capital city, home to not one but two teams in
Roma and Lazio. As the other major Italian teams conquered at
home and abroad, what was happening in the Eternal City?

Roma had started the 1990s with the earlier discussed UEFA
Cup Final where they suffered defeat to Inter, Rudi Völler's goals
having taken them there, along with winning the Coppa Italia.
But from that point on it had just been continual frustration. The
1990s saw Roma finish no higher than fourth in Serie A and their
only European involvement was a few UEFA Cup campaigns,
where they progressed no further than the quarter-finals. Between
1990 and 1999, four different managers failed to bring success
to the *Giallorossi*, unable to even win another Coppa Italia. The
only excitement that Roma fans would enjoy during this barren
period was the two seasons of 1998 and 1999 when Zdeněk Zeman
was manager.

Brought in from city rivals Lazio, Zeman came with an attacking
philosophy, setting Roma up in a 4-3-3, rare in an Italian league
that was still predominantly defensively minded. His first season
in charge would see Roma finish fourth, their best performance

since 1988, as they scored 67 Serie A goals, making them joint-top scorers alongside champions Juventus. It meant that Roma finished above Lazio for the first time in five years, despite Lazio winning both head-to-head games during the season, as well as eliminating Roma from the Coppa Italia. Notably, 13 of those goals had come from a young 21-year-old who, in his first breakout season, had made himself a first-team regular under Zeman. Those 13 would be just a drop in the ocean as Francesco Totti would go on to score 250 goals across 619 appearances for the *Giallorossi*, making him a fully fledged Roma legend.

* * *

Lazio, meanwhile, spent the 1990s gradually building a strong team. Having suffered the indignation of playing the majority of the 1980s in Serie B, due to both poor performances and punishment for involvement in 1986's *Totonero* scandal, they had started the new decade under the management of Dino Zoff. Over the first two seasons, Lazio continued to stagnate, finishing 11th and tenth. But then, in March 1992, came the moment that would change Lazio's world.

Sergio Cragnotti was an Italian businessman who headed the food conglomerate Cirio. Like so many successful Italian businessmen before him, he wanted to invest his wealth in a sexier product, so, in March 1992, he acquired Lazio. Like other Italian clubs of this era, Lazio now had an owner who wasn't afraid to spend big on attracting star talent. A new era would commence for the Eagles.

Cragnotti's first full season as owner saw the earlier discussed high-profile signing of Paul Gascoigne but it would be a lower-profile signing that summer that would have a greater impact on the team. Giuseppe 'Beppe' Signori had been making a name for himself at Foggia, where his 37 goals over 100 appearances convinced Lazio to buy him. A hard-working, fast, left-footed striker, his goals would spark the initial Lazio revolution.

Zoff's first season under Cragnotti saw Lazio finish a respectable fifth as Signori hit the track running, banging in 26 Serie A goals to earn the *Capocannoniere* by five clear goals, ahead of such talent as Roberto Baggio, Rubén Sosa and Gabriel Batistuta.

That was sufficient to earn Lazio a UEFA Cup place, thus making their first foray into Europe since 1977, and earn Zoff another season at the helm.

Unfortunately for Lazio, that first UEFA Cup excursion saw them eliminated in the second round by Boavista. They also suffered an embarrassing first-round Coppa Italia elimination at the hands of lowly Avellino. Despite Cragnotti financing the purchases of strikers Pierluigi Casiraghi and Alen Bokšić, they were still completely reliant on Signori, whose 23 Serie A goals compared to five from the next-highest Lazio goalscorer, Roberto Cravero, helped them to a fourth-place Serie A finish. It wasn't enough for the ambitious owner, leading to the end of Zoff's four seasons in charge. Lazio fans would now experience Zemanball.

Zdeněk Zeman was a Czech who had never played the game professionally yet started a coaching career in Sicily before taking over at Serie C club Foggia in 1989. He immediately put in place his favoured 4-3-3 formation, with a high back line, encouraging attacking, entertaining football, which he always believed was more important than the result. The three front players weren't traditional wingers and a striker but more like three strikers playing close together. His approach yielded immediate results as Foggia won back-to-back promotions to Serie A, after which they stunned pundits by finishing ninth in their debut season, earning them the nickname *Foggia dei Miracoli* as they became press darlings with their attacking style, even flirting with a European place for a while. That style also earned its own nickname, becoming identified as *Zemanlandia*. The kamikaze nature of their games was demonstrated by their season-end statistics: 58 goals for (second behind champions Milan), 58 goals against (second behind last-placed Ascoli). A perfect example was their last game of the season where, leading 2-1 at half-time against Milan, they proceeded to lose 8-2. Whatever you thought of *Zemanlandia*, it was entertaining.

Zeman kept Foggia in Serie A over the next two seasons, despite his best players being poached and having insufficient funds to replace them adequately. And it was that continued success, along with the playing style, that attracted him to Cragnotti. With Zoff out, Zeman made the jump from managing Foggia to the big league.

His first season in charge saw him exploit Lazio's attacking potential to the full, continuing to play his brand of attack and high defensive line. He also brought along his tough training regime, which created friction between himself and Gascoigne. While Signori continued to be the main man, hitting 17 Serie A goals, Casiraghi and Bokšić now both contributed materially, with 12 and nine, respectively.

Lazio tore into opponents, thrashing Napoli 5-1, Milan 4-0, Fiorentina 8-2, Juventus 3-0 and, most ironically, Foggia 7-1, with all seven goals scored in the second half. By the season's end, they had scored a league-leading 69 goals over 34 games. It was a huge improvement but not enough to prevent Lippi's Juventus lifting the title, yet Cragnotti could proudly reflect on a second-place finish. The football had been exciting, yielding results, and finally Lazio fans could dream of pushing on and challenging for a first Scudetto since 1974.

Considering Signori's 76 goals during his three seasons with Lazio, Cragnotti, ever the businessman, thought it might be the ideal time to cash out, while the striker's stock was high. A deal was put in place to sell Signori to Parma for 25 billion lire as well as Pippo Inzaghi and Dino Baggio. However, Cragnotti hadn't factored in the reaction of others to losing their talisman, as 5,000 fans demonstrated against the move in the streets, sporting director Zoff pointed out what a loss it would represent and even banks assured Cragnotti that they would cover debts if Signori stayed. Signori wanted to stay, too – so stay he did.

While Zeman's football continued to entertain during 1995/96, Lazio couldn't build on the previous campaign. Their UEFA Cup adventure ended early when eliminated by Lyon in the second round, while Inter defeated them in the Coppa Italia quarter-finals. The league continued to see them in free-scoring mode, putting six past Sampdoria, five past Atalanta and four past Juventus and Fiorentina as they again ended the season as top scorers with 66 goals. Signori continued his hot streak, netting another 24 Serie A goals to end as joint *Capocannoniere* alongside Bari's Igor Protti, but it still only earned Lazio a third-place finish, behind Capello's Milan and Lippi's Juventus. It was good by historic Lazio standards, but was it good enough for Cragnotti?

If you already own the season's joint-top goalscorer, then what could be better than partnering him with the season's other joint-top goalscorer? Well, that's what Cragnotti thought too, as Lazio swooped to add Protti to their line-up, as well as signing emerging star Czech international Pavel Nedvěd, coming off the back of an impressive Euro performance. Everything was in place for a strong 1996/97 as the season commenced.

The remainder of 1996 couldn't have gone worse for Lazio. In the Coppa Italia, they were eliminated in the quarter-finals by Napoli. In the UEFA Cup, they fell at the second hurdle, eliminated by Spanish minnows Tenerife when, having won their home leg 1-0, they travelled to Spain and were 3-3 early in the second half, only to keep pushing forward in true Zeman style, allowing Tenerife to win 5-3. And their Serie A form wasn't much better. Losing four of their first eight games left Lazio in 14th, which only improved to tenth by the time 1996 ended. They weren't even scoring many goals anymore. The Zeman magic had worn off and Cragnotti was quick to act, when, on 27 January 1997, he relieved Zeman of his duties, and Zoff, the club's sporting director, returned to guide Lazio to the end of the season until a permanent replacement could be appointed.

Zoff's return did lead to an improvement on the pitch as Lazio started scoring again, allowing them to finish fourth and secure a UEFA Cup spot, while Signori once again finished top scorer with 15 Serie A goals. The question now was who would be in charge for the upcoming campaign?

* * *

Swede Sven-Göran Eriksson had established himself as a top coach in Italy since arriving at Roma in 1984. His résumé to date included Roma, Fiorentina and Sampdoria, during which time he had won two Coppa Italia trophies, while also returning briefly to Benfica and taking them to a European Cup Final. In December 1996, he announced his intention to leave as Sampdoria coach at the season's end and head over to England and Blackburn Rovers, who had won the Premier League in 1995. But he then went back on his word, affirming in February that he would stay in Italy to become manager of Lazio, stating family reasons. Therefore, as the 1997/98 season began, the Swede sat in charge.

The first thing he did was bring over his Sampdoria captain, Roberto Mancini, as well as signing Vladimir Jugović from Juventus and bringing back Alen Bokšić, also from the Old Lady. Tactically, Zeman's attacking 4-3-3 was also ditched, replaced by Eriksson's more pragmatic 4-4-2.

Unsurprisingly, it took a while for the Lazio squad to adapt to Eriksson's leadership, losing four of their first 11 Serie A matches to place them ninth but at least securing a 3-1 victory away at Roma. Playing Mancini, Casiraghi and Bokšić saw Eriksson move Signori to the bench, something the Lazio hitman found hard to stomach. The breaking point came after a disagreement over a substitution in late November when Lazio travelled to Vienna to play Rapid Wien in the UEFA Cup, with Signori told to warm up for 30 minutes and then not used. Relations had broken down irrevocably, Eriksson recalling in an interview with *The Guardian*: 'I couldn't have him at the club. A very good striker, but he had a negative attitude.' A loan to Sampdoria followed, where he would ironically slot into Mancini's old position, before being sold to Bologna at the end of the season.

It was a sad end for such a great Lazio servant, three-time *Capocannoniere* and finisher of 126 goals, predominantly over five seasons, placing him third in the list of Lazio's all-time goalscorers. Known particularly for his one-step penalty, he put his technique down to watching darts players, who employed no 'run-up'. Being brought into the team to replace Sosa was a big challenge but one that he met admirably. He hadn't even started his career as a striker. Instead, it was Zeman while at Foggia who moved him into the role and his scoring had probably kept Zeman in his job during a lean spell for the club. His goals were rarely dramatic, but he had the knack of being at the right place at the right time, exhibiting great speed of thought.

But while Lazio's 1997/98 Serie A start was spluttering, they had progressed to the quarter-finals of both the UEFA Cup and Coppa Italia. It was then, following a 2-1 Serie A loss to Juventus, that the Eagles suddenly took off. The next three and a half months would represent an incredible time for Lazio supporters.

Their Serie A campaign saw them go on a 16-game unbeaten streak, including 12 wins, propelling them up to third in the standings, just two points behind leaders Juventus, who they were scheduled to face next on 5 April. Within the run was another satisfying victory over Roma, but even sweeter than that was eliminating the *Giallorossi* in the Coppa Italia with wins in both home and away legs, before then defeating Juventus to book an April final against Milan. And if that wasn't enough, a UEFA Cup semi-final spot had also been secured by dispatching Auxerre. For over 100 days, everything went perfectly for Eriksson, and as they emerged for the league game against Juventus, fans could even dream of a possible treble. Sadly, it's the hope that kills.

With over 70,000 Lazio fans filling the Stadio Olimpico, and under the experienced eye of referee Pierluigi Collina, the top-of-the-table clash got underway. An impressive Lazio *tifo* had greeted the players as the supporters whipped up a red-hot atmosphere. But it was Juventus, through Inzaghi, who took the lead after an hour. To compound their troubles, Nedvěd then earned himself a second yellow with 14 minutes remaining. Juventus left Rome with a vital win and, with that, Lazio's league form completely dissolved. With six games left, they lost five and drew the other, dropping from third to finish the season in seventh – a spectacular collapse. Fans could only watch in horror, turning their attention instead to the cup competitions.

First up was the UEFA Cup semi-final against Atlético Madrid, where a Jugović goal in Spain was enough to see Lazio through to the final. Then came the two-legged Coppa Italia Final. Playing first in Milan, it looked like Lazio would come away with a credible goalless draw until George Weah grabbed a last-minute winner. Back in Rome, things looked even bleaker after Demetrio Albertini doubled Milan's aggregate lead early in the second half. But a spirited fightback from the Eagles saw them turn the game around with three goals in ten minutes, securing Lazio's first trophy since the 1974 Scudetto. Eriksson had given Cragnotti his first silverware as owner.

The UEFA Cup Final was an all-Italian affair as Lazio faced Inter and, as discussed, the first single-legged final saw Inter completely dominate Lazio, running out 3-0 winners with Ronaldo playing in his pomp. But Eriksson, and more importantly Cragnotti, could look back on a strong season. After so long in the doldrums,

Cragnotti's investment and Eriksson's leadership had delivered a Coppa Italia trophy, a UEFA Cup Final appearance and a league campaign that had seen Lazio compete until late in the season. Lazio had joined the list of Italian clubs performing strongly on the European stage.

* * *

Despite Signori's sale to Bologna, Lazio's strike force still consisted of Mancini, Casiraghi and Bokšić. The summer of 1998 would see Eriksson's attacking options strengthened even further. While Casiraghi departed for Chelsea, he was replaced by two talented strikers. Christian Vieri had moved from Juventus to Atlético Madrid in the summer of 1997 for £12.5m as chairman Jesús Gil went on a spending spree, and his initial season there had seen him win the Pichichi Trophy with 24 league goals in 24 appearances, five ahead of Barcelona's Rivaldo. However, he wasn't happy in Spain, leading Cragnotti to splash out £17m to bring him to Rome.

Chilean striker Marcelo Salas, meanwhile, had started his career at local team Universidad de Chile, where a strong 1996 Copa Libertadores saw him earn a move to River Plate. Two seasons there saw him help them win several trophies, while also being named South American Footballer of the Year in 1997. Out came Cragnotti's chequebook again and in came Salas for a cool $20.5m.

Add to those the signings of Siniša Mihajlović from Sampdoria, Sérgio Conceição from Porto and Dejan Stanković from Red Star Belgrade and Eriksson had a formidable squad for the campaign ahead. However, Lazio were unconvincing for the first three months of the new season, losing three of their first 11 Serie A games to sit in tenth, while at least getting through the first two rounds of the Cup Winners' Cup, albeit narrowly against Lausanne-Sport and Partizan. November ended with a painful *Derby della Capitale*, which saw Lazio leading ten-man Roma 3-1 with 12 minutes remaining, only to end in a draw.

While alarm bells may have been ringing at this stage, everything suddenly then clicked for the Eagles. Across the next four months from the start of December to the end of March, Lazio played 15 Serie A games and won 13 of them, while drawing the other two. While Mancini, Salas and Vieri led the goalscoring, Mihajlović also contributed through his incredible ability at free kicks. As Eriksson once commented, 'With him, having a free kick was like having a penalty. When players used to get fouled near the box they would scream for a penalty, but Siniša would say, "What are you worried for? I'll score," and usually he did!' Mihajlović would end his career as the leading scorer of free kicks in Serie A history. The run took Lazio to the top of the Serie A standings, five points ahead of Fiorentina and seven ahead of Milan, with eight games remaining.

April saw Lazio facing three vital games in successive weeks. First up was a home game against third-placed Milan, which ended goalless, cementing the seven-point gap. But next was the *Derby della Capitale* in front of 75,000 at the Stadio Olimpico, Roma playing as the nominal home team – a Roma team that would enjoy nothing more than derailing Lazio's Scudetto dream. The atmosphere was off the charts, even by Italian football standards.

Roma got off to a dream start when Marco Delvecchio rifled them ahead after just 13 minutes to send the Roma faithful into ecstasy. Then, just before half-time, Delvecchio placed himself into Roma legend, sliding home from close range after a Totti short-corner routine. As the game heated up and Lazio grew more desperate, Mihajlović and Roma's Paulo Sérgio received their marching orders, before Vieri tapped home with 11 minutes remaining to give Lazio a lifeline. It wasn't to be. Alessandro Nesta joined Mihajlović in the Lazio changing room after receiving a straight red for a professional foul, before Totti inflicted the final wound, scrambling home Roma's third in the final minute. It was a devastating loss, allowing Milan to move to just four points behind them, made worse by being against their mortal enemies.

Lazio desperately needed to bounce back in their next fixture, at home to Juventus, but a Thierry Henry double saw the Eagles defeated 3-1 again, while Milan thrashed Udinese 5-1 to pull to within a point of them. With five games remaining, it looked like Lazio were cracking. But three wins in succession got them back on track, although Milan matched them to maintain the one-point gap. Two games remaining – all Lazio had to do was win both and the Scudetto was theirs.

On 15 May 1999, the Eagles travelled up to Florence for their last away game. It took just 14 minutes for Fiorentina to open the scoring, inevitably through the ever-reliable Batistuta, lashing the ball into the corner. But Lazio didn't panic, Mihajlović floating a free kick into Vieri for a first-half equaliser. With Milan winning their game, though, Lazio needed to push for a victory.

The second half saw Vieri hit the crossbar before Batistuta drew a penalty with 18 minutes remaining. With Lazio staring at possible defeat, Marchegiani saved from Rui Costa to keep the dream alive, but, try as they might, Lazio couldn't find a winner. As news filtered through that Milan had beaten Empoli 4-0, the fate of the Scudetto no longer lay in Lazio's hands. They would need to beat Parma on the final day and pray that lowly Perugia could prevent a Milan win.

But before that, the Lazio players had to pick themselves up to play a Cup Winners' Cup Final. Since the turn of the year, they had thrashed Greek side Panionios in the quarter-finals by a 7-0 aggregate, Stanković netting three and Nedvěd two, before then getting past a tough Lokomotiv Moscow side on away goals. That set up a final against Mallorca, who had somewhat surprisingly overcome Chelsea in the semi-finals.

Both teams lined up in a 4-4-2 at Villa Park for what would be the last-ever Cup Winners' Cup Final. Starting at a frantic pace, it took just seven minutes for Vieri to chase down a long ball and send a lobbed header over Mallorca's keeper, and it took just four minutes more for Dani to poke in an equaliser. From then on, the game became cagier, both sides creating chances until the deadlock was broken with just nine minutes remaining. A loose ball on the edge of the area fell to Nedvěd, who spun and volleyed into the bottom corner. Lazio had won their first, and at time of writing still only, European trophy. With their Serie A title hopes fading, it represented a great moment for the club and Eriksson, who summed it up thus:

> I feel very happy. This is Lazio's first win in Europe. This is also the last Cup Winners' Cup so the trophy is ours forever. No one can take it away from us. It was a very good game. Mallorca are a very good team but we deserved it. We've only lost one match in Europe in the last two seasons and that was last year's UEFA Cup Final against Inter.

With the knowledge that they had at least secured European glory, thoughts turned back to the final-day Serie A drama. Ahead of the weekend, Eriksson mused:

> We'll try to beat Parma and see if it's enough for us to be champions of Italy; whatever happens, we've had an extremely good season. We're undefeated in Europe, we won the Italian Super Cup and we're fighting for the league title to the end.

Going into half-time, Lazio were one up against Parma through Salas, but Milan sat 2-0 up at Perugia. Parma equalised early in the second half, but Salas restored Lazio's advantage with 14 minutes remaining. From that point on, all Lazio fans could do was sit glued to their radios, and with 11 minutes remaining, a glimmer of hope appeared as Perugia pulled a goal back through a penalty. One more, Lazio fans prayed for just one more Perugia goal. It didn't come and Zaccheroni's Milan took the title by a single point.

Despite their Serie A disappointment, Lazio fans could bask in European glory, especially considering Roma's continued drought. Lazio had added another Italian club to the list of European champions during this period, continuing the country's dominance on the biggest stages. And as for the Serie A heartbreak, they would only have to wait another 12 months for that to be rectified.

* * *

While the final season of the decade had seen Lazio winning the Cup Winners' Cup, another Italian club was also making waves in Europe. Following on from their 1994/95 UEFA Cup glory discussed earlier, the following season saw Parma eliminated in the quarter-finals of the Cup Winners' Cup by PSG in a year when they finished a respectable sixth in Serie A. The start of the season had seen some notable additions to the squad, particularly Hristo Stoichkov from Barcelona, Fabio Cannavaro from Napoli and Filippo Inzaghi from Piacenza, as well as the debut of a young goalkeeping talent on 19 November 1995, who made his mark by saving a penalty in a 0-0 draw against Milan – 17-year-old Gianluigi Buffon.

The 1996/97 season saw Nevio Scala step down as manager, replaced by Carlo Ancelotti, and several material changes to the squad. Significant talent came in, including Lilian Thuram from AS Monaco, Enrico Chiesa from Sampdoria and a young Hernán Crespo arriving from River Plate, while key players leaving included Hristo Stoichkov and Fernando Couto heading to Barcelona, Filippo Inzaghi heading to Atalanta and Faustino Asprilla heading off on loan to Newcastle. The season started badly, with Parma eliminated in the first round of both the Coppa Italia by Pescara and then the first round of the UEFA Cup by Portuguese side Vitória de Guimarães, and sitting 14th in Serie A just before the end of the year.

To add to new manager Ancelotti's woes, he had changed Parma's formation, switching to a rigid 4-4-2 in which new boys Chiesa and Crespo played up front, meaning less game time for Parma hero Zola, given a wide midfield position when in the team. Parma were having problems adapting to this new set-up, as proven by their early results, and it also caused resentment from Zola. Over in London, Ruud Gullit was busy starting an international revolution at Chelsea and, having already signed Gianluca Vialli from Juventus over the summer, he saw an opportunity to swoop in and add Zola to his squad, paying £4.5m for the Sicilian wizard in November 1996. It would prove to be a masterstroke of business for the Blues, Zola playing for seven seasons in West London, where he attained cult status.

December would also see the return of a familiar face to the Stadio Ennio Tardini as Tomas Brolin returned home from Leeds United, where he was having a torrid time. Injuries, poor performances and clashes with management had seen the Swede effectively frozen out, leading to Brolin funding a loan back to Italy from his own pocket. It wouldn't work out well for him back in Parma either, playing only sporadically across the rest of the season before ending the loan agreement.

Although 14th towards the end of December, the Parma players eventually began to adapt to Ancelotti's ways and proceeded to tear through the remainder of the season. They won 15 of their last 21 league matches, losing only three, to almost chase down Juventus, finishing just two points behind them in second place. It was an extraordinary turnaround, driven by the emergence of the Chiesa/ Crespo partnership, who ended up scoring 26 Serie A goals between them, although the *Capocannoniere* went to old boy Ingazhi in his first season at Atalanta. To this day, it's still Parma's highest Serie A placing.

Asprilla returned in 1997/98, while the most significant new signing was the £9m paid for Jesper Blomqvist from Milan. Their second-place finish the season before had earned Parma a place in the Champions League qualifying second round, where they easily dispatched Widzew Łódź to reach the lucrative group phase. There they would finish second behind a strong Borussia Dortmund, who reached the semi-finals, thus ending Parma's European journey, in a season that would also see them come sixth in Serie A and reach the semi-final of the Coppa Italia, denied a place in the final by a stoppage-time Kluivert goal for Milan. But by pipping Lazio to the sixth-placed finish by just one point, Parma had ensured more European football the following season, albeit back in the UEFA Cup.

However, that finish was not seen as adequate by the Parma management, so Ancelotti was dismissed and replaced by Alberto Malesani, a former photocopier salesman turned manager, poached from Fiorentina. Following on from the 1998 World Cup in France, Parma again splashed the cash, this time investing £15m to bring over Argentine midfielder Juan Sebastián Verón from Sampdoria. The squad was now ready for another attempt at European success.

Their 1998/99 UEFA Cup campaign began with straightforward wins over Fenerbahçe of Turkey and Wisła Kraków of Poland before overcoming stronger opposition in Glasgow Rangers in the third round. That earned Parma a quarter-final tie against Bordeaux where they hit their first road bump, losing 2-1 in France, while also losing Antonio Benarrivo for the second leg to a red card. However, the second leg would prove to be a notable night in Parma's history.

Parma initially had trouble breaking down a well-organised Bordeaux defence. But as half-time loomed, Crespo levelled the tie on aggregate. Bordeaux needed to hold on to the break and reassess but, just three minutes after Crespo's opener, Enrico Chiesa (father of ex-Juventus and now Liverpool striker Federico Chiesa) rifled a low shot from distance into the bottom corner to double Parma's advantage.

The second half immediately continued in the same vein as Roberto Sensini headed home a Verón free kick. With the Stadio Ennio Tardini bouncing, Chiesa grabbed his second after Bordeaux gave the ball away in midfield, allowing him to break away. Bordeaux were struggling to stay afloat, and Parma continued to take advantage, Crespo next grabbing his second and Parma's fifth with 25 minutes still remaining. The final humiliation came in the dying minutes, when Parma were awarded an unjust penalty that Abel Balbo converted. A historic European night had seen Parma put six unanswered goals past the French.

Parma's reward for such a fine performance was a semi-final clash against Atlético Madrid. The trip to the Calderón opened with a magnificently chipped goal from Chiesa before a questionable penalty allowed Juninho to level. Then, just before half-time, Chiesa struck again, his header hitting the bar before then converting the rebound. The tie was all but settled when Crespo added a typical goal poacher's third, allowing Parma to return to Italy with a significant advantage. An uneventful 2-1 return leg saw Parma once again in a UEFA Cup Final, just four years after defeating Juventus.

Ahead of the final, Parma secured their second-ever Coppa Italia, defeating Fiorentina on away goals, Crespo grabbing two of their three goals. With a fourth place in Serie A also locked up, they had secured Champions League football for the following season. Could the UEFA Cup be the icing on the cake?

There was the possibility of another all-Italian final as Bologna met Marseille in the other semi-final. After a goalless draw in France, Bologna were four minutes from facing Parma, holding a 1-0 lead, until Marseille were awarded a penalty that Laurent Blanc converted to deprive Bologna at the death. It was a questionable decision and, unsurprisingly, tempers then boiled over, as a huge post-game fight broke out between both sets of players, also involving officials and fans, which required the intervention of riot police among a sea of flares.

UEFA were not amused. Bologna's Amedeo Mangone was suspended for five European games, and team-mate Giampiero Maini was suspended for three games. Marseille star forward

Christophe Dugarry was barred for five matches, and team-mate Hamada Jambay for four. Meanwhile, the French club's coach, Rolland Courbis, was fined $3,300 for statements made to the media, while his son, Stephane, was briefly held by police for his role in the fight and suspended from all functions connected with UEFA matches for one year. Finally, Bologna's Giancarlo Marocchi received a four-match suspension for the red card he received during the match itself. What it meant was that, in the final, Marseille would be without Dugarry and Jambay, as well as three other key players who had received second yellow suspensions in the semi-final second leg.

The final took place at the Luzhniki Stadium in Moscow, attracting a crowd of 61,000. Given their absentees, Marseille started in a defensive nature, only sporadically venturing out of their own half. But eventually, after 25 minutes, they made a mistake, captain Laurent Blanc trying a casual header back to his keeper, only for Crespo to steal in and lob Stéphane Porato. Parma continued to dominate and went two ahead just 11 minutes later through a powerful header from Paolo Vanoli. From then on, Marseille had no way back, Chiesa lashing a third past a deflated Porato early in the second half to wrap up the match. Malesani had led Parma to their third European trophy of the decade – and Italian clubs had won two of the three European trophies in 1998/99. It appeared that the 1990s were ending just as they had started – Italian football on top of the world. No other European country could touch them.

LAZIO (1997–1999)
Cup Winners' Cup winners – 1998/99
UEFA Cup runners-up – 1997/98
European Super Cup winners – 1999
Coppa Italia winners – 1997/98

PARMA (1995–1999)
UEFA Cup winners – 1998/99
Coppa Italia winners – 1998/99

Chapter 24
The Facts and Nothing but the Facts

The 1990s Serie A is 100 per cent better than today's Premier League without a doubt. Teams like Man United don't have great players. Compare that to Serie A ... people know about Baggio, Batistuta, Zidane, Conte, Roberto Carlos, Weah, Baresi and Paolo Maldini. They were great, great players!

Paul Ince, former Inter player

HOPEFULLY THE preceding chapters on Italian football between 1988 and 1999 have convinced you that this was indeed a special time for *Calcio*. We've looked at the teams and how they each came to the fore across the 11 seasons, hitting in waves. Whenever one team faded, another came along to take up the mantle, suffocating the rest of Europe. But, like anyone presenting their thesis, I would like to take the opportunity to summarise the case, backed up by some cold, hard statistics. So here, gentlemen and ladies of the jury, is why Italian football from 1988 to 1999 should be venerated and why it remains the Sistine Chapel of the game, alongside the Sagrada Familia that is 2010s Spanish football.

1970 until Heysel

	European Cup				Cup Winners' Cup				UEFA Cup			
1970/71	Ajax	2	Panathinaikos	0	Chelsea	2	Real Madrid	1	Leeds	3	Juventus	3
1971/72	Ajax	2	Inter Milan	0	Rangers	3	Dynamo Moscow	2	Tottenham	3	Wolves	2
1972/73	Ajax	1	Juventus	0	AC Milan	1	Leeds	0	Liverpool	3	Borussia Mönchengladbach	2
1973/74	Bayern Munich	4	Atlético Madrid	0	Magdeburg	2	AC Milan	0	Feyenoord	4	Tottenham	2
1974/75	Bayern Munich	2	Leeds	0	Dynamo Kyiv	3	Ferencvaros	0	Borussia Mönchengladbach	5	Twente	1
1975/76	Bayern Munich	1	St Étienne	0	Anderlecht	4	West Ham	2	Liverpool	4	Brugge	3
1976/77	Liverpool	3	Borussia Mönchengladbach	1	Hamburg SV	2	Anderlecht	0	Juventus	2	Athletic Bilbao	2
1977/78	Liverpool	1	Brugge	0	Anderlecht	4	Austria Vienna	0	PSV Eindhoven	3	SEC Bastia	0
1978/79	Nottm Forest	1	Malmo	0	Barcelona	4	Fortuna Dusseldorf	3	Borussia Mönchengladbach	2	Red Star Belgrade	1
1979/80	Nottm Forest	1	Hamburg SV	0	Valencia	0	Arsenal	0	Eintracht Frankfurt	3	Borussia Mönchengladbach	3
1980/81	Liverpool	1	Real Madrid	0	Dinamo Tbilisi	2	Carl Zeiss Jena	1	Ipswich	5	AZ	4
1981/82	Aston Villa	1	Bayern Munich	0	Barcelona	2	Standard Liege	1	IFK Göteberg	4	Hamburg	0
1982/83	Hamburg SV	1	Juventus	0	Aberdeen	2	Real Madrid	1	Anderlecht	2	Benfica	1
1983/84	Liverpool	1	Roma	1	Juventus	2	Porto	1	Tottenham	2	Anderlecht	2

309

As discussed in the early chapters, the early 1970s saw supremacy of the European Cup rest with just two teams: Ajax and Bayern Munich. For each to win the toughest European competition three times successively was an impressive feat. In fact, since that era, the only other team who have managed this is Real Madrid from 2015/16 to 2017/18. Those six years from 1971 to 1976 saw Italy win only one trophy, Milan's success in the 1973 Cup Winners' Cup, while British teams, despite no success in the European Cup, were proving their worth with two Cup Winners' Cup and four UEFA Cup wins. But those trophies would act as the springboard for success in the big one.

From 1976/77 to 1983/84, English teams enjoyed outstanding success in the European Cup. Liverpool had been knocking at the door with their two UEFA Cup wins and now converted that European experience into winning four European Cups in the space of eight seasons under the leadership of Bob Paisley and Joe Fagan, both of whom had come through the fabled Boot Room developed by the inspirational Bill Shankly. Incredibly, Nottingham Forest also won back-to-back European Cups in a manner that beggars belief today. Narrowly promoted to the English First Division, they won the English league at their first attempt and then immediately added two successive European Cups, all under the eyes of the great Brian Clough, along with Peter Taylor. To this day, they have won more European Cups than league titles, an amazing statistic. Even Aston Villa got in on the act, defeating a strong Bayern Munich. Seven finals involving English clubs and seven wins. Remarkable.

And it wasn't just the European Cup that British clubs were lifting. Teams such as Alex Ferguson's Aberdeen, Bobby Robson's Ipswich and Keith Burkinshaw's Tottenham Hotspur enjoyed success in the other two competitions. Meanwhile, the only Italian team to make any serious impact during this time was Juventus. But even when reaching the only European Cup Final that didn't involve the English, they still spurned the opportunity, losing to Hamburg.

The 1984/85 season saw Liverpool once again reach the European Cup Final, while city rivals Everton secured the Cup Winners' Cup under Howard Kendall. The chance to make it eight out of nine English final wins. And then came the horrific events of Heysel.

The subsequent five-year ban from all European competition for English clubs changed the landscape completely. With the dominant nation suddenly sidelined, a vacuum existed for others to occupy.

1985/86 to 1987/88

European Cup				Cup Winners' Cup				UEFA Cup			
1985/86	Steaua Bucherest 0	Barcelona	0	Dynamo Kyiv	3	Atlético Madrid	0	Real Madrid	5	FC Köln	3
1986/87	Porto 2	Bayern Munich 1		Ajax	1	Lokomotive Leipzig	0	IFK Göteberg	2	Dundee Utd	1
1987/88	PSV Eindhoven 0	Benfica	0	Mechelen	1	Ajax	0	Bayer Leverkusen	3	Espanyol	3

Immediately following the English ban, European football entered a period where no major country took control. For three seasons, it felt like any team from anywhere could succeed. The European Cup was won by sides from Romania, Portugal and the Netherlands, where all three clubs had never lifted the trophy before. In the Cup Winners' Cup, Dynamo Kyiv and Belgian side Mechelen enjoyed triumphs, while Lokomotive Leipzig reached a final. The UEFA Cup saw finals involving IFK Gothenburg, Dundee United and Espanol. No Italian teams reached any of the nine finals – not even Juventus. There was no clue of what was about to befall European football.

1988/89 to 1998/99

European Cup				Cup Winners' Cup				UEFA Cup			
1988/89	AC Milan	4	Steaua Bucherest 0	Barcelona	2	Sampdoria	0	Napoli	5	Stuttgart	4
1989/90	AC Milan	1	Benfica	0	Sampdoria	2	Anderlecht	0	Juventus	3	Fiorentina	1
1990/91	Red Star Belgrade	0	Marseille	0	Man Utd	2	Barcelona	1	Inter Milan	2	Roma	1
1991/92	Barcelona	1	Sampdoria	0	Werder Bremen	2	Monaco	0	Ajax	2	Torino	2
1992/93	Marseille	1	AC Milan	0	Parma	3	Royal Antwerp	1	Juventus	6	Borussia Dortmund	1
1993/94	AC Milan	4	Barcelona	0	Arsenal	1	Parma	0	Inter Milan	2	Austria Salzburg	0
1994/95	Ajax	1	AC Milan	0	Real Zaragoza	2	Arsenal	1	Parma	2	Juventus	1
1995/96	Juventus	1	Ajax	1	PSG	1	Rapid Wien	0	Bayern Munich 5		Bordeaux	2
1996/97	Borussia Dortmund 3		Juventus	1	Barcelona	1	PSG	0	Schalke 04	1	Inter Milan	1
1997/98	Real Madrid	1	Juventus	0	Chelsea	1	Stuttgart	0	Inter Milan	3	Lazio	0
1998/99	Man Utd	2	Bayern Munich	1	Lazio	2	Mallorca	1	Parma	3	Marseille	0

You could say it all began with ownership and money. If you look at the start of this successful era, it starred three clubs, all of whom took on owners willing to invest in the team. Napoli kicked things off, when they raised enough to make Diego Maradona the highest transfer in football history at the time, £3m. Where exactly the money came from is still somewhat of a mystery, but owner Corrado Ferlaino coordinated it somehow. Then there was the famous purchase of Milan by Silvio Berlusconi, whose funding permitted bringing in the likes of Ruud Gullit, Marco van Basten and Frank Rijkaard. Sampdoria, meanwhile, had their benefactor in owner Paolo Mantovani. And the list would continue – Parmolat at Parma, the Agnelli family at Juventus, Moratti at Inter and Cragnotti at Lazio. Serie A was awash with money. It could afford to attract top talent from around the world. But the other side of that equation was whether top talent would want to come to Italy.

Let's consider the Italian lifestyle. If you're a young talented footballer, making good money, Italy has a lot going for it. Nightlife, glamour, food, culture, weather – there's a reason that playboys live in Italy and the south of France rather than Berlin. And then it becomes a snowball effect. Italy has the money and lifestyle to attract top talent, top talent comes to play in Serie A, Serie A teams become the best in the world, winning trophies, and therefore top talent wants to play in the best league and for the best teams in the world. If you're a talented player in, say, Argentina or Uruguay, Italy or Spain are going to be your natural destinations, similar in culture and close in language.

So, for these reasons, Serie A took off. It could have been Spain, but they didn't have the level of ownership investment that Italian clubs had. Consider for a moment the evolution of the world record transfer fee from 1984 to 2000:

Year	Player	From	To	Fee
1984	Diego Maradona	Barcelona	**Napoli**	£5m
1987	Ruud Gullit	PSV	**Milan**	£6m
1990	Roberto Baggio	Fiorentina	**Juventus**	£8m
1992	Jean-Pierre Papin	Marseille	**Milan**	£10m
1992	Gianluca Vialli	Sampdoria	**Juventus**	£12m
1992	Gianluigi Lentini	Torino	**Milan**	£13m
1996	Ronaldo	PSV	Barcelona	£13.2m
1996	Alan Shearer	Blackburn	Newcastle	£15m
1997	Ronaldo	Barcelona	**Inter**	£19.5m
1998	Denílson	São Paulo	Real Betis	£21.5m
1999	Christian Vieri	Lazio	**Inter**	£32m
2000	Hernán Crespo	Parma	**Lazio**	£35.5m

In 16 years, 12 records were broken, of which nine were purchases by Italian clubs. If there was a star player around, he was moving to Italy. And, of course, those star players produced teams that were the envy of all. Again, just consider the statistics for Italian clubs across 1988 to 1999:

11 European Cup/Champions League competitions
**Four champions (Milan 1988/89, 1989/90, 1993/94,
Juventus 1995/96)**
Five runners-up (Sampdoria 1991/92, Milan 1992/93,
1994/95, Juventus 1996/97, 1997/98)

11 Cup Winners' Cup competitions
**Three champions (Sampdoria 1989/90, Parma 1992/93,
Lazio 1998/99)**
Two runners-up (Sampdoria 1988/89, Parma 1993/94)

11 UEFA Cup competitions
**Eight champions (Napoli 1988/89, Juventus 1989/90,
1992/93, Inter 1990/91, 1993/94, 1997/98, Parma
1994/95, 1998/99)**
Six runners-up (Fiorentina 1989/90, Roma 1990/91, Torino
1991/92, Juventus 1994/95, Inter 1996/97, Lazio 1997/98)

Think about that for a moment. In the top European
competition, contested by the best within the continent, only
two of the 11 finals didn't involve an Italian club. In the UEFA
Cup, there were four all-Italian finals and only one final
that didn't involve an Italian club. Looking at the 33 finals
combined, the 66 combatants included the following numbers
from each key country:

Italy (Serie A)	28
Germany (Bundesliga)	8
Spain (La Liga)	7
France (Ligue 1)	7
England (Premier League)	5
Netherlands (Eredivisie)	3

In other words, Italy had more finalists than Germany, Spain,
France and England combined! And those finalists came from a
range of clubs, in fact ten different teams – Milan, Inter, Juventus,
Napoli, Sampdoria, Parma, Roma, Lazio, Fiorentina and Torino.

Next, thinking about all the great players strutting their stuff in Serie A, let's consider the annual Ballon d'Or winners during this period:

Year	Player	Club
1988	Marco van Basten	**Milan**
1989	Marco van Basten	**Milan**
1990	Lothar Matthäus	**Inter**
1991	Jean-Pierre Papin	Marseille
1992	Marco van Basten	**Milan**
1993	Roberto Baggio	**Juventus**
1994	Hristo Stoichkov	Barcelona
1995	George Weah	**Milan**
1996	Matthias Sammer	Borussia Dortmund
1997	Ronaldo	**Inter**
1998	Zinedine Zidane	**Juventus**
1999	Rivaldo	Barcelona

Eight of the 12 awards went to players within Italian clubs at the time. And of the other four, Papin would move thereafter to Milan, Stoichkov to Parma and Rivaldo to Milan, while Sammer had played for Inter before heading back to Germany. And on top of all that, the 1988, 1989 and 1990 Ballon d'Or each had all the top three players plying their trade in Italy.

Oh, and if anyone thinks that Italian football prevailed by just bringing in the best foreign players that money could buy, let's not forget that for much of the period there were restrictions on how many imported players could take to the pitch. And the Italian national team wasn't too bad either – semi-finalists in the 1990 World Cup and finalists in the 1994 edition, only losing on penalties. Then there's my personal hero. If anyone says that all the best players in Serie A during the era were non-Italians, I have two things to say to you: Roberto Baggio and the Milan back four.

Between 1988 and 1999, Italian football ruled Europe – the defence rests its case, Your Honour.

Chapter 25

The Fall of the Italian Empire

Wherever we go at Parmalat, at Parma Calcio
... we find false documents and debt and people
tell us of other false documents and debt.

Italian investigator

SO, 28 Italian participants in European finals across the 11 seasons up to 1998/99. Winning both the UEFA Cup and Cup Winners' Cup in that final season. It seemed that everything was set for another decade of continued success. Only that wasn't to be the case. The future would see a huge drop-off for Italian clubs.

With the Cup Winners' Cup now over, European competition dropped to just the Champions League and UEFA Cup. And over the next decade no Italian club would reach any of the ten UEFA Cup finals. Remember, during the last 11 seasons of the UEFA Cup, there were four all-Italian finals and only one final that didn't involve an Italian club. Their participation had dropped from 14 finalists to zero. Incredibly, that drought would last until Inter lost to Sevilla in 2020, by which time it was now the Europa League. The 20 seasons of non-participation was an incredible decline.

In the Champions League, meanwhile, Italy did enjoy some success over the next decade, but mainly due to Milan. They would participate in three finals, winning two and losing that epic encounter against Liverpool, while Juventus would lose out against Milan, and Inter would win right at the end of the decade. But still, five finalists in ten seasons (of which three were Milan) versus nine in the prior 11 seasons, another significant decrease.

So why the fall? A lot of it came down to the collapse in financial strength of several of the clubs. After all, this is Italy, so you're never too far away from financial scandal or mismanagement. Let's summarise some of the woes that befell Italian teams after the 1990s ended.

* * *

The first major club to run into trouble was Fiorentina, who had reached third in Serie A in 1998, managed by the great Trapattoni and fuelled by the goals of Batistuta. In 2001, it was revealed that the finances of the club were in a terrible state, with debts of around $50 million. Unable to pay wages, club owner Vittorio Cecchi Gori was incapable of raising sufficient funds to keep the club afloat. Relegation at the end of 2001/02 compounded the problem, leading to administration in June 2002. The club ceased to exist and had to be reformed as a Serie C2 club.

They did at least return to Serie A swiftly, but then, in 2006, they became embroiled in the *Calciopoli* scandal, resulting in a 15-point penalty for the next season. But since then they have recovered to the point that in 2023 and 2024, they reached back-to-back European Conference League finals, losing out to West Ham United and Olympiacos.

The following year saw Lazio join Fiorentina in financial distress. Cirio, run by Sergio Cragnotti, owner of Lazio, had to declare default on its bonds, creating significant losses for many small investors, including Lazio supporters. In 2002, Cragnotti was forced to sell his stake in the club and, with that, Lazio's huge financial backing of the 1990s was significantly reduced. Their 2000 Serie A title would be their last to date, with no European final appearances registered either up to the time of writing.

One of the most shocking falls occurred at Parma. Having won the UEFA Cup and Coppa Italia in 1999, they went on to lift another Coppa Italia in 2002. All seemed well as the financial backing of Parmalat continued to be strong, on the back of a market value of £2.5 billion in April 2002, until everything unravelled the following year. Two attempts to issue bonds collapsed, leading to the resignation of the chief finance officer (CFO), after which questions started to arise about their financing, causing a share price collapse and the new CFO to also resign. Repayments were missed, the third CFO quit and then, shockingly, at the end of 2003, founder Calisto

Tanzi resigned, as it was claimed that an offshore bank account of €3.9 billion was forged.

Parmalat's market capitalisation fell from £2.5 billion in 2002 to just £60 million a year later – a 98 per cent drop – putting the company into administration. The company was no more, massive fraud being discovered that led to the trial of Calisto Tanzi and 15 other Parmalat officials. While some settled out of court, Tanzi was sentenced to ten years' imprisonment for fraud. It was Europe's biggest bankruptcy at the time, with many citizens impacted as pension funds were harmed.

Unsurprisingly, Parma football club was declared insolvent and placed into special administration before emerging as a reformed club. From that time forwards, its highest finish would be sixth in Serie A. They spent time in Serie B before again going bankrupt in March 2015, the situation becoming so bad that many of the trophies that they won in the 1990s had to be auctioned off. Bankruptcy meant reforming as a Serie D club and, although they secured three successive promotions to get back to Serie A, they then fell again. At the time of writing, they have just clinched a place back in Serie A.

Once Maradona departed, Napoli's fortunes were never the same again. The 1997/98 season would see them relegated, winning only two matches all season. Returning to Serie A two years later, they immediately got relegated again before declaring bankruptcy in August 2004, with debts of around €70 million. Like Fiorentina, they had to legally reform as a Serie C club, supported by the new ownership of film producer Aurelio De Laurentiis. Despite this, the Napoli fans kept the faith, 51,000 attending one Serie C game.

From 2010 onwards, Napoli became a contender once more in Italy. But it seemed like they were cursed never to win the Scudetto again, finishing twice four times and third three times from 2011 to 2019. And then, in 2023, it finally happened. For the first time since the glory days of Maradona, Luciano Spalletti guided Napoli back to the holy land. Needless to say, quite the party broke out across the city for many days.

Torino had reached the 1992 UEFA Cup Final under Mondocino before they also hit financial problems, resulting in frequent changes in ownership and manager in the mid-90s. They were eventually relegated in 1996, after which they spent the next

16 years yo-yoing between Serie A and Serie B. They have now stabilised in Serie A but, since that 1992 final, have never placed higher than seventh and have only played in Europe twice since 1994. Like the other clubs mentioned here, they too went through bankruptcy in 2005, having to reform within Serie B.

Following on from their 1991 Scudetto, Sampdoria have never hit the highs again. Becoming a mid-table team, they have rarely played in Europe and even suffered an ownership scandal of their own when, late in 2021, their owner, film producer Massimo Ferrero, was arrested as part of an ongoing investigation into bankruptcy and corporate crimes. Since then, they have been relegated down to Serie B, where they currently still play at the time of writing.

* * *

That leaves four of the ten teams discussed in detail within this book as unaffected by bankruptcy or major financial issues.

From 2000 onwards, Roma have been so often the bridesmaid and only once the bride. Having won the Scudetto in 2001 under Capello, they have since come second an incredible nine times. For most of that period, however, they continually underperformed in Europe, until eventually winning the 2022 Europa League under José Mourinho, who also took them to the same competition's final the following year.

That leaves Inter, Juventus and Milan as the key teams that have enjoyed some success in European competition since 1999. Milan won the Champions League in 2003 and 2007 under Ancelotti, while Juventus, although dominating Serie A, have suffered three final defeats, against Borussia Dortmund, Real Madrid and Milan. Inter finally won one Champions League title, in 2010, defeating Bayern Munich under Mourinho. These clubs have not been immune to controversy either, most notably the 2006 *Calciopoli* scandal that resulted in Juventus being stripped of their title and demoted to Serie B, while also costing Milan, Lazio and Fiorentina material point deductions.

As Italian teams suffered financially, England and Spain became the new destination of choice for many star players. With the Premier League getting into its stride after 1999 and the value of TV rights ballooning, Chelsea, Manchester United and Liverpool regularly reached Champions League finals. If players preferred sunnier climes than England, then Spain was the ideal destination. Barcelona and Real Madrid virtually monopolised the Champions League from 2009 onwards, while Atlético Madrid and Sevilla decided to carve up the Europa League. And finally, major foreign ownership enriched PSG, Chelsea and Manchester City. Italian teams now don't have the financial muscle to compete with these clubs, given the gap in wealth and TV rights valuations.

But while Italian clubs may not enjoy the prestige that they did between 1988 and 1999, they are storied institutions and, given the lifestyle, the major clubs of Juventus, Inter and Milan can still attract talent. They can also compete at the top level, as demonstrated by Inter reaching the 2023 Champions League Final and giving Manchester City a decent run for their money. But gone are the days when any one of ten Italian clubs could compete for European honours, but that doesn't mean that those days should be forgotten. For those of us who lived through them, they were fantastic years – seasons in the sun, where we could watch the world's finest strut their stuff in futuristic stadia before a backdrop of ultras and *tifos*. Italian football was cool. Italian football was sexy.

And watching old Roberto Baggio clips will still bring a lump to my throat. *Grazie mille, Il Divin Codino!*